Celebrate Recovery®

A recovery program based on
8 principles from the Beatitudes

LEADER'S GUIDE

T0387981

John Baker along with his wife Cheryl, founded Celebrate Recovery˚, a ministry that began at Saddleback Church in 1991. John was on staff from the time Celebrate Recovery started until he went home to be with Jesus in 2021. He served as the Pastor of Membership, the Pastor of Ministries, and the Pastor of Saddleback Church's Signature Ministries. He also served as one of the nine Elder Pastors at Saddleback. John was a nationally known speaker and trainer in helping churches start Celebrate Recovery ministries.

John's writing accomplishments include Celebrate Recovery's *The Journey Begins* curriculum, *Life's Healing Choices*, the *NIV Celebrate Recovery Study Bible* (general editor), *The Landing* and *Celebration Place* (coauthor), *Your First Step to Celebrate Recovery* and the *Celebrate Recovery Daily Devotional* (coauthor).

John and Cheryl, were married for more than five decades and served together in Celebrate Recovery since the beginning. They have two adult children, Laura and Johnny, and five grandchildren.

Johnny Baker is the Global Executive Director of Celebrate Recovery, along with his wife Jeni. He has been on staff at Celebrate Recovery since 2004 and has been the Pastor of Celebrate Recovery at Saddleback Church since 2012.

As an adult child of an alcoholic who chose to become an alcoholic himself, Johnny is passionate about breaking the cycle of dysfunction in his family and helping other families find the tools that will lead to healing and openness. He knows that because of Jesus Christ, and by continuing to stay active in Celebrate Recovery, Maggie, Chloe, and Jimmy—his three children—will never see him drink. Johnny is a nationally recognized speaker, trainer, and teacher of Celebrate Recovery. He is the author of *Road to Freedom*, a coauthor of the *Celebrate Recovery Daily Devotional*, *Celebration Place*, and *The Landing*, and is an associate editor of the *NIV Celebrate Recovery Study Bible*. Johnny and Jeni have been married since 2000.

REVISED AND UPDATED EDITION

Celebrate Recovery®

A recovery program based on
8 principles from the Beatitudes

LEADER'S GUIDE

JOHN BAKER & JOHNNY BAKER

FOREWORD BY RICK WARREN

Harper*Christian*
Resources

This book is dedicated to my Lord and Savior, Jesus Christ.
To my wife, Cheryl, and my children, Laura and Johnny,
for loving me no matter what.

To Pastors Rick Warren and Glen Kreun,
for trusting and believing in me.

To the Saddleback Church staff, for their support.

To the thousands of courageous men and women who have celebrated
their recoveries with me over the last twenty years!

AUTHOR'S NOTE

Because I have picked up a variety of quotes and slogans from numerous recovery meetings, tapes, and seminars, I have not been able to provide some sources for all of the material here. If you feel that I have quoted your material, please let me know and I will be pleased to give you the credit.

Celebrate Recovery Leader's Guide, Revised and Updated
©1998, 2012, 2025 by John Baker and Johnny Baker

Published in Grand Rapids, Michigan, by HarperChristian Resources. HarperChristian Resources is a registered trademark of HarperCollins Christian Publishing, Inc.

Requests for information should be sent to customercare@harpercollins.com.

ISBN 978-0-310-17601-5 (softcover)
ISBN 978-0-310-17602-2 (ebook)

All Scripture quotations are taken from the Holy Bible, New International Version®, NIV®. Copyright © 1973, 1978, 1984, 2011 by Biblica, Inc.® Used by permission. All rights reserved worldwide.

Any internet addresses (websites, blogs, etc.) and telephone numbers in this study guide are offered as a resource. They are not intended in any way to be or imply an endorsement by HarperChristian Resources, nor does HarperChristian Resources vouch for the content of these sites and numbers for the life of this study guide.

HarperChristian Resources titles may be purchased in bulk for church, business, fundraising, or ministry use. For information, please e-mail ResourceSpecialist@ChurchSource.com.

First Printing March 2025 / Printed in the United States of America

Contents

PRINCIPLE ONE   51

Realize I'm not God. I admit that I am powerless to control my tendency to do the wrong thing and that my life is unmanageable.

Blessed are the poor in spirit. (Matthew 5:3)

PRINCIPLE TWO 69

Earnestly believe that God exists, that I matter to Him, and that He has the power to help me recover.

Blessed are those who mourn, for they will be comforted. (Matthew 5:4)

PRINCIPLE THREE 83

Consciously choose to commit all my life and will to Christ's care and control.

Blessed are the meek. (Matthew 5:5)

PRINCIPLE FOUR 97

Openly examine and confess my hurts, hang-ups, and habits to myself, to God, and to someone I trust.

Blessed are the pure in heart. (Matthew 5:8)

PRINCIPLE FIVE 141

Voluntarily submit to every change God wants to make in my life and humbly ask Him to remove my character defects.

Blessed are those who hunger and thirst for righteousness. (Matthew 5:6)

PRINCIPLE SIX 155

Evaluate all my relationships. Offer forgiveness to those who have hurt me and make amends for harm I've done to others, except when to do so would harm them or others.

Blessed are the merciful. (Matthew 5:7)

Blessed are the peacemakers. (Matthew 5:9)

PRINCIPLE SEVEN 173

Reserve a daily time with God for self-examination, Bible reading, and prayer in order to know God and His will for my life and to gain the power to follow His will.

PRINCIPLE EIGHT 197

Yield myself to God to be used to bring this Good News to others, both by my example and by my words.

Blessed are those who are persecuted because of righteousness. (Matthew 5:10)

THE JOURNEY CONTINUES 217

Preface

As we put together this latest edition of the *Celebrate Recovery Leader's Guide* you will see some exciting updates and changes. While the lessons have stayed the same, there are some changes to both content and format. Most noticeably, the Getting Started section of the Leader's Guide has been updated to help you start and grow your Celebrate Recovery ministry. There are some new tools such as DNA Group Formats, new ways to start a Celebrate Recovery Ministry, changes in the Appendices, and much more.

We have also made some changes to the *Celebrate Recovery Participant's Guides*. We are now combining the individual Participant's Guides 1–4 (*The Journey Begins*) into one single Participant's Gude with four volumes and a new trim size. And Participant's Guides 5–8 (*The Journey Continues*) will also be combined into one single Participant's Guide with a new trim size. Here are some of the key changes:

- Both of the combined participant's guides will now allow for more room to write.
- We have also updated Principle 4 of the RECOVERY Principles in all of the guides. The new Principle now reads, *Openly examine and confess my **hurts**, **hang-ups**, and **habits** to myself, to God, and to someone I trust.*
- Also, all Scripture references are now in the NIV translation and correspond to the *NIV Celebrate Recovery Study Bible.* Please note, this applies to the 8 Principles and 12 Steps as well.
- The Inventory Worksheet has also been updated to help make the process clearer to participants. There is new information in the Inventory Lesson in both the Leader's Guide and each newly combined Participant's Guide.

We are praying these updates help you start and grow your Celebrate Recovery ministry!

Foreword by Rick Warren

The Bible clearly states "all have sinned" (Romans 3:23). It is my nature to sin, and it is yours too. None of us is untainted. Because of sin, we've all hurt ourselves, we've all hurt other people, and others have hurt us. This means each of us needs repentance and recovery in order to live our lives the way God intended.

You've undoubtedly heard the expression "Time heals all wounds." Unfortunately, it isn't true. As a pastor I frequently talk with people who are still carrying hurts from thirty or forty years ago. The truth is, time often makes things worse. Wounds that are left untended fester and spread infection throughout your entire body. Time only extends the pain if the problem isn't dealt with.

What we need is a biblical and balanced program to help people overcome their hurts, hang-ups, and habits. Celebrate Recovery® is that program. Based on the actual words of Jesus rather than psychological theory, this recovery program is unique, and it is more effective in helping people change than anything else I've seen or heard of. Over the years I've witnessed how the Holy Spirit has used this program to transform literally thousands of lives at Saddleback Church and to help people grow toward full Christlike maturity.

Most people are familiar with the classic 12-Step program of AA and other groups. While undoubtedly many lives have been helped through the 12 Steps, I've always been uncomfortable with that program's vagueness about the nature of God, the saving power of Jesus Christ, and the ministry of the Holy Spirit. So I began an intense study of the Scriptures to discover what God had to say about "recovery." To my amazement, I found the principles of recovery—in their logical order—given by Christ in His most famous message, the Sermon on the Mount.

My study resulted in a ten-week series of messages called "The Road to Recovery." During that series my associate pastor John Baker developed the participant's guides, which became the heart of our Celebrate Recovery program. I believe that this program is unlike any recovery program you may have seen. There are seven features that make it unique.

1. *Celebrate Recovery is based on God's Word, the Bible.* When Jesus taught the Sermon on the Mount, He began by stating eight ways to be happy. Today we call them the Beatitudes. From a conventional viewpoint, most of these statements don't make sense. They sound like

contradictions. But when you fully understand what Jesus is saying, you'll realize that these eight principles are God's road to recovery, wholeness, growth, and spiritual maturity.

2. *Celebrate Recovery is forward-looking.* Rather than wallowing in the past or dredging up and rehearsing painful memories over and over, Celebrate Recovery focuses on the future. Regardless of what has already happened, the solution is to start making wise choices now and depend on Christ's power to help make those changes.

3. *Celebrate Recovery emphasizes personal responsibility.* Instead of playing the "accuse and excuse" game of victimization, this program helps people face up to their own poor choices and deal with what they can do something about. We cannot control all that happens to us, but we can control how we respond to everything. That is a secret of happiness. When we stop wasting time fixing the blame, we have more energy to fix the problem. When we stop hiding our own faults and stop hurling accusations at others, then the healing power of Christ can begin working in our mind, will, and emotions.

4. *Celebrate Recovery emphasizes spiritual commitment to Jesus Christ.* The third principle calls for people to make a total surrender of their lives to Christ. Lasting recovery cannot happen without this step. Everybody needs Jesus. Celebrate Recovery is thoroughly evangelistic in nature. In fact, the first time I took our entire church through this program, over 500 people prayed to receive Christ on a single weekend. It was an amazing spiritual harvest. And during the ten-week series that I preached to kick off this program, our attendance grew by over 1,500! Don't be surprised if this program becomes the most effective outreach ministry in your church. Today, nearly 73 percent of the people who've been through Celebrate Recovery have come from outside our church. Changed lives always attract others who want to be changed.

5. *Celebrate Recovery utilizes the biblical truth that we need each other in order to grow spiritually and emotionally.* It is built around small group interaction and the fellowship of a caring community. There are many therapies, growth programs, and counselors today that operate around one-to-one interaction. But Celebrate Recovery is built on the New Testament principle that we don't get well by ourselves. We need each other. Fellowship and accountability are two important components of spiritual growth. If your church is interested in starting small groups, this is a great way to get started.

6. *Celebrate Recovery addresses all types of hurts, hang-ups, and habits.* Some recovery programs deal only with alcohol or drugs or another single problem. But Celebrate Recovery is a "large umbrella" program under which a limitless number of issues can be dealt with. At

Saddleback Church, only one out of three who attend Celebrate Recovery are dealing with alcohol or drugs. We have several other specialized groups too.

7. *Finally, Celebrate Recovery is a leadership factory.* Because it is biblical and church-based, Celebrate Recovery produces a continuous stream of people moving into ministry after they've found recovery in Christ. Eighty-five percent of the people who've gone through the program are now active members of Saddleback Church, and an amazing 42 percent are now using their gifts and talents serving the Lord in some capacity in our church.

In closing, let me say that the size of your church is no barrier to beginning a Celebrate Recovery ministry. You can start it with just a small group of people and watch it grow by word of mouth. You won't be able to keep it a secret for long!

I'm excited that you have decided to begin a Celebrate Recovery ministry in your church. You are going to see lives changed in dramatic ways. You are going to see hopeless marriages restored and people set free from all kinds of sinful hurts, hang-ups, and habits as they allow Jesus to be Lord in every area of their lives. To God be the glory! We'll be praying for you.

Dr. Rick Warren
Founder of Saddleback Church

The Road to Recovery

EIGHT PRINCIPLES BASED ON THE BEATITUDES

By Pastor Rick Warren

1. **R**ealize I'm not God. I admit that I am powerless to control my tendency to do the wrong thing and that my life is unmanageable.
   Blessed are the poor in spirit, for theirs is the kingdom of heaven. (Matthew 5:3)
2. **E**arnestly believe that God exists, that I matter to Him, and that He has the power to help me recover.
   Blessed are those who mourn, for they will be comforted. (Matthew 5:4)
3. **C**onsciously choose to commit all my life and will to Christ's care and control.
   Blessed are the meek, for they will inherit the earth. (Matthew 5:5)
4. **O**penly examine and confess my hurts, hang-ups, and habits to myself, to God, and to someone I trust.
   Blessed are the pure in heart, for they will see God. (Matthew 5:8)
5. **V**oluntarily submit to every change God wants to make in my life and humbly ask Him to remove my character defects.
   Blessed are those who hunger and thirst for righteousness, for they will be filled. (Matthew 5:6)
6. **E**valuate all my relationships. Offer forgiveness to those who have hurt me and make amends for harm I've done to others, except when to do so would harm them or others.
   Blessed are the merciful, for they will be shown mercy. (Matthew 5:7)
   Blessed are the peacemakers, for they will be called children of God. (Matthew 5:9)
7. **R**eserve a daily time with God for self-examination, Bible reading, and prayer in order to know God and His will for my life and to gain the power to follow His will.
8. **Y**ield myself to God to be used to bring this Good News to others, both by my example and by my words.
   Blessed are those who are persecuted because of righteousness, for theirs is the kingdom of heaven. (Matthew 5:10)

Twelve Steps and Their Biblical Comparisons[1]

1. We admitted we were powerless over our addictions and compulsive behaviors, that our lives had become unmanageable.

   For I know that good itself does not dwell in me, that is, in my sinful nature. For I have the desire to do what is good, but I cannot carry it out. (Romans 7:18)

2. We came to believe that a power greater than ourselves could restore us to sanity.

   For it is God who works in you to will and to act in order to fulfill his good purpose. (Philippians 2:13)

3. We made a decision to turn our lives and our wills over to the care of God.

   Therefore, I urge you, brothers and sisters, in view of God's mercy, to offer your bodies as a living sacrifice, holy and pleasing to God—this is your true and proper worship. (Romans 12:1)

4. We made a searching and fearless moral inventory of ourselves.

   Let us examine our ways and test them, and let us return to the LORD. (Lamentations 3:40)

5. We admitted to God, to ourselves, and to another human being the exact nature of our wrongs.

   Therefore confess your sins to each other and pray for each other so that you may be healed. (James 5:16)

---

1. Throughout this material, you will notice several references to the Christ-centered 12 Steps. Our prayer is that Celebrate Recovery will create a bridge to the millions of people who are familiar with the secular 12 Steps (I acknowledge the use of some material from the 12 Suggested Steps of Alcoholics Anonymous.) and in so doing, introduce them to the one and only true Higher Power, Jesus Christ. Once they begin that relationship, asking Christ into their hearts as Lord and Savior, true healing and recovery can begin!

6. We were entirely ready to have God remove all these defects of character.

    Humble yourselves before the Lord, and he will lift you up. (James 4:10)

7. We humbly asked Him to remove all our shortcomings.

    If we confess our sins, he is faithful and just and will forgive us our sins and purify us from all unrighteousness. (1 John 1:9)

8. We made a list of all persons we had harmed and became willing to make amends to them all.

    Do to others as you would have them do to you. (Luke 6:31)

9. We made direct amends to such people whenever possible, except when to do so would injure them or others.

    "Therefore, if you are offering your gift at the altar and there remember that your brother or sister has something against you, leave your gift there in front of the altar. First go and be reconciled to them; then come and offer your gift." (Matthew 5:23–24)

10. We continued to take personal inventory and when we were wrong, promptly admitted it.

    So, if you think you are standing firm, be careful that you don't fall! (1 Corinthians 10:12)

11. We sought through prayer and meditation to improve our conscious contact with God, praying only for knowledge of His will for us and power to carry that out.

    Let the message of Christ dwell among you richly. (Colossians 3:16)

12. Having had a spiritual experience as the result of these steps, we try to carry this message to others and to practice these principles in all our affairs.

    Brothers and sisters, if someone is caught in a sin, you who live by the Spirit should restore that person gently. But watch yourselves, or you also may be tempted. (Galatians 6:1)

From My Heart to Yours

My name is John Baker, and I'm a believer who struggles with alcoholism. In 1992, I joined the Saddleback Church staff as the Director of Small Groups and Recovery. Over the years, I have also have had the honor of serving as the Pastor of Membership and Ministry. In 2001, I became the Pastor of Celebrate Recovery. That's what I do, but God is really more interested in who I am, when there is no one else around. He's interested in my character, my values.

So as a way of introducing who I am, I would like to share my testimony by relating my experiences, as I have traveled my personal "road to recovery."

I was raised in a Christian home in the Midwestern town of Collinsville, Illinois, population 10,000. I had a so-called "normal" childhood, whatever that is. My parents were members of a small Baptist church pastored by a very young Gordon MacDonald. I asked Christ into my heart at age thirteen. In high school I was class president and lettered in basketball, baseball, and track. I felt called into ministry at age sixteen and applied to several Christian universities. Up to this point, everything sounds normal—almost boring.

But I had a problem: I had to be the best in everything. Deep down inside I never felt good enough for my parents, my teammates, my girlfriends, or anyone. If I wasn't good enough for them, I wondered how I could ever be good enough for God. I must have missed the Sunday sermons on God's mercy and Jesus' unconditional love and undeserved and unearnable grace. I was a walking, talking paradox—a combination of the lowest possible self-esteem and the world's largest ego. Believe me, that's not a very comfortable feeling inside. The best way that I can describe the feeling is a burning emptiness—a hole—right in the gut.

I wrestled with God's call and judged myself unworthy to enter the ministry. Instead, after high school I went to the University of Missouri. When I packed for my freshman year, I took my nonexistent self-esteem with me. I joined a fraternity and soon discovered the solution—or what I believed to be the solution—for my life's pain: alcohol. It worked! I fit in! For the first time in my life, I felt like I belonged.

While attending the university as a business administration major (with a minor in partying), I met my wife, Cheryl. We were married during my senior year. Because the Vietnam War was in full swing, we knew that after college I would be called into the service. Little did Cheryl know what else the next nineteen years would have in store.

In 1970 I graduated from college, joined the Air Force, and was chosen to be a pilot. I attended Officers' Training School, and in ninety days learned how to act like an officer and drink like a gentleman. I continued to abuse alcohol, viewing it as a cure for my pain, certainly not a sin!

In the service, I quickly found the proper use for 100 percent oxygen—a cure for hangovers! The service is a great place to discover one's talents. Soon I was selected as my squadron's social officer. Perfect! A job that required a lot of hours planning functions at the officers' club bar. Then the war ended, and I was assigned to a reserve unit.

After the service, I joined Scott Paper Company. I earned my MBA degree at night school and God gave us our first child, a daughter, Laura. Two years later we were blessed with our son, John Jr.

I was promoted eight times in the first eleven years of my business career. I was the vice president of sales and marketing for two large consumer food manufacturers. I had reached all my life's career and financial objectives and goals by the time I was thirty! Along with all this business success, however, came several relocations. Moving every two years made it difficult for us to establish a home church, but as my drinking continued, church became less and less important to me. I knew that if I died I was saved, but my Christianity was not reflected in my lifestyle, business practices, and priorities.

Still, I thought my life appeared normal to casual observers. I was a leader in my church's Awana ministry for youth. I thought nothing of leaving work early to stop by a bar before the Wednesday night meeting so I could relax and relate better to the kids. Didn't everybody do that? I was also my son's Little League coach for five years, but I always stopped by the pizza joint with my assistant coach for a few pitchers of beer after every game. Again, didn't everybody? Talk about insanity!

Slowly I became more and more uncomfortable with the lifestyle I was leading. I faced a major decision. I had a choice: do it my way—continue drinking and living by the world's standards—or surrender, repent, and do it God's way. I wish I could tell you that I saw the light and did it God's way, but the truth is, I chose my way. My drinking increased and I turned my back on God. Proverbs 14:12 says, "There is a way that appears to be right, but in the end it leads to death."

I was on that road. I was what is known as a functioning alcoholic. I never lost a job, never got arrested for drunk driving. No, the only things my sin-addiction cost me were my close relationships with the Lord and my family. Cheryl and I separated, after nineteen years of marriage. I lost all purpose for living. You see, what I had considered the solution for my life's problem, alcohol, became the problem of my life!

My life was out of control. I had created my own hell on earth! On an October morning, I was in Salt Lake City on a business trip when I woke up and knew I couldn't take another drink. But I also knew that I couldn't live without one! I had finally hit my bottom. I was dying physically, emotionally, mentally, and most important, spiritually. I was at **Principle 1**.

Principle 1: Realize I'm not God. I admit that I am powerless to control my tendency to do the wrong thing and that my life is unmanageable.

Blessed are the poor in spirit, for theirs is the kingdom of heaven. (Matthew 5:3)

Step 1: We admitted we were powerless over our addictions and compulsive behaviors, that our lives had become unmanageable.

For I know that good itself does not dwell in me, that is, in my sinful nature. For I have the desire to do what is good, but I cannot carry it out. (Romans 7:18)

When I got back home from that business trip, I went to my first AA meeting. But that was only the beginning. All in all, I went to over ninety meetings in ninety days. As time passed, I was ready for **Principle 2**.

Principle 2: Earnestly believe that God exists, that I matter to Him, and that He has the power to help me recover.

Blessed are those who mourn, for they will be comforted. (Matthew 5:4)

Step 2: We came to believe that a power greater than ourselves could restore us to sanity.

For it is God who works in you to will and to act in order to fulfill his good purpose. (Philippians 2:13)

This is where I found my first glimmer of hope! God loves me unconditionally. I was finally able to understand Romans 11:36: "From him and through him and for him are all things. To him be the glory forever!"

Today my life with Christ is an endless hope: My life without Him was a hopeless end! My own willpower left me empty and broken, so I changed my definition of willpower. Now I know that true willpower is the willingness to accept God's power over my life.

This led me to **Principle 3**.

Principle 3: Consciously choose to commit all my life and will to Christ's care and control.

Blessed are the meek, for they will inherit the earth. (Matthew 5:5)

Step 3: We made a decision to turn our lives and our wills over to the care of God.

Therefore, I urge you, brothers and sisters, in view of God's mercy, to offer your bodies as a living sacrifice, holy and pleasing to God—this is your true and proper worship." (Romans 12:1)

In working the first three principles I said, "I can't; God can," and I decided to let Him. One day at a time. If we don't surrender to Christ, we will surrender to chaos!

I thought the first three principles were hard, but now came **Principle 4**.

Principle 4: Openly examine and confess my hurts, hang-ups, and habits to myself, to God, and to someone I trust.

Blessed are the pure in heart, for they will see God. (Matthew 5:8)

Step 4: We made a searching and fearless moral inventory of ourselves.

Let us examine our ways and test them, and let us return to the LORD. (Lamentations 3:40)

Step 5: We admitted to God, to ourselves, and to another human being the exact nature of our wrongs.

Therefore confess your sins to each other and pray for each other so that you may be healed. (James 5:16)

At this point I had to go back to visit the young John Baker, to face the hurts, hang-ups, and habits I had attempted to drown with alcohol. I had to face the loss of my infant brother. I had to accept my part in all the destruction that my alcoholism had caused to all those who were once close to me. After I 'fessed up, I was able to face the truth and accept Jesus' forgiveness and healing, which led me out of the darkness of my secrets and into His wonderful light!

I thank God for providing me with a sponsor who helped me stay balanced and didn't judge me during the sharing of my inventory. I cannot begin to tell you the burden God lifted off me when I completed the instructions found in James 5:16! I now knew I was forgiven by the work of Jesus Christ—the one and only true Higher Power—on the cross and that all the sins and wrongs of my past were no longer a secret. Now I was finally willing to have God change me. I was ready to submit to any and all changes God wanted me to make in my life. You see, not much changed in my life—just everything changed!

Principle 5 made me realize that it was time to "let go and let God." By this time, I was happy to do so! I had seen enough of myself to know that I was incapable of changing my life on my own.

Principle 5: Voluntarily submit to every change God wants to make in my life and humbly ask Him to remove my character defects.

Blessed are those who hunger and thirst for righteousness, for they will be filled. (Matthew 5:6)

Step 6: We were entirely ready to have God remove all these defects of character.

Humble yourselves before the Lord, and he will lift you up. (James 4:10)

Step 7: We humbly asked Him to remove all our shortcomings.

If we confess our sins, he is faithful and just and will forgive us our sins and purify us from all unrighteousness. (1 John 1:9)

For me, completing Principle 5 meant three things: (1) I allowed God to transform my mind—its nature, its condition, its identity; (2) I learned to rejoice in steady progress—patient improvement that allowed others to see the changes in me that I could not see; (3) God rebuilt my self-worth based on His love for me rather than my always trying to measure up to the world's standards.

During this time God gave me His definition of humility: "My grace is sufficient for you, for my power is made perfect in weakness" (2 Corinthians 12:9). Then I could say with the apostle Paul, "I will boast all the more gladly about my weaknesses, so that Christ's power may rest on me . . . . For when I am weak, then I am strong" (vv. 9–10).

I was now ready to work on **Principle 6**, my favorite:

Principle 6: Evaluate all my relationships. Offer forgiveness to those who have hurt me and make amends for harm I've done to others, except when to do so would harm them or others.

Blessed are the merciful, for they will be shown mercy. (Matthew 5:7)

Blessed are the peacemakers, for they will be called children of God. (Matthew 5:9)

Step 8: We made a list of all persons we had harmed and became willing to make amends to them all.

Do to others as you would have them do to you. (Luke 6:31)

Step 9: We made direct amends to such people whenever possible, except when to do so would injure them or others.

"Therefore, if you are offering your gift at the altar and there remember that your brother or sister has something against you, leave your gift in front of the altar. First go and be reconciled to them; then come and offer your gift." (Matthew 5:23–24)

I said this is my favorite principle, but certainly not the easiest! I had quite a list of names on my amends list. They ranged from former employers and employees to friends and neighbors. But my most special amends were to my family, especially to my wife, Cheryl. We were still separated.

I told her that my drinking was not her fault. I was truly sorry for the pain I had caused in her life, that I still loved her, and that if I could ever do anything for her—anything—she only had to ask.

Over the months of separation, Cheryl had seen the changes God was making in my life, changes that occurred as I worked my program. (This is where it really gets interesting!) She and the kids had started attending a church that met in a gym. It was called Saddleback. One Saturday night I was visiting the kids and they asked me to join them on Sunday morning. Much to their surprise, I said yes! It had been five years since I had last attended a church service, but when I heard the music and Pastor Rick Warren's message, I knew I was home. Cheryl and I began to work in earnest on our problems and five months later, God opened our hearts and we renewed our marriage vows. Isn't that just like God!

As a family we were baptized and later took all the church's classes: 101 Membership, 201 Maturity, and 301 Ministry. In Class 301, I found one of my life's verses:

But you are a chosen people, a royal priesthood, a holy nation, God's special possession, that you may declare the praises of him who called you out of darkness into his wonderful light. Once you were not a people, but now you are the people of God; once you had not received mercy, but now you have received mercy. (1 Peter 2:9–10)

As Pastor Rick Warren says, "God never wastes a hurt." All the pain and heartache of my addiction finally made sense!

However, at my AA meetings I was mocked when talking about my Higher Power—the only true Higher Power, Jesus Christ. And at church I couldn't find a small group where individuals could openly relate to my struggle with my sin-addiction to alcohol. I knew they had to be there because in a church the size of Saddleback, I couldn't be the only one struggling with a hurt, hang-up, or addictive habit.

So I wrote Pastor Rick Warren a short, concise, thirteen-page, single-spaced letter outlining the vision that God gave me—

The vision of Celebrate Recovery, a Christ-centered recovery program.

The next thing I knew, Pastor Rick called me into his office and said, "Great, John—you do it!" From that meeting Celebrate Recovery was born.

I finally was able to accept God's call. I entered Golden Gate Baptist Seminary and committed my life to God, to serve Him wherever and whenever He chose.

I have dedicated my life to serving Jesus Christ. I intend to work the last two principles on a daily basis for the remainder of my time on this earth.

Principle 7: Reserve a daily time with God for self-examination, Bible reading, and prayer in order to know God and His will for my life and to gain the power to follow His will.

Principle 8: Yield myself to God to be used to bring this Good News to others, both by my example and by my words.

Blessed are those who are persecuted because of righteousness, for theirs is the kingdom of heaven. (Matthew 5:10)

Step 10: We continued to take personal inventory and when we were wrong, promptly admitted it.

So, if you think you are standing firm, be careful that you don't fall! (1 Corinthians 10:12)

Step 11: We sought through prayer and meditation to improve our conscious contact with God, praying only for knowledge of His will for us and power to carry that out.

Let the message of Christ dwell among you richly. (Colossians 3:16)

Step 12: Having had a spiritual experience as the result of these steps, we try to carry this message to others and to practice these principles in all our affairs.

Brothers and sisters, if someone is caught in a sin, you who live by the Spirit should restore that person gently. But watch yourselves, or you also may be tempted. (Galatians 6:1)

God has blessed me richly, and I gratefully pass on these blessings to you. It is my prayer that this book will help your church start a Celebrate Recovery program where your people can safely work together on their hurts, hang-ups, and habits—a program where Christ's love, truth, grace, and forgiveness are demonstrated in all things.

In His steps,
John Baker

Getting Started

The purpose of Celebrate Recovery is to help individuals experience healing from their hurts, hang-ups and habits through a relationship with Jesus Christ. We are transformed as we share our experiences, strengths, and hopes with one another and find healing and restoration through God's grace.

By working through the principles, we grow spiritually, and we are freed from our hurts, hang-ups, and habits. This freedom creates peace, serenity, joy, and most importantly, a stronger personal relationship with others and our personal, loving, and forgiving Higher Power, Jesus Christ.

On November 21, 1991, Celebrate Recovery held its first meeting at Saddleback Church, Lake Forest, California, with 45 attendees. The program continues to grow beyond our greatest expectations, as thousands of individuals around the world have found transformation, freedom, and healing from their hurts, hang-ups, and habits.

Over the years, we tried a variety of new ideas and concepts to help the ministry grow. Of course, not everything we tried worked, but from the very beginning, I told the leadership team that the one thing we could not change in Celebrate Recovery is the truth that Jesus Christ is the one and only Higher Power.

This Leader's Guide is a compilation of what we have learned over the years. As you read through the book, you will find the basics or "how-tos" of starting and running a healthy Celebrate Recovery ministry, including Large Group, Open Share Groups, and Step Study Groups.

This Leader's Guide includes the CR Start-up Strategy, the foundational "7 Keys," CR group formats, 25 Lessons for your Large Group Meeting, training for your potential leaders, and much more.

DNA of Celebrate Recovery

The Celebrate Recovery® name is a registered trademark.

In a desire to protect the integrity of the broader ministry, Celebrate Recovery® requires that if you use the Celebrate Recovery® name, the DNA is an irreducible minimum of your program.

Following the DNA allows individual CR ministries to use the name Celebrate Recovery and to be connected to the growing community of Christ-centered, bible-based Celebrate Recovery ministries all over the world. While you are helping individuals at your church overcome their hurts, hang-ups or habits, your CR ministry is also part of an international community reaching people for Christ.

By calling your ministry Celebrate Recovery and following the DNA you receive connection to other groups, support from the Global team and local representatives, identification with the CR name and promotion on the CR Locator.

A church or organization may decide to use Celebrate Recovery curriculum and mix it with other materials, or programs. This is certainly up to their discretion. HOWEVER, they are prohibited from using the Celebrate Recovery name.

Items produced for commercial sale using the Celebrate Recovery name or any part of the Celebrate Recovery curriculums is strictly prohibited. This is a trademark and copyright violation.

To view the most up-to-date version of the Celebrate Recovery DNA, go to celebraterecovery.com.

The DNA of an Authentic Celebrate Recovery Ministry

1. Jesus Christ is the one and only Higher Power. The program is a Christ-centered ministry.
2. The Bible and *Celebrate Recovery curriculum is to be used exclusively. The twenty-five Large Group Lessons, found in this Leader's Guide, are taught in Large Group according to the Yearly Lesson and Testimony Schedule (found in Appendix 9), keeping at least the acrostic and the Scriptures as the key points in the lessons. This is to keep consistency within groups, allowing teachers to be creative with the remainder of each lesson.

3. The ministry is "group based." All Open Share and Step Study groups are gender-specific, implement and follow "The Celebrate Recovery Small Group Guidelines" every time, and all groups adhere to the CR DNA Group Formats:
   - Small Group Guidelines (Appendix 10)
   - Extended Small Group Guidelines (Appendix 10)
   - DNA Group Formats (Appendix 8)
4. A Celebrate Recovery ministry can be in person or online. If a local Celebrate Recovery ministry chooses to offer an online Large Group Meeting, please do the following:
   1. Use the CR parameters for online Large Groups to ensure anonymity and confidentiality are followed.
   2. Please follow copyright licensing procedures per your church copyright permissions.
   3. Before posting testimonies online, all testimonies must have written signed consent in accordance with your church.
   4. Teaching and posting Celebrate Recovery Lessons online is permitted. Again, your local group must follow proper copyright licensing procedures per your church copyright permissions.
5. We expect each group (local CR ministry) to be accountable to Christ, the local church, and the Celebrate Recovery Global Team.
6. Celebrate Recovery is a ministry of the local church. Therefore, Celebrate Recovery will not attempt to dictate any doctrine or policy to a local church. A local Celebrate Recovery ministry should follow the policies of their local church and continue to be grateful for their continued support.

*Celebrate Recovery curriculum consists of the *Celebrate Recovery Study Bible*, the *Celebrate Recovery Curriculum Kit*, the *Celebrate Recovery Leader's Guide*, *The Journey Begins*, *The Journey Continues*, *Advanced Leadership Training Guide*, *Celebrate Recovery Program Bundle*, *Your First Step to Celebrate Recovery*, *Life's Healing Choices*, *The Road to Freedom*, *Celebrate Recovery Daily Devotional*, *Celebrate Recovery Booklet: 28 Devotions*, *Celebrate Recovery Journal*, *Celebrate Recovery Prayer Journal*, *Testimonies to Go*, *Testimonies to Go: Special Edition with John and Cheryl Baker*, *Never Let Go*, *Senior Pastor Support* DVD, *Worship* DVDs, *Celebrate Recovery Words* DVD, *Celebrate Recovery Visual Kit*, *The Landing*, and *Celebration Place*, and are to be used exclusively.

The 3 Doors of Celebrate Recovery

There are 3 equally powerful elements of Celebrate Recovery to begin your ministry. We call them the 3 Doors of Celebrate Recovery. After prayerfully considering your resources, you may choose to start your Celebrate Recovery with all 3 Doors, or you may choose to start with 1, 2 or all 3 Doors. If you start with 1 Door we recommend you start with either Open Share or Step Study Groups, rather than Large Group.

The following illustration will help you understand the components of each of the 3 Doors of Celebrate Recovery: the Large Group, Open Share Group, and Step Study Group.

Large Group	Open Share Group	Step Study Group
• One-hour • In person or online • Mixed recovery issues • Mixed-gender • Open to newcomers • No sharing • Information table • Worship • 8 Principles or 12 Steps read • Announcements • Acknowledge sobriety (chips) • Lesson from the Celebrate Recovery Leader's Guide or a testimony • Serenity Prayer • Dismiss to Open Share Groups or Newcomers 101	• One-hour • In person or online • Mixed recovery issues and/or recovery issue-specific • Gender-specific • Open to newcomers • Share struggles and victories, free to pass • Acknowledge sobriety (chips) • Follow the Small Group Guidelines • Build relationships to find sponsor and/or accountability team	• 1 1/2 to 2-hour meeting • In person or online • Mixed recovery issues • Gender-specific • Open to newcomers at beginning, closed after a few weeks • Sharing expected, answer questions using The Journey Begins or The Journey Continues Participant's Guides • Follow the Small Group Guidelines • Weekly attendance expected • Build relationships to find sponsor and/or accountability team • High level of accountability

Large Group

- One-hour
- In person or online
- Mixed recovery issues
- Mixed-gender
- Open to newcomers
- No sharing
- Information table
- Worship
- 8 Principles or 12 Steps read
- Announcements
- Acknowledge sobriety (chips)
- Lesson from the Celebrate Recovery Leader's Guide or a testimony
- Serenity Prayer
- Dismiss to Open Share Groups or Newcomers 101

Open Share Group

- One-hour
- In person or online
- Mixed recovery issues and/or recovery issue-specific
- Gender-specific
- Open to newcomers
- Share struggles and victories, free to pass
- Acknowledge sobriety (chips)
- Follow the Small Group Guidelines
- Build relationships to find sponsor and/or accountability team

Step Study Group

- 1 1/2 to 2-hour meeting
- In person or online
- Mixed recovery issues
- Gender-specific
- Open to newcomers at beginning, closed after a few weeks

- Sharing expected, answer questions using *The Journey Begins* or *The Journey Continues Participant's Guides*
- Follow the Small Group Guidelines
- Weekly attendance expected
- Build relationships to find sponsor and/or accountability team
- High level of accountability

Implementing the Celebrate Recovery Start-Up Strategy

This simple yet effective start-up strategy will help you organize and plan your Celebrate Recovery ministry. The churches that have followed this strategy have been able to smoothly and effectively begin helping those in their church and community who are struggling with a hurt, hang-up, or habit. This strategy is broken up into three phases and each phase is designed to help you build a strong foundation to support your ministry both at the beginning and as it grows. The strategy can take as little as 90 days or as long as a year, depending on how you decide to handle your initial volunteers/leaders Step Study, which will be discussed in Phase 2.

Phase 1: Investigate, Communicate, and Invite

Investigate www.celebraterecovery.com

On the website you can:

- Search for Celebrate Recovery ministries in your local area. Visit as many of these as you can. Although each ministry will have its own unique personality, you will be able to see how the DNA of Celebrate Recovery is kept intact.
- Check out the free training videos available through the website for starting a Celebrate Recovery.
- Investigate all of the free and paid resources we offer to help you launch and grow your ministry and your leaders.
- It is highly recommended that you initially order the *Celebrate Recovery Curriculum Kit*, which includes a sample set of CR Curriculum and resources for getting a CR started:
    - ✓ 1 Leader's Guide
    - ✓ 1 copy of the *Celebrate Recovery Participant's Guide, Volumes 1–4* (The Journey Begins)

✓ 1 copy of the *Celebrate Recovery Participant's Guide, Volumes 5–8* (The Journey Continues)
✓ 1 copy of the *Celebrate Recovery Study Bible*
✓ 1 copy of *Your First Step to Celebrate Recovery*
✓ 1 copy of the *Celebrate Recovery Daily Devotional* booklet

Consider reading *Life's Healing Choices* by John Baker. It would be helpful to read it at this time to gain a broad understanding of the Celebrate Recovery principles of recovery. There are also free resources available for use at https://celebraterecovery.com/free-resources/ including video messages, mp3 files, and text from the Leader's Guide.

Communicate
Communicate with your CR Representative.

- Your CR Representative is a valuable resource who will come alongside you and can support and guide you along the way. They are Celebrate Recovery participants themselves who have experience in CR leadership and have served on a T.E.A.M. in their local ministries. (T.E.A.M. will be covered in a later section.)
- Go to celebraterecovery.com to find a CR Rep near you.

Communicate with your church.

- Set up an appointment to share your vision with your senior pastor and any of those who will be supervising this ministry. On celebraterecovery.com we offer a free videos of Pastors Rick Warren, John Baker, and Johnny Baker explaining the benefits of this program from a pastor's key point of view.
- Use church bulletin announcements, flyers, video, social media and your church website to communicate the plans to bring Celebrate Recovery to your church.

Invite

Invite anyone in your church who is interested to join you for an informational meeting. At this meeting:

- Share your plans and begin to recruit support. Christ-centered and/or secular recovery experience is helpful. Some people will be potential leaders; others may want to come alongside the ministry in other areas, such as worship or childcare.

- Create a sign-up sheet for those interested in possibly serving as leaders or volunteers for your Celebrate Recovery ministry.
- Invite those who signed up to begin working through Phase 2: Train, Plan, Prepare.

Phase 2: Train, Plan, and Prepare

Train

We suggest you meet twice a week with your potential leaders and volunteers; once a week for training and planning, and once a week to work through a Celebrate Recovery Step Study. This will provide your team with some Celebrate Recovery experience. Some may have 12 Step experience, but you want to ensure that all have experienced aspects of Celebrate Recovery so they may lead others with integrity.

Whether you launch with 1, 2, or 3 of The Doors of Celebrate Recovery, it is recommended that your team complete volume 1 in the Participant's Guide, at minimum, and then continue to meet after the launch of your Celebrate Recovery to complete your Step Study. However, you may decide to complete Volumes 2, 3, and/or 4 to gain more personal recovery experience before launching your ministry. You will continue to meet twice a week once your General Meeting Night Launches if your Step Studies have not been completed. Your planning and training night will transition to your General Meeting Night when you're ready to launch, and you will continue the Step Study on the other night.

If your Step Studies have not been completed by the time you launch, continue to meet twice a week. If you will be launching with all 3 Doors, your planning and training night will transition to what is called the General Meeting Night, consisting of Large Group and Open Share Groups. Please Note: for this reason, it's important that your training night be the same night of the week that you intend your General Meeting Night to be once you launch. You will continue the leader/volunteer Step Study on the second night of the week.

Once your Celebrate Recovery has been up and running for 6 months or more, you may decide to offer Step Studies to your participants. Step Studies are held on a different night of the week than the General Meeting Night. This will be discussed in later sections of this guide.

Before meeting with your potential leaders and volunteers:

- Familiarize yourself with the *Celebrate Recovery Curriculum Kit* and its components.
- Purchase a copy of *The Journey Begins Participant's Guide* and a Leader's Guide for each volunteer/leader.

Below is the suggested format for your weekly meetings:

Night 1: Planning & Training (1–1.5 hours)

- Open with prayer
- Train on topics from the Leader's Guide (use only those trainings necessary for your initial leaders/volunteers Step Study and the Doors that you will be implementing at your Celebrate Recovery):
  - ➤ Facilitating your General Meeting Night (page 20)
  - ➤ Large Group Format (page 267, and APPENDIX 9)
  - ➤ Open Share Group Format (page 267 and APPENDIX 9)
  - ➤ Step Study Group Format (page 267 and APPENDIX 9)
  - ➤ Guidelines (page 275 and APPENDIX 11)
- Plan: (Outlined in the next section)

Night 2: Step Study Group (1.5–2 hours)

- Meet in separate men's and women's Step Study Groups.
- Refer to page 22 for the DNA Step Study Group Format.

Plan

Some of the components discussed below will be described in more detail in later sections of this chapter. This will simply give you an idea of what elements to consider for your Celebrate Recovery ministry.

Things to consider for your Celebrate Recovery ministry, whether you will launch with 1, 2, or 3 Doors:

- Childcare: Although childcare is not mandatory, it is HIGHLY recommended. Determine the ages that will be included. Refer to your family ministries director/pastor for proper procedures for your church.
- Fellowship Events: Decide if you will be offering fellowship events, before and/or after your Large Group and/or Open Share Groups. These are optional elements that will help to build community and improve the experience for participants.
- Food: Decide if you will serve dinner/snacks and/or coffee/desserts during your fellowship events.
- Just keep it simple and do what is appropriate for your ministry.

Things to consider for Large Group:

- Worship: Determine if the worship component will consist of lyric videos, acoustic with a single person, or a full band, etc.
- Teaching/Testimony: Decide who will be teaching the twenty-five lessons from this Leader's Guide along with who will be sharing their written testimonies. Consider scheduling these components on a quarterly basis.

Things to consider for Open Share Groups:

- Initial Open Share Groups: Determine which groups you will offer. If you only have enough leaders for one women's and one men's group, start with a women's mixed issues group and a men's mixed issues group. If you are able to have two of each group, a suggestion would be to add a men's chemically-dependent group and women's chemically-dependent group.
- Leaders: We recommend two Open Share Group leaders per group according to their recovery experience, leadership skills, and training.

Prepare

- Set the date and location for your Celebrate Recovery ministry.
- Contact your CR Rep if you have questions as you prepare to launch.
- Confirm commitments from those assisting in facilities, worship, childcare, and food.
- Finalize assignments for roles in the Large Group Meeting and Open Share Groups.
- Invite the church. Put information about Celebrate Recovery in the church bulletin and/or set up an information table during church services. Consider creating an informational brochure. You could also use church announcements to show the pastor's support and approval of the program. This will let everyone know that your church is a safe place to deal with their hurts, hang-ups, and habits. *Emphasize that Celebrate Recovery is NOT just for chemical dependency.
- An excellent way to help your church learn about your upcoming Celebrate Recovery ministry is to consider having your church use the *Life's Healing Choices* book. This book will greatly enhance your congregation's understanding of the scope of Celebrate Recovery's hurts, hang-ups, and habits.
- Invite the outside community. Consider having a soft launch or dress rehearsal first. This will give you a few meetings to have things running smoothly before the public arrives.
- Open the doors on your launch date—well equipped and ready.

- Have fun!
- PRAY CONTINUOUSLY!

Phase 3: Continuing Growth

Continue to stay in touch with your CR Rep. He or she will guide you in the process of getting your program listed on the Celebrate Recovery Locator.

Check the Celebrate Recovery website to find online and in-person training events and Summit dates.

Consider purchasing the *Celebrate Recovery Advanced Leadership Training Guide* once your ministry has been going for 6 months or so. This resource is next level training that will be valuable to your ministry to further equip and empower your leaders once they have some experience in leading groups and other components of the ministry. One way the ALT helps with this is by explaining how to start and conduct regular monthly leader's meetings.

The *Advanced Leadership Training Guide* includes:

- Ministry and Leader Resources
- Training scripts and handouts for: Sponsor training, Writing Your Testimony training, New Leader Orientation, Small Group Guidelines Training, Open Share Group Leader training, Newcomers 101 Leader training, Step Study Leader training, 4th and 5th Step training, and Mental Health training.
- Additional Leader training for monthly leaders meeting or special lesson nights.
- Celebration Place/The Landing training.

We recommend waiting six months or so after you launch before offering Step Study Groups to your Celebrate Recovery participants. This will accomplish four things:

1. Leaders will have time to complete the initial Step Study if they did not complete it before your launch.
2. Your Celebrate Recovery will have a chance to grow and develop.
3. Your participants will have a chance to get comfortable in Open Share Groups before going deeper in a Step Study.
4. Your leaders will gain experience in leading Open Share Groups, preparing them to be effective Step Study leaders.

As your ministry and leadership grow, consider starting *Celebration Place* and *The Landing*. Go to celebraterecovery.com for resource options.

- *Celebration Place* is created for children ages five to eleven. The beauty of *Celebration Place* is that it addresses the very same topics adults are learning about in Celebrate Recovery—but in kid-friendly ways. This approach initiates positive, fun, faith-filled conversations between kids and parents that let them practice open communication and sharing in ways they may never have before.
- *The Landing*: *The Landing* is a dynamic resource that targets and assists students. Young people can break patterns of unhealthy behavior through the community, teaching, and experiences they'll discover at The Landing. They'll examine the past decisions that led them to where they are today; talk about the patterns and behaviors that keep them trapped; pursue the life-changing truths of freedom found throughout the Bible; and commit to living differently and building healthy relationships with family members, adult leaders, and trusted peers.

Final Thoughts

This Start-Up Strategy is meant to help you prepare, launch, and maintain a healthy Celebrate Recovery ministry. You may need to spend more time in one area than another. Some ministries complete the CR Start-Up Strategy in 90 days, others take up to a year or longer if they choose to complete their initial Step Study with their potential leaders and volunteers before launching their ministry. There is no right or wrong amount of time to take. It's up to you to decide what is best for your church and Ministry. The important thing is that you take advantage of the years of experience of the CR Global Team and thousands of others that have paved the way. Stay connected and don't be afraid to ask questions. You have lots of support!

Seven Keys for a Healthy Celebrate Recovery

There are seven keys to a healthy Celebrate Recovery Ministry: **(1) senior pastor support, (2) leadership training, (3) worship, (4) groups, (5) fellowship, (6) curriculum, and (7) outreach.** Think of the seven keys this way: Jesus Christ is the one and only true Higher Power. He is the rock, the foundation, of the Celebrate Recovery program. Proverbs 9:1 tells us, "Wisdom has built her house; she has set up its seven pillars." Each of the seven keys act like a pillar built on the foundation and supported by the foundation—Jesus Christ. The seven keys, in turn, are the pillars that help support your Celebrate Recovery ministry.

It's important to note that not every CR will start with all 7 keys. You will most likely add them as your ministry grows and matures. The more keys you have in place the more secure your CR ministry will be.

Senior Pastor Support

The first key for a healthy CR ministry is senior pastor support. We can't emphasize the importance of this key enough.

So Christ himself gave the apostles, the prophets, the evangelists, the pastors and teachers, to equip his people for works of service, so that the body of Christ may be built up until we all reach unity in the faith and in the knowledge of the Son of God and become mature, attaining to the whole measure of the fullness of Christ. (Ephesians 4:11–13)

Your pastor's support of the CR ministry at your campus makes it acceptable and safe for someone to be in recovery. It is not just "those" people anymore—it's "us"!

This support goes both ways. It's just as important for the CR ministry at your church to support your pastor(s). The ministry, first and foremost, is there to serve the needs of the church community. If you want your CR to be supported by the church as a whole, it needs to act as a regular ministry of the church, not as something separate. Celebrate Recovery should participate in all church-wide events, as this is a great way to support your church, and get the word out about CR to the church community.

If you feel you need help in obtaining your senior pastor's or elder board's support, a great tool is the video found in the videos found on the Celebrate Recovery website (under Free Resources). Make an appointment with your senior pastor or elders and watch the video together. It is a concise overview of the Celebrate Recovery ministry. They will have an opportunity to hear from the hearts of Pastor Rick Warren, John Baker, and Johnny Baker about how God has changed lives through the ministry of Celebrate Recovery.

Leadership Training

The second key to a healthy Celebrate Recovery Ministry is leadership training. Proverbs 23:12 says, "Apply your heart to instruction and your ears to words of knowledge." It has been said, "Once you stop learning, you stop leading."

If we had to choose one word that would describe the leadership training for Celebrate Recovery, it would be consistent. Consistency with how often we train our leaders, and what we train our leaders are both vital. Scheduling monthly leader's meetings to provide ongoing training for our leaders and to discuss recovery issues and group dynamics keep our leaders learning and growing. These leader's meetings include four elements: planning, training, sharing, and fellowship time.

- Planning time includes assigning the lessons that will be taught by the teaching team and lining up the testimonies for the next month. In addition, assignments for the General Meeting Night and other special events are given out at this time.

- The training time will be conducted by the Training Coach and/or Ministry Leader. More about these roles and others will be explained in a later section. The trainings found in this CR Leader's Guide are to train and equip leaders for a new Celebrate Recovery start-up. As your ministry grows you can add trainings from the CR *Advanced Leader Training Guide*, as well as trainings found through the Celebrate Recovery Website. These resources, as well as any additional training provided by the CR Global Team, are how we keep our training consistent.
- During sharing time we encourage the leaders to break into small groups. This gives them an opportunity to share different ideas for handling a conflict in their group, implementing the Small Group Guidelines, or any general tips or strategies that have worked in their groups. They can also use this time to share their experiences, strengths, hopes, and especially their struggles with one another.
- We use the fellowship time in our leader's meetings to allow the leaders time to connect with each other. This is a great time to share what Christ has done in each of our lives and to bond us as a ministry team in purpose and spirit.

We recommend your leader's sign an annual leadership covenant and that they meet the following minimum qualifications. However, every church has different requirements to serve as a leader in the ministries of that church, so discuss it with your church leadership and adapt accordingly.

1. They are a growing Christian, not a new believer.
2. They have worked hard on their own recovery and are able to talk comfortably about their own victories and struggles.
3. They have completed a Step Study using the Celebrate Recovery *Participant's Guides*.
4. They have a strong personal support network.
5. They agree to attend ongoing monthly leader's meetings.

<u>Worship</u>

The third key for a healthy Celebrate Recovery Ministry is worship. We begin every Large Group Meeting with twenty minutes of praise and worship through music. This time is important for the following reasons:

- Worship music is a major strength and difference between a Christ-centered and a secular recovery program.

    And you will sing as on the night you celebrate a holy festival; your hearts will rejoice as when people playing pipes go up to the mountain of the LORD, to the Rock of Israel. (Isaiah 30:29)

- Worship music provides a time for everyone to put aside the busyness and hassles of the world and get in touch with the true Higher Power, Jesus Christ. It allows time for the power of the Holy Spirit to fill all those who attend with a peace and a safety that only He can provide. There will be people present who are hurting so badly that they may be able to express their pain only through silent prayer and worship.

- Worship music gives us a vehicle in which to celebrate our recoveries! I suggest keeping the praise songs upbeat to build up, strengthen, and encourage those who attend, and to focus on the joy of God's presence, peace, and power in their recoveries.

It doesn't matter what size your Celebrate Recovery ministry is; a twenty-piece band is not necessary to incorporate worship music into your recovery program. When Celebrate Recovery started in 1991, we had two singers and a three-piece band. Whether you use a full band, a video, stream music, or simply find someone who can lead while playing a guitar, just be sure to include worship music as a key part of your recovery program.

Groups

The fourth key for a healthy CR ministry is groups.

Two are better than one, because they have a good return for their labor: If either of them falls down, one can help the other up. But pity anyone who falls and has no one to help them up. Also, if two lie down together, they will keep warm. But how can one keep warm alone? Though one may be overpowered, two can defend themselves. A cord of three strands is not quickly broken. (Ecclesiastes 4:9–12)

We have three different groups in Celebrate Recovery: Large Group, Open Share Group, and Step Study. To keep consistency and safety in all CR ministries, all three groups have a DNA format. The Large Group is mixed-gender, and Open Share Group and Step Study are gender-specific.

The two main reasons we do not have co-ed Open Share and Step Study Groups are:

- We have found that the level of sharing is not as deep when men and women are in the same group. For example, how can someone struggling with sexual addiction share in a mixed group? It would be inappropriate for them to share in a mixed group to the level that they need to.
- We believe it increases the level of safety for the individuals in the group as some participants may try to use the vulnerability of sharing during group time as a means to connect romantically with another participant.

It is important to start your recovery ministry slowly. In the beginning, the four Open Share Groups we recommend starting are Men's Mixed Issues, Men's Chemical Dependency, Women's Mixed Issues and Women's Chemical Dependency. However, if you only have enough leaders to start with two groups, start with Men's Mixed Issues, and Women's Mixed Issues. You can help the most people by starting with these two groups because anyone can join the Mixed Issue Group.

As you grow, you can add new issue-specific groups as you have leaders able to facilitate them. It's likely you'll have people coming to you saying, "Why don't you have an Open Share Group for this addiction or this compulsion or behavior?" or "Don't you consider this other struggle as important as your chemically-dependent group?" And you might find it hard not to say, "We'll start it next week!" Then go off and try to find someone to lead it. But there is a better way to grow your recovery ministry.

We recommend the following system for starting new Open Share Groups. When someone comes and asks to start a new Open Share Group, ask them if they have at least a consecutive year of recovery in this area. (This experience could be Christ-centered or secular.) If they say yes, and are a trained leader, this may be a good opportunity to start that new Open Share Group. If they say no, ask them if they know of anyone who does have recovery in that area. You can possibly pursue it with that other person, if they are a trained leader. If the response to both of those questions is no, then you can offer to notify them if you're able to offer that Open Share Group at a later time.

A good best practice when starting a new Open Share Group is to have one of the leaders of the new group give their testimony in the Large Group Meeting around the time you are launching the Open Share Group.

We recommend having two trained leaders ready to lead the group, if possible.

It is better to have fewer healthy Open Share Groups than many unhealthy Open Share Groups. We would rather disappoint people by not having a group when they want it than cause someone great harm by having a group without trained and qualified leaders.

Fellowship Events

The fifth key for a healthy Celebrate Recovery Ministry is fellowship events. "And if anyone gives even a cup of cold water to one of these little ones who is my disciple, truly I tell you, that person will certainly not lose their reward" (Matthew 10:42).

At Celebrate Recovery, the main focus of every fellowship event is to help participants develop healthy relationships that will grow into a support team of sponsors and accountability partners. We want to provide a place where people in recovery can join together, fellowship with one another, and share God's answer on how to overcome their struggles by His power.

At Celebrate Recovery we have two main fellowship events, a meal before Large Group and/or a cafe time following Open Share Groups. Both of these fellowship events are designed to encourage individuals to meet and provide a forum for the building of accountability teams and sponsorship relationships. We don't assign sponsors; it is each person's responsibility to find Accountability Partners and Sponsors. Also, these fellowship events are a great way to get everyone involved in 12-Step service. Someone may not meet all the requirements of being a Celebrate Recovery leader. However, he or she can start serving and giving back by volunteering to help out at one of the fellowship events.

Curriculum

The sixth key for a healthy Celebrate Recovery ministry program is curriculum. Romans 15:4 tells us, "For everything that was written in the past was written to teach us, so that through the endurance taught in the Scriptures and the encouragement they provide we might have hope."

The Celebrate Recovery curriculum is effective because it fulfills the following four requirements:

- First, the foundation of our curriculum is the Bible. God's Word needs to be at the center of your recovery ministry. And it can't be if it is not the center of your curriculum.
- Second, our curriculum is applicable to all groups, all areas of recovery, and all ages. At Celebrate Recovery, we want to break the family's cycle of dysfunction at the youngest

level—the kids. That's why we have The Landing for students and Celebration Place for five- to eleven-year-olds. Both programs are based on Celebrate Recovery.

- Third, our curriculum is easy to use. Remember, it's impossible to eat an elephant in one bite, but if you cut it up in small pieces it becomes much easier. Though not necessarily any tastier!
- Fourth, our curriculum creates movement through the Steps. Our curriculum creates a clear path through the recovery process.

The Celebrate Recovery curriculum fulfills all four of these curriculum requirements! It is built on God's Word, it can be used in all areas of recovery, it's easy to use, and it moves participants through the steps.

Outreach

The last of the seven keys for keeping your recovery ministry healthy and growing is outreach. Matthew 5:14–16 tells us that we are to be " 'the light of the world. A town built on a hill cannot be hidden. Neither do people light a lamp and put it under a bowl. Instead they put it on its stand, and it gives light to everyone in the house. In the same way, let your light shine before others so that they may see your good deeds and glorify your Father in heaven.' "

There are two groups of people we are looking to reach with Celebrate Recovery. The first group is those who know Jesus, but don't know they struggle with hurts, hang-ups, or habits, or maybe they don't feel they have a safe place to share their struggles. This group is your church community. There are so many people in your church each weekend who are silently suffering because they don't yet know CR is a safe option for them. This is why it's so important to have a presence in the church and be active in church events, so you can get the word out to your church community that CR is a safe place to find healing. This is also why it is important to stress that Celebrate Recovery is NOT just for drug addicts and alcoholics, but anyone with a hurt, hang-up, or habit!

The second group is those who know they're hurting/struggling and need help, but don't know Jesus. We have a great opportunity to provide a safe place for people to find healing, but more importantly for them to find Jesus. When people come to your CR who don't know Jesus and are not a member of your church, you have a great opportunity to help them find a church home. Some ways to do this are to make announcements during the Large Group Meeting about what the sermon will be about the next weekend, and to invite them to any community events your church will be hosting. Always invite them to attend the weekend service during your Large Group Meeting. Have a slide with the service times for your church, along with any other important info for the weekend service.

Once you have established that your CR ministry is part of and for your local church community, it's time to begin to look outside your church walls to the second group of people through community outreach.

We recommend you inform local Christian counselors/therapists about your CR ministry. They may be looking for more tools to offer their clients. Other outreach opportunities include reaching out to local recovery houses, rescue missions, and prisons/jails. You can either bring CR to them, or invite them to attend your Celebrate Recovery ministry. For even more outreach opportunities, go to celebraterecovery.com.

The most effective way to practice this key is to share your story. This can be done by offering to share your Celebrate Recovery testimony at other local CR ministries, or just by letting people in your life know how Jesus has impacted your life through CR. Even just wearing a hat or t-shirt from your local group can be a great way to get a conversation started.

The best outreach tool is word of mouth! Just like the woman at the well who, after she had an encounter with Jesus, ran through her town yelling, "Come, see a man who told me everything I ever did. Could this be the Messiah?" (John 4:29) She couldn't keep the good news to herself, and as a result many believed in Jesus. John 4:39 tells us, "Many of the Samaritans from that town believed in him because of the woman's testimony, 'He told me everything I ever did.' "

Facilitating Your Celebrate Recovery Groups

Fellowship Dinner

You may choose to offer dinner as a Fellowship Event before your Open Share Group, Step Study Group, or Large Group. This can be done in different ways; every week, bi-monthly, monthly, or quarterly, as a full meal, or just appetizers or finger foods. There is a lot of flexibility to fit the needs of your ministry. If you use the same space for dinner and the Large Group Meeting for a General Meeting Night, clear all food away fifteen minutes before the Large Group Meeting starts.

A General Meeting Night consists of two Doors of Celebrate Recovery: the Large Group and Open Share Groups. As discussed in the Start-up Strategy, your Celebrate Recovery may include one Door with Open Share or Step Study Groups.

Now, we'll cover some information about the different elements of the General Meeting Night. Some of the components below may also be included in a Celebrate Recovery that offers one Door. You decide which components to include depending on the resources available to you. As your CR grows you may decide to include additional components.

Greeters

Greeters are extremely important both in making a positive first impression on all newcomers and in encouraging regular attendees. This is a great service opportunity for anyone who is new to recovery and looking to serve.

Have Greeters stationed and ready fifteen minutes before they are scheduled to serve. If your CR passes out handouts and/or a bulletin, have them ready for the Greeters to give to participants as they arrive.

Information Table

The information table is a key part of helping the newcomer feel welcome. The info table should be inviting and its location clearly marked. Having a table banner, overhead banner, or sign clearly marks its location and purpose for newcomers.

The table should be staffed by at least one man and one woman. (We do this to be sensitive to those in attendance. A woman with abuse issues, for example, would find it difficult to seek information from a man.) Info table volunteers should arrive early to be ready to connect with participants. They can answer questions, give directions, make connections, and handle resource sales. Make sure whoever will be handling the resource sales is trustworthy and knows and follows your church policies for handling monies.

The following are some examples of the resources that may be available at the information table:

- CR Resources and Curriculum for sale (cannot sale for profit)
- Welcome Newcomers (Appendix 6)
- 8 Recovery Principles Based on the Beatitudes
- Celebrate Recovery's 12 Steps and Their Biblical Comparisons
- Things We Are, Things We Are Not (Appendix 7)
- CR Issue Pamphlets[1]

The DNA of Celebrate Recovery states that only approved CR Curriculum and resources may be used at a Celebrate Recovery ministry. Therefore, please do not include other recovery resources at your information table. No exceptions for other literature! While there are

---

1. If you display CR Issue Pamphlets, please use only the most up-to-date versions available at celebraterecovery.com. These are the only CR approved issue pamphlets. If they're not on the CR official website, they're not DNA approved. This includes outdated CR Info sheets included in older CR Curriculum.

many wonderful recovery resources available, having them on your info table will confuse and distract people from the primary purpose of learning about and following the 12 Step recovery process.

*If you display CR Issue Pamphlets, please use only the most up-to-date versions available at celebraterecovery.com. These are the only CR approved issue pamphlets. If they are not on the CR official website, they are not DNA approved. This includes outdated CR Info sheets included in older CR Curriculum.

Large Group

The Large Group is designed to enable participants to set aside the busyness and the stresses of the outside world. It includes a time of worship music, and alternates each week with one of the twenty-five lessons from the *Celebrate Recovery Leader's Guide* or a testimony. This time begins to unfold the safe environment essential for recovery. It allows those present to get in touch with the one and only Higher Power, Jesus Christ, to hear lessons that help them learn how to work through the 8 Recovery Principles and 12 Steps, and to hear testimonies of those who have found healing through Jesus Christ in Celebrate Recovery. These elements bring hope to those who attend.

Praise the LORD. Praise God in his sanctuary; praise him in his mighty heavens. Praise him for his acts of power; praise him for his surpassing greatness. Praise him with the sounding of the trumpet, praise him with the harp and lyre, praise him with timbrel and dancing, praise him with the strings and pipe, praise him with the clash of cymbals, praise him with resounding cymbals. Let everything that has breath praise the LORD. Praise the LORD. (Psalm 150:1–6)

DNA Format for Large Group

One hour in length

(The order of the format is flexible. As long as the components are included, you may adjust the flow of events as you desire.)

- Welcome and Open in Prayer
- Worship Music
- Read the 8 Principles or Christ-centered 12 Steps, with Biblical comparisons

- Lesson or Testimony*
  > Testimonies are to be written in advance, edited and approved by the Ministry Leader or Team Member, and must be read using the approved edited version.
- Closing Prayer (It is optional to close with the Serenity Prayer; however, it is highly recommended.)
- Dismissal to Open Share Groups

Optional best practice elements:
- Announcements
- Chip ceremony
- Special music with offering or invitation
- Guest speaker or special lesson a few times a year.

Opening Song, Welcome, and Prayer

It is important to begin and end each Large Group promptly. This will ensure that you have a full hour for the Open Share Group Meetings immediately following Large Group. Choose an opening praise song that is very upbeat and familiar. An opening song helps bring people into the worship area. After the song, someone on the leadership team welcomes everyone, especially newcomers, then prays the opening prayer. This is a good opportunity to have participants greet one another if you like.

8 Principles or 12 Steps and Their Biblical Comparisons

Two individuals are selected to read the 8 Principles or the 12 Steps and their biblical comparisons. The purpose is twofold: (1) to reinforce the biblical foundation for the program, and (2) to allow increased participation for Celebrate Recovery attendees. One person is asked to read the principle/step and another reads the Bible verse for that principle/step until all 8 principles/12 Steps are completed.

Example:

First reader: "Principle 1: Realize I'm not God. I admit that I am powerless to control my tendency to do the wrong thing and that my life is unmanageable."

Second reader: "Blessed are the poor in spirit, for theirs is the kingdom of heaven." (Matthew 5:3)

Announcements

The primary purpose of the announcements is to help the newcomers feel welcome and inform them about Newcomers 101 (if you offer it). You may also invite participants to your weekend services at this time if they do not have a church home and announce upcoming events both at your CR and your church. Announcements can be shared at any time during your meeting; at the beginning, after worship music, at the end, or split up at different times in the meeting. Determine what works best for your ministry.

While an important part of the program, announcements can be rather "dry," so we attempt to make them light, fun and keep them short. Welcome the Newcomer (without singling them out individually—they will not feel safe). Remind everyone that CR is a safe place. You may also invite participants to your weekend services at this time if they do not have a church home and announce upcoming events both at your CR and your church. Include Step Study announcements and fellowship events.

Worship

At Celebrate Recovery, one of the many ways we choose to worship is through singing. Including two to three worship songs allows participants to lean in and focus on Jesus as their higher power and to prepare their hearts and minds for the lesson or testimony and Open Share Groups.

During one of the worship songs, you may choose to take a collection or love offering. Announce that the money collected supports childcare, pays for special speakers, and/or offsets regular expenses. Make it clear that no one is obligated to give to this offering!

You may also choose to close with a worship song to give participants an opportunity to respond to what they've heard.

Lesson or Testimony

As mentioned previously, we teach the twenty-five lessons from the *Celebrate Recovery Leader's Guide*. Typically, we follow a teaching week with a testimony week. Appendix 4 is a guide to help you generate healthy testimonies, and Appendix 5 has three sample testimonies for you to review. These sample testimonies are not meant to be read in your Large Group Meeting, but to give you an example of written and edited testimonies.

When lessons are taught, you may use the lesson handout notes provided on celebraterecovery.com. The lesson handout notes also provide the Leader's Focus Question for Open Share Groups.

We strongly recommend using the lessons, as is, from the Leader's Guide the first time a new teacher teaches the lesson. Once they become more comfortable, however, they may come up with their own introductions, illustrations, and closings while the acrostic and scriptures must be used, unchanged, every time according to the DNA. They can be creative and teach from their own experience, adding personal stories. This makes the lesson real for everyone while modeling transparency and honesty. We have created videos, available at celebraterecovery.com > resources, to help with:

- How to teach the lessons
- How to be creative with teaching the lessons
- Actual lessons taught by the Global CR team that you may show at your Large Group Meeting, or watch to get an idea on how to teach a lesson

On testimony night, consider asking the person's Sponsor, or a member of their Accountability Team, to introduce them, and ask them to keep the introduction brief.

Testimonies are to be completely written out, word for word. The Ministry Leader reads, reviews, and approves them, and participants read the final approved version as it is written. This may feel restrictive, but this keeps the Large Group safe.

Why Is It Necessary to Have Testimonies Written and Reviewed?

- It helps the presenter prepare with confidence.
- It avoids triggers.
- It prevents unnecessary offense.
- It eliminates "churchy" language.
- It ensures that the testimony focuses on recovery principles and experiences.
- It provides a working text for preparing short testimonies for other venues.

What Are the Reasons for Reading a Testimony from a Script?

- It places the focus on what God has done.
- It ensures that what has been approved is what is shared.
- It feels safer and is consistent for all, as everyone reads their testimony. No one needs to be a public speaker.

- It frees the emotions of the participant.
- It ensures the length of the testimony enables the Large Group Meeting to end on time.

New Celebrate Recovery ministries may find it challenging to include a live testimony every other week. Contact neighboring churches with Celebrate Recovery ministries to invite them to share their testimonies at your Celebrate Recovery. Also consider using the "Testimonies to Go" DVDs or testimonies found through celebraterecovery.com.

Yearly Lesson and Testimony Schedule

The DNA Yearly Lesson and Testimony Schedule can also be found in Appendix 9. This plan is designed to cover the twenty-five Large Group lessons (which are the same lessons covered in the *The Journey Begins Participant's Guides*) over a one-year period, alternating with testimonies, and allowing a few nights for special music, lessons, events, or speakers. You may choose to invite a special guest speaker such as a Christian counselor in the area, or a pastor from your church. We recommend sharing with them which Step was taught the week prior, and ask them to focus on that step. Be sure to preview their talk to keep your group safe.

A lesson is taught one week and a testimony is shared the following week. This schedule is repeated annually, as we teach the same lessons every year.

Week	Principle	Large Group Teaching
1		Introduction/Overview of Program
2	1	Lesson 1: Denial
3	1	Testimony
4	1	Lesson 2: Powerless
5	1	Testimony
6	2	Lesson 3: Hope
7	2	Testimony
8	2	Special Music, Lesson, Event or Speaker
9	2	Lesson 4: Sanity
10	2	Testimony
11	3	Lesson 5: Turn
12	3	Testimony
13	3	Lesson 6: Action
14	3	Testimony
15	4	Lesson 7: Sponsor
16	4	Testimony
17	4	Lesson 8: Moral
18	4	Testimony
19	4	Lesson 9: Inventory
20	4	Testimony
21	4	Special Music, Lesson, Event or Speaker
22	4	Lesson 10: Spiritual Inventory Part 1
23	4	Testimony
24	4	Lesson 11: Spiritual Inventory Part 2
25	4	Lesson 12: Confess

Prayer and Dismissal to Open Share Groups

If you have a guest speaker or a testimony, you may have the leader return to the stage to thank them, and then introduce the person closing in prayer. One option is to end the Large Group with reading the complete version of Reinhold Neibuhr's Serenity Prayer. We recommend displaying the prayer on a screen so everyone can join in reading it together.

After the closing prayer, remember to announce where the Men's and Women's Open Share Groups will be meeting if you did not already. If you offer Newcomers 101 announce it at this time as well. Remind them, if anyone is unsure of where to go for Open Share Group, to find a leader and they will be happy to help. And that if they have questions, they can stop by the Celebrate Recovery information table or ask one of the Celebrate Recovery leaders.

Chips

Some Celebrate Recovery ministries may choose to hand out chips to celebrate and recognize sobriety dates, while others offer recovery chips during Open Share Groups. It's up to your CR ministry to decide how often and in which groups you will offer chips.

Example Large Group Runsheet

Below is an example of what your Large Group Meeting might look like. Again, you know your worship culture. You will also find a Large Group runsheet template to use for scheduling, or your church might use a scheduling app or software. Whatever you use, we recommend the Worship Leader, audio/tech Person, and anyone assigned a task to receive a copy of the week's Large Group runsheet before start time. When everyone is informed, the evening runs smoother.

Note: The Celebrate Recovery Visual Kit contains PowerPoint® presentations and many helpful tools that will save you hours of work for your Large Group.

Remember to keep all the required DNA elements, and start and end on time. We recommend that you schedule volunteers and communicate ahead of time who will be handling the different elements for the night so that they can be prepared. Have any materials and information they will need ready for them. For those who will be a part of the Large Group experience, ask them to sit in the front row so they are ready when Large Group begins. It can be helpful to have a dedicated person who makes sure all volunteers are present, have everything they need, and are given any necessary instructions.

Sample Large Group Format

Time	Length	Element/Notes
7:00 pm	4-5 min	Opening worship song
7:05 pm	2 min	Welcome and Opening Prayer
7:07 pm	12 min	Worship music
7:19 pm	3-4 min	Read the 8 Principles or 12 Steps
7:23 pm	3-4 min	Announcements
7:26 pm	3-4 min	Special Music and Offering
7:30 pm	20 min	Teaching or Testimony (includes introducing the testimony)
7:50 pm	1 min	Closing
7:51 pm	2 min	Serenity Prayer or The Lord's Prayer
7:53 pm	5 min	Worship music (Response)/Dismissal to Open Share Groups

Large Group Runsheet Template

Elements (*CR DNA Format Elements)		Volunteer Assignments
(60 minute service)*	Offering	Greeters
Welcome	Teaching or Testimony*	Resource Table
8 Principles or 12 Steps*	Chips	
Music*	Serentiy Prayer*	
Announcements	Closing	
Prayer/Scripture	Dismiss	

Time	Element/Notes	Assigned

31

Transition to Open Share Groups

After the Large Group Meeting, the Ministry Leader or the person who taught the lesson may want to stand by the door to greet people as they exit. This helps the Newcomer connect. If you offer a General Meeting Night, the Open Share Groups meet immediately after the Large Group concludes.

Note: As your Celebrate Recovery grows, you may decide to have leader notebooks available, one for each Open Share Group Leader, near/at the Info Table. The notebooks may include the Open Share Group format, the Small Group Guidelines, and the Issue Pamphlet for the group. Leaders can pick up their binders before the Open Share Groups.

Open Share Groups

As a reminder, Open Share Groups are gender-specific.

We call them Open Share Groups for two reasons:

- First, they are always open to newcomers. Anyone is able to join an Open Share Group at any time, the only requirement is they identify with the issue of that Open Share Group.
- Second, the Open Share Group is open for participants to share about whatever they wish, or they may choose to pass. There is no specific question or topic they have to share about. We recommend participants share about their struggles, their recovery, and/or a victory in their lives.

Simple DNA Format for Open Share Groups:

(In Person or Online, One Hour, Follows CR DNA)

1. Welcome and Leader Introductions
2. Open in Prayer
3. Read the CR Small Group Guidelines
4. Group Open Sharing
5. Wrap-Up
6. Close in Prayer

Below is an extended DNA Format with Optional Elements, which can be helpful if your Celebrate Recovery is only offering Open Share Groups. This allows you to bring in some of the powerful elements of the Large Group.

Extended DNA Format for Open Share Groups:

(In Person or Online, One Hour, Follows CR DNA)
Bolded Points = Non-optional Elements

1. **Welcome and Leader Introductions**
2. **Open in Prayer**
3. *Optional*: Read through the 8 Principles or 12 Steps
4. **Read the CR Small Group Guidelines**
   a. *Online Groups*: also read the 3 additional online guidelines
5. *Optional*: Include a 5–10 minute (max) devo or minimony
6. *Optional*: Read the issue pamphlet related to the groups issue focus
7. *Optional*: Ask participants to introduce themselves
8. *Optional*: Share Focus question
9. **Group open sharing**
10. **Wrap up the meeting**
    a. *Optional* In-Person: Hand out recovery chips
    b. *Optional* Online: acknowledge sobriety/recovery time
    c. *Optional*: Take prayer requests
    d. *Optional*: Ask for potential sponsors to raise their hand
    e. *Optional*: Invite participants to after-group fellowship and/or church events
11. **Close in prayer**

If you have more than one Open Share Group meeting at a time, elements 1–5 in the **Extended DNA Format for Open Share Groups** can be done all together before breaking out into gender-specific share time without breaking gender-specific CR DNA.

PLEASE NOTE: The 5–10 minute devo/minimony is not a teaching moment. Options for this time include reading a devo, character study, or testimony from the CR Bible, reading a devo from the CR 365 Devotional, watching a minimony found through celebraterecovery.com, or a leader or participant sharing a reviewed personal devo or minimony.

Welcome, Opening Prayer, and Leader Introductions

This time allows the Open Share Group to again focus their attention to the Lord and to feel the bond of their group. It is also another opportunity to softly welcome newcomers. It is not necessary to ask participants in Open Share Groups to introduce themselves. It may help newcomers who are feeling uncomfortable to know that they do not have to introduce themselves. If you choose not to have all participants introduce themselves here, please ask them to introduce themselves when they share.

Reading of Celebrate Recovery's Small Group Guidelines

Read at every Open Share group meeting, these simple rules are designed to keep the group safe! If your recovery meetings are not safe, they will fail! It is the responsibility of the group leaders to ensure that these guidelines are followed. The guidelines and explanations will be covered later in this section. To reinforce their importance, the guidelines can also be read every four to six weeks during the Large Group time if you choose.

Open Sharing

The participant can choose to share whatever is on their heart, or they can choose to pass. You may also use a focus question, which can be found on the Celebrate Recovery lesson handout notes, found at celebraterecovery.com. When the leader opens up sharing time, ask for those who will be sharing to start by introducing themselves. This can be a full CR introduction, or just their name. They can introduce themselves however they choose.

It is important that even if you have a small group, you do not go around the group and share twice. One main reason is if the group gets bigger, as we all hope it will, there won't be time for everyone to share twice, and they will already be in the habit of sharing twice. This can also create an unhealthy situation where someone dominates the group sharing time.

Wrap-Up and Closing Prayer

Wrapping up the session is the leader's responsibility. It is up to him or her to see that the group has enough time for closure—that the meeting does not just come to an abrupt halt or go on and on and on. If there were any major issues raised in the group, the leader should be sure to follow-up.

Invitation to the Cafe Fellowship Time

The meeting can now continue "unofficially" at the place designed specifically for fellowship. At the cafe, individuals have an opportunity to continue to share with those with whom they feel safe. It is a time for participants to develop accountability partners and/or sponsorship relationships.

Newcomers 101

Praise be to the God and Father of our Lord Jesus Christ, the Father of compassion and the God of all comfort, who comforts us in all our troubles, so that we can comfort those in any trouble with the comfort we ourselves receive from God. (2 Corinthians 1:3–4)

It is essential to remember that when a person comes to Celebrate Recovery for the first time, he or she may be overwhelmed with feelings of pain, humiliation, sadness, and hopelessness. The whole concept of recovery may be unfamiliar and a little frightening. Selecting and identifying with an Open Share Group may seem to be an impossible task.

With the newcomers' feelings in mind, the most important thing to remember about leading Newcomers 101 is to project a friendly, open, approachable demeanor.

You will need two Leaders, a man and a woman, to facilitate the Newcomers 101 Open Share Group. This remains the same whether you have two or 20 first-time attendees. An exception is when only one Newcomer man or woman attends. In this instance, only the one gender-specific leader will need to stay, and the other leader can go to Open Share Group. We recommend the leaders wear a Celebrate Recovery leader's shirt or leader's badge to identify themselves as someone who has worked the program and achieved credibility with their Church.

Newcomers 101 group starts with everyone together for the first part of the hour, and then participants break into gender-specific groups for share time. It is imperative to go through the first part quickly, twenty minutes at most, in order to move to the Open Share Group time that is so important for the newcomer. The purpose of this sharing time is to help the participant choose the group to attend next week. An audiovisual presentation is advisable, but not required, so the participants can follow along. A welcome slide would be appropriate as the newcomers enter the room.

Set Up
1. Make sure the room is ready 15 minutes prior to the Newcomers 101 group's arrival.
2. Directions and signage — make sure it is easy for a Newcomer to find.
3. Remember to have ready:
    > Chairs in a semicircle, making sure that everyone can see the video.

> ➤ Television or laptop ready — plugged in, with DVD working and in place and ready to start.
>
> ➤ Any curriculum that you will be presenting.
>
> ➤ Have a few Issue Pamphlets available. You can get these from the Information Table.

Welcome the Newcomers

Begin walking around the room and greeting the men and women who are new to the program. During this time, if there are other leaders present, do not stand in groups talking to one another! Move around, smile, and look approachable. Give the impression that you are looking forward to Newcomers 101. What a wonderful opportunity to share what Jesus has done in your life!

Open in Prayer

Wait until all of the newcomers are settled and then open in prayer. Keep the prayer upbeat. We want to give hope and victory!

Welcome Participants; Show a Newcomers' Video

We strongly suggest that your program develop its own newcomers' video. This video should show leaders from different areas of recovery talking about the changes the program has made in their lives. If your senior pastor is willing to be a part of the video, the newcomers know, right from the start, that your program has senior pastor support. Examples of newcomers' videos can be found through celebraterecovery.com.

Introduce the Leaders

Leaders can rotate into Newcomers 101 so that they may continue to attend their own meetings. However, they must elect other strong leaders to run the groups in their absence.

In order to get through all of the information needing to be covered during the first part of the evening, the introductions need to be very concise—one to two minutes maximum. The emphasis should focus on the important difference between Celebrate Recovery and a secular program: that we believe in the one and only true Higher Power, Jesus Christ. We also want to make it clear that our lives have changed as a result of this program.

An example of a leader introduction for this group is: "Hi, my name is _____ and I'm a believer who struggles with codependency. After attending this program, my marriage was reconciled, and I love to give back to this ministry."

In this example, newcomers learn the name of the leader; that they are a Christian who struggles with codependency; and that they feel they have been changed enough to give back to the program. The underlying message is upbeat and gives hope to newcomers.

These introductions help the newcomers to relax, without the fear of having to speak in front of the entire group while also being able to relate to the leaders.

Very Briefly State the Goal of Newcomers 101

Summarize briefly the goal of Newcomers 101. For example, you might say, "The goal of Newcomers 101 is to explain how Celebrate Recovery works and to help you find a group to attend next week. The Newcomers group is a one-time attendance group only."

Explain that the group will be divided into a men's group and a women's group during the second half of the meeting—just like the Open Share Groups that are meeting throughout the church.

Again, we want to help the newcomers feel comfortable in our program. So for this evening only, you can explain that questions will be welcomed after the Open Share Group, and that questions are not a part of the regular Open Share Groups.

Announce Time and Place for Celebration Place and The Landing

Announcing the provision of programs for elementary school, junior high/middle school, and high school students emphasizes that the entire family can find healing in one program. This will open up your Celebrate Recovery ministry to more people.

Explain the Different Components of the Program

Very briefly mention that the tools of Celebrate Recovery are the *Celebrate Recovery Study Bible*, the participant's guides, and the *Celebrate Recovery Journal*. *Life's Healing Choices* is the recommended book to better understand the 8 Recovery Principles and to be encouraged by the sixteen great testimonies. (Slides showing these tools are recommended for familiarity.)

Although Step Study Groups are an important part of Celebrate Recovery, it might be too confusing to explain at this point. A long explanation about sponsors and accountability partners might also take up too much time. The participants will learn more about different components of the program as they begin to attend regularly. For now keep the information to the basics so they do not become overwhelmed

In conclusion, finish with a quick review of what your Celebrate Recovery offers.

Next Read the Small Group Guidelines

Mention that these guidelines are to protect the participants of Celebrate Recovery and to provide a safe place for sharing.

Divide into Men's and Women's Groups

Couples who have come together might be uncomfortable splitting up. Gently explain that this division makes the program a safe place for people to share.

Once divided, explain that in the Open Share Groups participants abide by the Small Group Guidelines and then read through them. Share how your groups keep time and signal to wrap up sharing.

Ask newcomers if they would like to share their name and a specific issue they are struggling with if they can identify with one already, or to say what brought them to Celebrate Recovery for the first time. Explain that we say "Hi" and the person's name after they have introduced themselves in order to get better acquainted, and that we affirm their sharing by saying, "Thank you for sharing" or clapping. Give them the opportunity to pass if they are not ready to share.

After the group has completed their sharing, open up for questions, again emphasizing that this will not happen in their regular Open Share Groups.

Encourage attendance in an Open Share Group for several weeks before deciding to try a different group. Explain it may take some time to feel comfortable, that it's a part of the process and will get easier. Suggest trying another group if after several weeks the group still feels uncomfortable. Leaders will not be offended.

Wrap up by letting the group know that you are always available to answer any questions they may have in the future. If you offer it, invite them to the cafe fellowship time and mention that these fellowship events are great opportunities to meet others in the program.

Close in Prayer

While the rest of the group talks informally, the leaders may want to meet one-on-one with anyone who decided to pass during sharing. However, if they do not want to share, we need to let them know that we understand how difficult it is to share for the first time. Encourage them to go to the Open Share Group the following week, emphasizing that they are not required to share until they are ready.

Step Study Groups

The Step Study Group participants work through the *Celebrate Recovery: The Journey Begins Participant Guide* by reading through the lessons and answering the questions at the end of each lesson together. Step Study Groups close (i.e., no new participants) after they have completed the lessons for the third principle. Step Study Groups meet together for approximately twelve months. They are gender specific, but not issue specific.

In addition to *The Journey Begins Participant's Guide*, *The Journey Continues Participant's Guide* takes participants even further in their recovery. To check out one of the twenty-five lessons from *The Journey Continues'* Participant's Guide, please see pages 221 in this Leader's Guide.

<u>DNA Format for Step Study Groups:</u>

1 ¹/₂ to 2 hours

1. Welcome and Open in Prayer
2. Leader and Participant Introductions
3. Read the 8 Principles or Christ-centered 12 steps
4. Read the CR Small Group Guidelines
5. Read the lesson acrostic from the *Participant's Guide* (when starting a new lesson) and take turns sharing answers to the questions.
6. Wrap Up and Close in Prayer

**Optional best practice elements:*

- Small Group Expectations (Initially when a new Step Study begins, can be found in the ALT)
- Worship song at the beginning of the meeting
- Share a devo from the CR 365 Daily Devo or the Celebrate Recovery Bible (no more than 5 minutes, remember, no outside curriculum)
- Assign the homework questions from the workbook for next week's meeting.
- Announcements
- Share written prayer requests

With the exception of #3 and #5, The DNA Format for Step Study Groups are the same as for Open Share Groups. Please refer to the training for Open Share Groups to cover any of those points. #3 and #5 will be covered below.

Read the 8 Principles or Christ-centered 12 Steps

Alternate reading through the 8 Principles or 12 Steps and their biblical comparisons each week, allowing the participants to take turns reading. This can be done in different ways. For example, one participant reads a Principle or Step and the biblical comparison, or one participant reads the Principle or Step and the next participant reads the biblical comparison. Another option is to have the participants take turns reading the Principle or Step and everyone reads the biblical comparison together.

Read the lesson acrostic and take turns sharing answers to the questions

Start by reading through the lesson when the group starts a new lesson. Then, go around the group and let all members have a chance to answer each question. Adhering to Guideline #1 is very important so everyone has a chance to share. Depending on the size of the Step Study Group, it may take two weeks to get through one lesson. Sharing in a Step Study is not optional, everyone who joins agrees to share their answers to the lessons each week.

Advanced trainings for Large Group, Open Share Groups, and Step Study Groups can be found in the *Advanced Leadership Training Guide,* available through celebraterecovery.com.

Small Group Guidelines

READ AT EVERY OPEN SHARE AND STEP STUDY GROUP MEETING, no matter how long you have been together! Continue to read the guidelines even if you have been together six months or a year. In fact, the guidelines become even more important if your group is extremely bonded.

The guidelines are designed to keep the groups safe! If your recovery meetings are not safe, they will fail! It is the responsibility of the group leaders to ensure that these guidelines are followed.

Below are the Extended Group Guidelines, which include the basic Guideline in bold, and an explanation of the guideline below it. For Step Studies, we recommend reading the Extended Group Guidelines for a few weeks, or as long as new participants are still joining the group. Once the group closes, or when no more new participants are joining the group, you may read through just the basic Guidelines each week. For Open Share Groups, we recommend reading the Extended Group Guidelines at minimum whenever a newcomer joins the group.

Thank your group in advance for honoring these guidelines. As your group matures, if one particular guideline starts to be a problem, reemphasize that particular guideline at the next meeting by reading the extended guideline. This might be all it will take to refocus the group. If it continues to be a problem with one particular person, address it with him or her individually.

1. **Keep your sharing focused on your own thoughts and feelings, using "I" and "Me" statements. Limit your sharing to three to five minutes.**

    This is a very important guideline. Using "I" and "Me" statements keeps us focused on our own thoughts, feelings, and actions, allowing us to take responsibility for our own recovery. Please adhere to the three-to-five-minute rule, so that everyone has an opportunity to share; and to ensure that one person does not dominate the group sharing time.

2. **There is NO cross talk. Cross talk is when two individuals engage in conversation excluding all others. Each person is free to express his or her feelings without interruptions.**

    Cross talk is also making comments or asking questions while someone is sharing, speaking to another member of the group while someone is sharing or responding to what someone has shared during his or her time of sharing. This guideline is about respect. When other participants are sharing, we don't want to interrupt their thoughts and feelings, which may be very deep, painful, scary, sad, etc. It's their time about them, not us. Basically, anything that would give the speaker the impression that we don't care about what they have to share, could be considered cross talk.

3. **We are here to support one another, not "fix" another.**

    We do not give unsolicited advice or attempt to solve someone else's problems. This includes sharing scriptures for the purpose of preaching or teaching, during our time of sharing. We also do not offer book recommendations or counselor referrals. This helps us stay focused on our own issues.

4. **Anonymity and confidentiality are basic requirements. What is shared in the group stays in the group. The only exception is when people threaten to injure themselves or others.**

    It can be very hurtful to discover that someone's sharing is being discussed outside of the group time. Most of the people in recovery have never been able to "tell the secret"— they need to be assured that this is the safe place to do it. When communicating with group members, be careful about protecting anonymity and confidentiality.

Please be advised, if anyone threatens to hurt themselves or others, the group Leader has the responsibility to report it to the Celebrate Recovery Ministry Leader.

5. **Offensive language has no place in a Christ-centered recovery group.**

The main issue here is that the Lord's name is not used inappropriately.

We also avoid graphic descriptions. If anyone feels uncomfortable with how explicitly a speaker is sharing regarding his/her behaviors, then you may indicate so by simply raising your hand. The speaker will then respect your boundaries by being less specific in his/her descriptions.

The following guidelines are to be used in all online Open Share Groups and Step studies.

1. **All members must use headphones.**

This will ensure that no one else can overhear what is shared in the group if others are present in the home. Even if you are alone in your home/car it helps all participants feel safe as they cannot ensure you are completely alone. So, we just keep this guideline consistent for everyone.

2. **All members must be alone in the room with their camera on and facing them during the entire meeting.**

If you have any backgrounds on, please turn those off. However, a blurred background is fine. Again, we ask that your camera be on, and that you face the camera for the entire group time.

3. **This meeting will not be recorded.**

This protects the confidentiality and anonymity of the participants.

TEAM Structure

If you try to run the CR ministry at your church all by yourself, you will burn out. And not only will you burn out as a leader, but eventually your own recovery will begin to suffer. The way to be an effective Celebrate Recovery Ministry Leader is to start giving the responsibilities of your leadership away.

We learn this from Moses and his father-in-law in Exodus 18:13–21: "The next day Moses took his seat to serve as judge for the people, and they stood around him from morning till evening.

When his father-in-law saw all that Moses was doing for the people, he said, 'What is this you are doing for the people? Why do you alone sit as judge, while all these people stand around you from morning till evening?' Moses answered him, 'Because the people come to me to seek God's will. Whenever they have a dispute, it is brought to me, and I decide between the parties and inform them of God's decrees and instructions.' Moses' father-in-law replied, 'What you are doing is not good. You and these people who come to you will only wear yourselves out. The work is too heavy for you; you cannot handle it alone. Listen now to me and I will give you some advice, and may God be with you. You must be the people's representative before God and bring their disputes to him. Teach them his decrees and instructions, and show them the way they are to live and how they are to behave. But select capable men from all the people-men who fear God, trustworthy men who hate dishonest gain-and appoint them as officials over thousands, hundreds, fifties and tens.' "

If you want to last, and have your ministry grow and be more effective in reaching and helping hurting, broken people, we strongly suggest that you build a T.E.A.M!

At Celebrate Recovery we suggest managing the ministry by the T.E.A.M. structure. We have one person minimum in each of the following roles:

T—Training Coach
E—Encourager Coach
A—Ambassador Coach
M—Ministry Leader

This is how we make Celebrate Recovery a truly volunteer-run ministry.

If you are a senior pastor or a church staff person, your task may be to assemble the T.E.A.M., which may or may not include you. As you form your T.E.A.M., follow the example of Jesus. Looking in Matthew, watch how Jesus formed His small group of leaders. After a night of intentional prayer, He called those who would follow and serve with Him.

As your Celebrate Recovery leadership grows, seek to fill the T.E.A. roles with one male and one female, especially in the role of the Encourager Coach.

The M may be a church staff or volunteer position appointed by the pastor. This role may be filled by one or two people.

It is not intended that each coach "does it all." It is the responsibility, however, of the coaches to supervise these areas. For example, you may have several people conducting training sessions who are responsible to the Training Coach.

We've provided descriptions for each role to assist you in evaluating leaders in your Celebrate Recovery to determine who might be a good fit for each one.

T = Training Coach

All Scripture is God-breathed and is useful for teaching, rebuking, correcting and training in righteousness, so that the servant of God may be thoroughly equipped for every good work. (2 Timothy 3: 16–17)

The Training Coach's role is to equip Celebrate Recovery leaders for ministry in an environment that allows each leader to grow in God and confidence. A key responsibility of the trainer is to ensure the DNA of an authentic Celebrate Recovery, which is vital in bringing accountability and credibility to the ministry.

An Effective Training Coach

- **Conducts NEW LEADER TRAINING and Orientation**

As discussed in the Start-up Strategy, when your CR has been up and running for 6 months or so, we suggest purchasing the Advanced Leadership Training Guide (ALT), which offers more in-depth training for leaders. The ALT includes training for:

- Writing Your Testimony
- Training Open Share Group Leaders
- Training Step Study Group Leaders
- Implementing the Small Group Guidelines
- Training Sponsors
- Additional Training for Great Leaders

- **Provides ONGOING LEADER Training**

Ongoing Leader Training is done during the monthly Leaders' Meetings. It is not necessarily the Training Coach's responsibility to conduct all of these sessions, but to work in conjunction with the Ministry Leader to determine the needs of the ministry.

- **Develops and oversees leadership for OPEN SHARE AND STEP STUDY GROUPS**

The Training Coach supports Open Share Group and Step Study Group leaders, being sensitive to any issues specific to a particular group dynamic, or leader conflicts.

- **Develops a Training Coach APPRENTICE**

Look for someone within your existing leadership to train and develop as an apprentice. A good trainer possesses the ability to see the vision and articulate it in a way that everyone can easily understand, training from personal experience. Motivation is caught, not taught.

E = Encourager Coach

Do not let any unwholesome talk come out of your mouths, but only what is helpful for building others up according to their needs, that it may benefit those who listen. (Ephesians 4:29)

The Encourager Coach's role is to funnel positive energy into Celebrate Recovery leaders so they can handle the struggles and stress that may come from working with people who are hurting. They also serve as a bridge for the participants, who begin to serve as volunteers on their pathway to becoming leaders.

An effective Encourager Coach:

- **Provides and oversees the SHEPHERDING CARE needs of the groups and Ministry Leaders**

The Encourager Coach speaks life into the leadership of the ministry and helps support the TEAM coaches by building them up, continually encouraging them with the Word of God and through prayer. The Encourager Coach recognizes milestones that have been reached by leaders, volunteers, and participants (as applicable) in their recovery.

- **Creates FELLOWSHIP OPPORTUNITIES for the leaders and groups**

In order to keep the leadership and ministry fun and friendly, the Encourager Coach plans fellowship events, both small and large. These events are different from the ones connected to your General Meeting Night (dinner, fellowship cafe), and are to be held other days/times during the week. This could also include adding a fun team building game at your monthly leaders' meeting. Encourager Coaches also support the Ambassador Coaches with Outreach fellowship events.

- **Recruits and interviews new LEADERSHIP CANDIDATES**

The "E" Coach may visit Step Studies on Step 12 to share the joy of serving as a leader and hand out Celebrate Recovery leader information sheets (Appendix 2) and share opportunities where participants can serve.

- **Develops an Encourager Coach APPRENTICE**

The Encourager Coach develops someone from within Celebrate Recovery to be an apprentice. This role will have both men and women serving the needs of the leadership team. A good Encourager Coach is naturally encouraging, relational, caring, and loves to pour into others.

A = Ambassador Coach

I will extol the LORD at all times; his praise will always be on my lips. I will glory in the LORD; let the afflicted hear and rejoice. Glorify the LORD with me; let us exalt his name together. (Psalm 34:1–3)

The Ambassador Coach's role is to get the word out about Celebrate Recovery by communicating favorably with church family and community. An Ambassador Coach will gain information and knowledge about churches and secular recovery groups in his/her area as well as local Christian counselors and probation departments.

An effective Ambassador Coach:

- **Effectively PROMOTES Celebrate Recovery to the church and the community**

Members of the Church:
- Create Celebrate Recovery brochures, business cards, and newsletters (for helpful resources go to celebraterecovery.com)
- Utilize your church's bulletin and website.
- Produce a video about your Celebrate Recovery and display pictures.
- Encourage your pastor to include Celebrate Recovery testimonies in sermons.
- Use Celebrate Recovery shirts, hats, etc.

The Community:
- Network with other ministries in your area.
- Use brochures, newsletters, and video.
- Utilize advertising in local newspapers and magazines.

- **Develops and maintains GROUP INFORMATION MATERIALS for groups and information tables**

The "A" Coach sets up and replenishes Celebrate Recovery information/resource table, including copies of: The Journey Begins Participant's Guides, the Celebrate Recovery Bible, the Celebrate Recovery journal, Life's Healing Choices books, and Issue pamphlets (only Issue pamphlets from celebraterecovery.com are DNA approved).

- **Develops an Ambassador Coach APPRENTICE**

Pray for God to provide the right person with a heart to get the word out about Celebrate Recovery; a "people" person, outgoing and good at developing relationships; someone with a passion for spreading the word that there is a place to find help from life's hurts, hangups, and habits.

M = Ministry Leader

Follow my example, as I follow the example of Christ. (1 Corinthians 11:1)

Roles of the Ministry Leader:

- They are the main leader, responsible for creating a safe environment, ensuring the DNA of CR is upheld, and the leaders are trained.
- Serves as the main contact between the ministry of CR and the church.
- Oversees the leaders, and the TEA coaches.
- Trains the other leaders at a monthly leaders' meeting, until they develop a T coach.
- Selects and schedules the lessons and testimonies. Not all Ministry Leaders like to teach, and some love it. It depends on the Ministry Leader. But they are in charge of scheduling the lessons and testimonies.
- Handles any pastoral care issues that come up, with the help and support of the Senior Pastor and leadership team at their church. For example, dealing with conflict resolutions between leaders or participants, or dealing with anyone who shows up under the influence.

The Ministry Leader has many important roles. However, the most important thing any effective Ministry Leader can do is to set the TONE in his or her Celebrate Recovery ministry. Let's look at some of the things a Ministry Leader can do to make Celebrate Recovery a great experience for everyone who attends.

An important way a Ministry Leader can set the TONE is Teaching by example. The Ministry Leader needs to be someone in recovery. While a pastor or staff person may oversee the ministry while not engaging in it, the Ministry Leader should be someone who recognizes the need for personal recovery, working the Celebrate Recovery Principles in his or her own life. That's one way to teach by example. When the Ministry Leader is involved in personal recovery, he or she is more effective in dealing with people who are in the same boat.

Teaching by example includes doing the things he or she is asking others to do. By showing up early to set up chairs or greeting newcomers, the Ministry Leader can show the rest of the TEAM, as well as other leaders, how they should interact on the General Meeting Night. In short, teach with more than just words. As Paul told the church in 1 Corinthians 11: 1, "Follow my example, as I follow the example of Christ."

Next, the Ministry Leader sets the TONE by Openly sharing his or her hurts, hang-ups, and habits. Ministry Leaders should be transparent, not unapproachable or "fixed." So, in teaching the lessons, they should use personal illustrations to show how Celebrate Recovery has and is helping them in their own lives. Yes, Ministry Leaders should be sure to share about how Jesus

Christ has changed them, but shouldn't shy away from sharing about the work they still have to do. This means Ministry Leaders should participate in Open Share and Step Study Groups at their local Celebrate Recovery ministry, and be part of the overall Celebrate Recovery ministry. Remember, there's no limitation. James 5:16 says, "Therefore confess your sins to each other and pray for each other so that you may be healed." That applies to all of us, from newcomer to Ministry Leader.

Setting the TONE also means to Never forget to keep the Celebrate in Celebrate Recovery. Recovery can be hard, especially at the beginning, but Jesus changes things. The Ministry Leader should make sure to help people remember the joy that is possible in Christ when He works in our lives. Pick uplifting, high-energy songs for worship, use jokes (even bad ones) in the lessons, have a smile on your face and ask the leaders and TEAM to do the same. Make sure every testimony has a section dedicated to celebrating what Christ has done. This will help us do what Paul instructs in Philippians 4:4: "Rejoice in the Lord always. I will say it again: Rejoice!" By remembering to celebrate the changes God will make in our lives, not just focusing on the problems of today, we can give the participants and newcomers hope.

Last, when the Ministry Leader sets the TONE we see that Everyone wants to be a part of something great. When the TEAM is in place, the leaders have been trained, and the TONE has been set, people will be drawn to your healthy Celebrate Recovery ministry. When pastors see lives changed, they will get behind Celebrate Recovery and send people in their congregation to it. When people share about what God has done for them, they will attract their friends and family to check it out.

In short, by putting the work in, and by setting the TONE, people will flock to Celebrate Recovery.

The 25 Celebrate Recovery Lessons

As stated earlier, this Leader's Guide includes the twenty-five lessons found in the four *Celebrate Recovery The Journey Begins Participant's Guides*, which covers all of the 8 Principles and 12 Steps. Each lesson has been written so that you can either read it in its entirety or "cut and paste" in your own illustrations. Just follow the basic format and be sure to include the recovery acrostic and Bible verses for each lesson. May God bless you and your ministry as you lead others on their road to recovery.

Principle 1

Realize I'm not God. I admit that I am powerless to control my tendency to do the wrong thing and that my life is unmanageable.

Blessed are the poor in spirit, for theirs is the kingdom of heaven. (Matthew 5:3)

Denial

_____

Principle 1: Realize I'm not God. I admit that I am powerless to control my tendency to do the wrong thing and that my life is unmanageable.

Blessed are the poor in spirit, for theirs is the kingdom of heaven. (Matthew 5:3)

Step 1: We admitted we were powerless over our addictions and compulsive behaviors, that our lives had become unmanageable.

For I know that good itself does not dwell in me, that is, in my sinful nature. For I have the desire to do what is good, but I cannot carry it out. (Romans 7:18)

_____

Introduction

Tonight we begin a journey together, a journey on the road of recovery. This journey begins with Principle 1, where we admit that we are powerless to control our tendencies to do the wrong thing and that our lives have become unmanageable, out of control. But before we begin this exciting journey together, we need to ask ourselves two questions:

- Am I going to let my past failures prevent me from taking this journey?
- Am I afraid to change? Or, what are my fears of the future?

Failures from the Past

Let's look at Hebrews 12:1–2:

Therefore, since we are surrounded by such a great cloud of witnesses, let us throw off everything that hinders and the sin that so easily entangles. And let us run with persever-ance the race marked out for us, fixing our eyes on Jesus, the pioneer and perfecter of faith.

There are two things I would like to point out in this verse. First, God has a particular race, a unique plan, for each of us. A plan for good, not a life full of dependencies, addictions, and obsessions.

The second thing is that *we need to be willing* to get rid of all the unnecessary baggage, the past failures, in our lives that keep us stuck. Again, it says, "Let us throw off everything that hinders and the sin that so easily entangles."

For many of us, our past hurts, hang-ups, and habits hold us back, trip us up! Many of us are stuck in bitterness over what someone has done to us. We continue to hold on to the hurt and we refuse to forgive the ones who have hurt us.

You may have been hurt deeply. Perhaps you were abused as a child, or maybe you were or are in a marriage where your spouse committed adultery.

I want you to know that I hurt for you. I'm truly sorry for you, sorry that you had to go through that hurt. But holding on to that hurt and not being willing to forgive the person who hurt you in the past is allowing them to continue to hurt you today, in the present.

Working this Christ-centered recovery program will, with God's power, allow you to find the courage and strength to forgive them. Now don't get all stressed out. You don't have to forgive them tonight! But as you travel your road to recovery, God will help you find the willingness to forgive them and be free of their hold on your life.

Some of you are bound by guilt. You keep beating yourself up over some past failure. You're trapped, stuck in your guilt. You think that no one anywhere is as bad as you are, that no one could love the real you, and that no one could ever forgive you for the terrible things that you have done.

You're wrong. God can. That's why Jesus went to the cross, for our sins. He knows everything you've ever done and everything you've ever experienced. And there are many here tonight that have faced similar failures and hurts in their life and have accepted Christ's forgiveness. They are here to encourage and support you.

The apostle Paul had a lot to regret about his past. He even participated in Stephen's murder. Yet in Philippians 3:13–14 he tells us, "Brothers and sisters, I do not consider myself yet to have taken hold of it. But one thing I do: Forgetting what is behind and straining toward what is ahead, I press on toward the goal to win the prize for which God has called me heavenward in Christ Jesus."

Here's the bottom line if you want to be free from your past hurts, hang-ups, and habits: You need to deal with your past bitterness and guilt once and for all. You need to do as Isaiah 43:18 tells us, "Forget the former things; do not dwell on the past." That doesn't mean *ignore* the past. You need to *learn* from your past, offer forgiveness, make amends, and then release it. Only then can you be free from your guilt, grudges, and grief!

Let's face it, we have all stumbled over a hurt, hang-up, or habit. But the race isn't over yet. God isn't interested in how we started, but how we finish the race.

Fears for the Future

You may worry about your future and be afraid to change. We all worry about things that we do not have any control over and do not have the power to change. And we all know worrying is a lack of trust in God.

The truth is, we can say without any doubt or fear, "The Lord is my helper; I will not be afraid. What can mere mortals do to me?" (Hebrews 13:6).

You may have been in your hurt, hang-up, or habit for so long that it has become your identity. You may be thinking, "What will happen if I really give recovery a chance? Will I change? If I give up my old hurts, hang-ups, and habits, what will I become? Who will I be?"

You may have been abusing alcohol, prescription drugs, or food. Perhaps you're afraid of what you will do without your substance of choice.

You may have been enabling someone in a dysfunctional relationship for years. Perhaps you wonder, "What if I change and my alcoholic husband gets mad at me?"

God doesn't want you to stay frozen in an unhealthy relationship or a bad habit. He wants you to do your part in becoming healthy.

Even if our past was extremely painful, however, we may still resist change and the freedom that can be found in really working this program. Because of our fear of the unknown or because of our despair, we just close our minds because we think that we don't deserve any better.

As you work the principles and steps, remember 1 John 4:18: "There is no fear in love. But perfect love drives out fear, because fear has to do with punishment. The one who fears is not made perfect in love."

You are not here by mistake tonight. This room is full of changed lives. It is my prayer for each of you that you will not let your past failures or your fear of your future stop you from giving Celebrate Recovery a real try.

Are you wearing a mask of denial tonight? Before you can make any progress in your recovery, you need to face your denial. As soon as you remove your mask, your recovery begins—or begins again! It doesn't matter if you're new in recovery or have been in recovery, working the steps for years. Denial can rear its ugly head and return at any time! You may trade addictions or get into a new relationship that's unhealthy for you in a different way than the previous one. So this lesson is for all of us.

We have a saying around here: "Denial isn't just a river in Egypt." But what is it?

What Is Denial?

Denial has been defined as "a false system of beliefs that are not based on reality" and "a self-protecting behavior that keeps us from honestly facing the truth."

As kids we all learned various coping skills. They came in handy when we didn't get the attention we wanted from our parents and others or to block our pain and our fears.

For a time these coping systems worked. But as the years progressed they confused and clouded our view of the truth of our lives.

As we grew, our perception of ourselves and our expectations of all those around us also grew. But because we retained our childish methods of coping, our perceptions of reality became increasingly more unrealistic and distorted.

Our coping skills grew into denial, and most of our relationships ended up broken or less fulfilling than they could have been.

Did you ever deny that your parents had problems? Did you ever deny that you had problems? The truth is, we can all answer yes to these questions to some extent. But, for some of us, that denial turned to shame and guilt.

Denial is the "pink elephant" sitting in the middle of the living room. No one in the family talks about it or acknowledges it in any way. Do any of the following comments sound familiar to you?

- "Can't we stop talking about it? Talking only makes it worse."
- "Billy, if we *don't* talk about it, it will go away."
- "Honey, let's pretend that it didn't really happen."
- "If I tell her that it hurts me when she says that, I'm afraid she will leave me."
- "He really doesn't drink that much."
- "It really doesn't hurt when he does that; I'm fine!"
- "Paul drinks more than I do."
- "Joan has been married three times; I've only been married twice."
- "I eat because you make me so mad!"
- "If you didn't nag me all the time, I wouldn't . . ."
- "Look honey, I have a tough job; I work hard. I need a few drinks to relax. It doesn't mean that I have a problem."

Folks, that's DENIAL.

As I said earlier, before we can take the first step of our recovery, we must first face and admit our denial.

Effects of Denial

Okay, let's look at tonight's acrostic:

DENIAL
Disables our feelings
Energy lost
Negates growth
Isolates us from God
Alienates us from our relationships
Lengthens the pain

The *D* in denial stands for DISABLES our feelings. Hiding our feelings, living in denial, freezes our emotions and binds us. Understanding and feeling our feelings is where we find freedom.

Second Peter 2:19 tells us: "They promise them freedom, while they themselves are slaves of depravity—for 'people are slaves to whatever has mastered them.' "

For me, the basic test of freedom is not what I'm free to do, it's what I'm free not to do! I'm free not to take that drink.

We find freedom to feel our true feelings when we find Christ and step out of denial.

The next letter in denial is *E*, which stands for ENERGY lost.

A major side effect of denial is anxiety. Anxiety causes us to waste precious energy dealing with past hurts and failures and the fear of the future. As you go through this program you will learn that it is only in the present that positive change can occur. Worrying about the past and dreading the future make us unable to live and enjoy God's plans for us in the present.

We let our fears and our worries paralyze us, but the only lasting way we can be free from them is by giving them to God. Psalm 146:7–8 says, "He upholds the cause of the oppressed and gives food to the hungry. The LORD sets prisoners free, the LORD gives sight to the blind, the LORD lifts up those who are bowed down, the LORD loves the righteous."

If you will transfer the energy required to maintain your denial into learning God's truth, a healthy love for others and yourself will occur. As you depend more and more on your Higher Power, Jesus Christ, you will see the light of truth and reality.

Let's move on to the *N* in denial.

Denial NEGATES growth.

We are as sick as our secrets and, again, we cannot grow in recovery until we are ready to step out of our denial into the truth. God is waiting to take your hand and bring you out. The Bible says, "Then they cried to the LORD in their trouble, and he saved them from their distress. He brought them out of darkness, the utter darkness, and broke away their chains" (Psalm 107:13–14).

As you travel the road of your recovery you will come to understand that God never wastes a hurt; God will never waste your darkness. But He can't use it unless you step out of your denial into the light of His truth.

Denial also ISOLATES us from God.

Adam and Eve are a great example of how secrets and denial separate us from true fellowship with God. After they sinned, their secret separated them from God. Genesis 3:7–8 tells us that Adam and Eve hid from God because they felt naked and ashamed.

Of course, good old Adam tried to rationalize. He said to God, "The woman you put here with me—she gave me some fruit from the tree" (Genesis 3:12). First he tried to blame God, saying, "The woman you put here with me . . . ." Then he tried to blame it on Eve: "*She* gave me some fruit" (emphasis added).

Remember, God's light shines on the truth. Our denial keeps us in the dark.

God is light; in him there is no darkness at all. If we claim to have fellowship with him and yet walk in the darkness, we lie and do not live out the truth. But if we walk in the light, as he is in the light, we have fellowship with one another, and the blood of Jesus, his Son, purifies us from all sin. (1 John 1:5–7)

Our denial not only isolates us from God, it ALIENATES us from our relationships.

Denial tells us we are getting away with it. We think no one knows, but they do. But while denial may shield us from the hurt, it also keeps us from helping ourselves or the people we love the most. We don't dare reveal our true selves to others for fear of what they will think or say if they knew the real us. We must protect ourselves—our secrets—at any cost. So we isolate ourselves and thereby minimize the risk of exposure and possible rejection from others. But at what price? The eventual loss of all our important relationships.

What's the answer? Listen to Ephesians 4:25: "Therefore each of you must put off falsehood and speak truthfully to your neighbor, for we are all members of one body."

Remember it is always better to tell the ugly truth rather than a beautiful lie. Finally, denial LENGTHENS the pain.

We have the false belief that denial protects us from our pain. In reality, denial allows our pain to fester and grow and to turn into shame and guilt. Denial extends your hurt. It multiplies your problems. Psalm 32:3–5 tells us, "When I kept silent, my bones wasted away through my groaning all day long. For day and night your hand was heavy on me; my strength was sapped as in the heat of summer. Then I acknowledged my sin to you and did not cover up my iniquity. I said, 'I will confess my transgressions to the LORD.' And you forgave the guilt of my sin."

Wrap-Up

Tonight I encourage you to *step out* of your denial! Walking out of your denial is not easy. Taking off that mask is hard. Everything about you shouts, "Don't do it! It's not safe!" But it is safe. It's safe at Celebrate Recovery. Here you have people who care about you and who love you for who you are—people who will stand beside you as truth becomes a way of life.

Jesus tells us, "Then you will know the truth, and the truth will set you free" (John 8:32). Step out of your denial so you can step into Jesus' unconditional love and grace and begin your healing journey of recovery.

Powerless

———————

Principle 1: Realize I'm not God. I admit that I am powerless to control my tendency to do the wrong thing and that my life is unmanageable.

Blessed are the poor in spirit, for theirs is the kingdom of heaven. (Matthew 5:3)

Step 1: We admitted we were powerless over our addictions and compulsive behaviors, that our lives had become unmanageable.

For I know that good itself does not dwell in me, that is, in my sinful nature. For I have the desire to do what is good, but I cannot carry it out. (Romans 7:18)

———————

Introduction

In Principle 1, we realize we're not God. We admit we are powerless to control our tendency to do the wrong thing and that our lives have become unmanageable. As soon as we take this step and admit that we are powerless, we start to change. We see that our old ways of trying to control our hurts, hang-ups, and habits didn't work. They were buried by our denial and held onto with our false power.

Tonight we are going to focus on four actions: two things we have to *stop* doing and two things we need to *start* doing in our recoveries. We need to take these four actions to complete Principle 1.

Four Actions

In Lesson 1 we talked about the first action we need to take.

1. Stop denying the pain.

We said that our denial had at least six negative effects: It disables our feelings, wastes our energy, negates our growth, isolates us from God, alienates us from our relationships, and lengthens our pain.

You are ready to accept Principle 1 when your pain is greater than your fear. In Psalm 6:2–3 David talks about a time when he came to the end of his emotional and physical resources: "Have mercy on me, LORD, for I am faint; heal me, LORD, for my bones are in agony. My soul is in deep anguish. How long, LORD, how long?" When David's pain finally surpassed his fear, he was able to face his denial and feel the reality of his pain. In the same way, if you want to be rid of your pain, you must face it and go through it.

The second action we need to take is to:

2. Stop playing God.

You are either going to serve God or self. You can't do both! Matthew 6:24 says, "No one can serve two masters. Either you will hate the one and love the other, or you will be devoted to the one and despise the other. You cannot serve both God and money."

Another term for serving "ourselves" is serving the "flesh." Flesh is the Bible's word for our unperfected human nature, our sin nature.

I love this illustration: If you leave the *h* off the end of flesh and reverse the remaining letters, you spell the word *self*. Flesh is the self-life. It is what we are when we are left to our own devices.

When our "self" is out of control, all attempts at control—of self or others—fail. In fact, our attempt to control ourselves and others is what got us into trouble in the first place. God needs to be the one in control.

There are two jobs: God's and mine! We have been trying to do God's job, and we can't!

On the flip side, He *won't* do our job. We need to do the footwork! We need to admit that we are not God and that our lives are unmanageable without Him. Then, when we have finally emptied ourselves, God will have room to come in and begin His healing work.

Let's go on now to the third action we need to take:

3. Start admitting our powerlessness.

The lust of power is not rooted in our strengths but our weaknesses. We need to realize our human weaknesses and quit trying to do it by ourselves. We need to admit that we are powerless and turn our lives over to God. Jesus knew how difficult this is. He said, "With man this is impossible, but with God all things are possible" (Matthew 19:26).

When we keep doing things that we don't want to do and when we fail to do the things we've decided we need to do, we begin to see that we do not, in fact, have the power to change that we thought we had. Life is coming into focus more clearly than ever before.

The last action we need to take is to:

4. Start admitting that our lives have become unmanageable.

The only reason we consider that there's something wrong, or that we need to talk to somebody, or that we need to take this step is because we finally are able to admit that some area—or all areas—of our lives have become unmanageable!

It is with this admission that you finally realize you are out of control and are powerless to do anything on your own. When I got to this part of my recovery I shared David's feelings that he expressed in Psalm 40:12: "For troubles without number surround me; my sins have overtaken me, and I cannot see. They are more than the hairs of my head, and my heart fails within me."

Does that sound familiar? Only when your pain is greater than your fear will you be ready to honestly take the first step, admitting that you are powerless and your life is unmanageable.

Tonight our acrostic will help us to focus in on the first half of Principle 1: POWERLESS.

Powerless

Our acrostic tonight demonstrates what happens when we admit we are POWERLESS. We begin to give up the following "serenity robbers":

Pride

Only ifs

Worry

Escape

Resentments

Loneliness

Emptiness

Selfishness

Separation

The first letter in tonight's acrostic is *P*. We start to see that we no longer are trapped by our PRIDE: "Pride brings a person low, but the lowly in spirit gain honor" (Proverbs 29:23).

Ignorance + power + pride = a deadly mixture

Our false pride undermines our faith and it cuts us off from God and others. When God's presence is welcome, there is no room for pride because He makes us aware of our true self.

Next we begin to lose the ONLY ifs. That's the *O* in Powerless.

Have you ever had a case of the "only ifs"?

Only if they hadn't walked out.

Only if I had stopped drinking.

Only if this. Only if that.

How reluctantly the mind consents to reality. But when we admit that we are powerless, we start walking in the truth, rather than living in the fantasy land of rationalization.

Luke 12:2–3 tells us: "There is nothing concealed that will not be disclosed, or hidden that will not be made known. What you have said in the dark will be heard in the daylight, and what you have whispered in the ear in the inner rooms will be proclaimed from the roofs."

The next letter in powerless is the *W*, which stands for WORRYING. And don't tell me that worrying doesn't do any good; I know better. The things I worry about never happen!

All worrying is a form of not trusting God enough! Instead of worrying about things that we cannot possibly do, we need to focus on what God can do. Keep a copy of the Serenity Prayer in your pocket and your heart to remind you.

By working this program and completing the steps, you can find that trust, that relationship, with the one and only Higher Power, Jesus Christ, so that the worrying begins to go away.

Matthew 6:34 tells us: "Therefore do not worry about tomorrow, for tomorrow will worry about itself. Each day has enough trouble of its own."

The next thing that happens when we admit we are powerless is that we quit trying to ESCAPE. That's the *E*.

Before we admitted we were powerless, we tried to escape and hide from our hurts, habits, and hang-ups by getting involved in unhealthy relationships, by abusing drugs such as alcohol, by eating or not eating, and so forth.

Trying to escape pain drains us of precious energy. When we take this first step, however, God opens true escape routes to show His power and grace.

But everything exposed by the light becomes visible—and everything that is illuminated becomes a light. This is why it is said: "Wake up, sleeper, rise from the dead, and Christ will shine on you." (Ephesians 5:13–14)

The *R* in powerless stands for RESENTMENTS.

If they are suppressed and allowed to fester, resentments can act like emotional cancer.

Paul tells us in Ephesians 4:26–27: "'In your anger do not sin': Do not let the sun go down while you are still angry, and do not give the devil a foothold."

As you continue to work the principles, you will come to understand that in letting go of your resentments, by offering your forgiveness to those who have hurt you, you are not just freeing the person who harmed you, you are freeing you!

But if we try to maintain our false power, we become isolated and alone. That's the *L* in powerless: LONELINESS.

When you admit that you are powerless and start to face reality, you will find that you do not have to be alone.

Do you know that loneliness is a choice? In recovery and in Christ, you never have to walk alone again.

Do you know that caring for the lonely can cure loneliness? Get involved! Get involved in the church or in your neighborhood or here at Celebrate Recovery! If you become a regular here, I guarantee that you won't be lonely.

> *Keep on loving one another as brothers and sisters. Do not forget to show hospitality to strangers, for by so doing some people have shown hospitality to angels without knowing it. Continue to remember those in prison as if you were together with them in prison, and those who are mistreated as if you yourselves were suffering. (Hebrews 13:1–3)*

When you admit you are powerless you also give up another *E*, the EMPTINESS.

When you finally admit that you are truly powerless by yourself, that empty feeling deep inside—that cold wind that blows through you—will go away.

Jesus said, "The thief comes only to steal and kill and destroy; I have come that they may have life, and have it to the full" (John 10:10). So let Him fill the emptiness inside. Tell Him how you feel. He cares!

Next you will notice that you are becoming less self-centered.

The first *S* stands for SELFISHNESS.

I have known people who have come into recovery thinking that the Lord's Prayer was "Our Father who art in heaven . . . Give me . . . give me . . . give me!" Luke 17:33 tells us, "Whoever tries to keep their life will lose it, and whoever loses their life will preserve it." Simply said, selfishness is at the heart of most problems between people.

The last thing that we give up when we admit that we are powerless is SEPARATION.

Some people talk about "finding" God—as if He could ever be lost.

Separation from God can feel real, but it is never permanent. Remember, He seeks the lost. When we can't find God, we need to ask ourselves, "Who moved?" I'll give you a hint. It wasn't God!

> *For I am convinced that neither death nor life, neither angels nor demons, neither the present nor the future, nor any powers, neither height nor depth, nor anything else in all creation, will be able to separate us from the love of God that is in Christ Jesus our Lord. (Romans 8:38–39)*

Wrap-Up

The power to change only comes from God's grace.

Are you ready to truly begin your journey of recovery? Are you ready to stop denying the pain? Are you ready to stop playing God? Are you ready to start admitting your powerlessness? To start admitting that your life has become unmanageable? If you are, share it with your group tonight.

I encourage you to start working and living this program in earnest. If we admit we are powerless, we need a power greater than ourselves to restore us. That power is your Higher Power—Jesus Christ!

Let's close in prayer.

Dear God, Your Word tells me that I can't heal my hurts, hang-ups, and habits by just saying that they are not there. Help me! Parts of my life, or all of my life, are out of control. I now know that I cannot "fix" myself. It seems the harder that I try to do the right thing the more I struggle. Lord, I want to step out of my denial into the truth. I pray for You to show me the way. In Your Son's name, Amen.

Principle 2

Earnestly believe that God exists, that I matter to Him, and that He has the power to help me recover.

Blessed are those who mourn, for they will be comforted. (Matthew 5:4)

Hope

———————————

Principle 2: Earnestly believe that God exists, that I matter to Him, and that He has the power to help me recover.

Blessed are those who mourn, for they will be comforted. (Matthew 5:4)

Step 2: We came to believe that a power greater than ourselves could restore us to sanity.

For it is God who works in you to will and to act in order to fulfill his good purpose. (Philippians 2:13)

———————————

Introduction

In Principle 2 we earnestly believe that God exists, that we matter to Him, and that He has the power to help us recover. Hebrews 11:6 tells us, "And without faith it is impossible to please God, because anyone who comes to him must believe that he exists and that he rewards those who earnestly seek him." Psalm 62:5 says, "Yes, my soul, find rest in God; my hope comes from him."

In the first principle, we admitted we were powerless. It is through this admission of our powerlessness that we are able to believe and receive God's power to help us recover. We do need to be careful, though, not to just cover the bottomless pit of our hurts, hang-ups, and habits with layers of denial or try some quick fix. Instead, we need to keep those hurts exposed to the light so that through God's power they can truly heal.

It's in the second principle that we come to believe God exists, that we are important to Him, and that we are able to find the one true Higher Power, Jesus Christ! We come to understand that God wants to fill our lives with His love, His joy, and His presence.

One of my very favorite parables is in Luke 15, the story of the prodigal son. Though the story is about a father's love for his lost son, it is really a picture of God the Father's love for you. God's love is looking for you, no matter how lost you feel. God's searching love can find you, no matter how many times you may have fallen into sin. God's hands of mercy are reaching out to pick you up and to love and forgive you.

Ladies and gentlemen, that's where you will find hope, and that's why I call Principle 2 the "hope" principle.

Hope

Let's look at what the word HOPE means in Principle 2:

Higher Power
Openness to change
Power to change
Expect to change

H stands for HIGHER Power. Our Higher Power is the one and only true Higher Power and He has a name: Jesus Christ!

In the past you may have believed in Jesus' existence and you may have even attended church. But what you will find in Principle 2 is a personal relationship with Christ. You will see that Jesus desires a hands-on, day-to-day, moment-to-moment relationship with us. For He can do for us what we have never been able to do for ourselves. Romans 11:33–36 says, "Oh, the depth of the riches of the wisdom and knowledge of God! How unsearchable his judgments, and his paths beyond tracing out! 'Who has known the mind of the Lord? Or who has been his counselor?' 'Who has ever given to God, that God should repay them?' For from him and through him and for him are all things. To him be the glory forever! Amen."

Many people today believe their doubts and doubt their beliefs! Have you ever seen an idea? Have you ever seen love? Have you ever seen faith? Of course not. You may have seen acts of faith and love, but the real things—the lasting things—in the world are the invisible spiritual realities.

This leads us to the first four words of the second step: "We came to believe . . ." Saying that we "came to believe" in anything describes a process. Belief is a result of consideration, doubt, reasoning, and concluding.

Second Corinthians 12:9 tells us, " 'My grace is sufficient for you, for my power is made perfect in weakness.' Therefore I will boast all the more gladly about my weaknesses, so that Christ's power may rest on me."

The next letter in hope is O, which stands for OPENNESS to change.

What is the process that leads to solid belief, which leads you to change your life? Let's look at the first four words in Step 2 again: "We came to believe . . ."

- "We came . . ." We took the first step when we attended our first recovery meeting!
- "We came to . . ." We stopped denying our hurts, hang-ups, and habits!
- "We came to believe . . ." We started to believe and receive God's power to help us recover.

Hope is openness to change. Sometimes we are afraid to change, even if our past was painful. We resist change because of our fear of the unknown, or, in our despair, we think we don't deserve anything better.

Here's the good news: Hope opens doors where despair closes them! Hope discovers what can be done instead of grumbling about what can't be done.

Throughout your life you will continue to encounter hurts and trials that you are powerless to change, but with God's help you can be open to allow those circumstances and situations to change you—to make you better—not bitter.

Ephesians 4:22–24 gives us a challenge to that end: "You were taught, with regard to your former way of life, to put off your old self, which is being corrupted by its deceitful desires; to be made new in the attitude of your minds; and to put on the new self, created to be like God in true righteousness and holiness."

How will you do that? The letter *P* tells us about POWER to change.

In the past, we may have wanted to change and were unable to do so; we could not free ourselves from our hurts, hang-ups, or habits. In Principle 2, we understand that God's power can change us and our situation. Philippians 4:13 confirms it: "I can do all this through him who gives me strength."

Power to change comes from God's grace. You see, hope draws its power from a deep trust in God, like that of the psalmist, who wrote, "Guide me in your truth and teach me, for you are God my Savior, and my hope is in you all day long" (Psalm 25:5).

In Principle 2, we begin to understand that God's power can change us and our situation. And once we tap into that power, right actions—Christlike actions—will follow naturally as by-products of working the principles and following the one and only Higher Power, Jesus Christ.

The last letter in hope is *E*: EXPECT to change.

Remember you are only at the second principle. Don't quit before the miracle happens! With God's help, the changes that you have longed for are just *steps* away. Philippians 1:4–6 expresses my heart: "In all my prayers for all of you, I always pray with joy because of your partnership in the gospel from the first day until now, being confident of this, that he who began a good work in you will carry it on to completion until the day of Christ Jesus."

You know, you can't do anything unless you get started, so how much faith do you need to get started?

Matthew 17:20 tells us, "If you have faith as small as a mustard seed, you can say to this mountain, 'Move from here to there,' and it will move. Nothing will be impossible for you."

It's reassuring to know that you do not need large amounts of faith to begin the recovery process. You need only a small amount, "as small as a mustard seed," to effect change, to begin to move your mountains of hurts, hang-ups, and habits.

Wrap-Up

Eternal life does not begin with death; it begins with faith! Hebrews 11:1 tells us what faith is: "Faith is confidence in what we hope for and assurance about what we do not see." Faith—even faith the size of a mustard seed so small you can hardly see it—is the avenue to salvation. You can't find salvation through intellectual understanding, gifts of money, good works, or attending church. No! The way to find salvation, is described in Romans 10:9: "If you declare with your mouth, 'Jesus is Lord,' and believe in your heart that God raised him from the dead, you will be saved."

Yes, all you need is just a little faith. If you will put the faith you have in Jesus, your life will be changed! You will find hope in the only Higher Power, Jesus Christ. His Spirit will come with supernatural power into your heart. It can happen to you! It happened to me!

Tonight I encourage you to take this step of hope. It will give you the courage to reach out and hold Christ's hand and face the present with confidence and the future with realistic expectancy.

Simply put, my life without Christ is a hopeless end; with Him it is an endless hope.

Sanity

Principle 2: Earnestly believe that God exists, that I matter to Him, and that He has the power to help me recover.

Blessed are those who mourn, for they will be comforted. (Matthew 5:4)

Step 2: We came to believe that a power greater than ourselves could restore us to sanity.

For it is God who works in you to will and to act in order to fulfill his good purpose. (Philippians 2:13)

Introduction

We spent our first month on Principle 1. We finally were able to face our denial and admit that we are powerless to control our tendency to do the wrong thing and that our lives had become unmanageable—out of control!

Now what do we need to do? How and where do we get the control? The answer is to take the second step on our journey of recovery.

The second step tells us that we have come to believe that a power greater than ourselves could restore us to sanity. "Wait a minute!" you're saying. "I spent an entire month hearing that to begin my recovery I had to face and admit my denial. Now you're telling me that I must be crazy? That I need to be restored to sanity? Give me a break!"

No, Step 2 isn't saying that you're crazy. Let me try to explain what the word *sanity* means in this step.

As a result of admitting our powerlessness in Principle 1, we can move from chaos to hope in Principle 2. We talked about that in our last teaching session. Hope comes when we believe that a power greater than ourselves, our Higher Power, Jesus Christ, can and will restore us! Jesus can provide that power where we were powerless over our addictions and compulsive behaviors. He alone can restore order and meaning to our lives. He alone can restore us to sanity.

Sanity

Insanity has been defined as "doing the same thing over and over again, expecting a different result each time."

Sanity has been defined as "wholeness of mind; making decisions based on the truth."

Jesus is the only Higher Power who offers the truth, the power, the way, and the life.

The following acrostic, using the word *sanity*, shows some of the gifts we receive when we believe that our true Higher Power, Jesus Christ, has the power and will restore us to SANITY!

Strength
Acceptance
New Life

Integrity

Trust

Your Higher Power

The first letter is *S*, which stands for STRENGTH.

When we accept Jesus as our Higher Power, we receive strength to face the fears that, in the past, have caused us to fight, flee, or freeze. Now we can say, "God is our refuge and strength, an ever-present help in trouble. Therefore we will not fear, though the earth give way and the mountains fall into the heart of the sea, though its waters roar and foam and the mountains quake with their surging" (Psalm 46:1–3), and "My flesh and my heart may fail, but God is the strength of my heart and my portion forever" (Psalm 73:26).

Relying on our own power, our own strength is what got us here in the first place. We believed we didn't need God's help, strength, or power. It's almost like we were disconnected from our true power source—God!

Choosing to allow my life to finally run on God's power—not my own limited power, weakness, helplessness, or sense of inferiority—has turned out to be my greatest strength. God came in where my helplessness began. And He will do the same for you!

The next letter, *A*, stands for ACCEPTANCE.

Romans 15:5–7 says, "May the God who gives endurance and encouragement give you the same attitude of mind toward each other that Christ Jesus had, so that with one mind and one voice you may glorify the God and Father of our Lord Jesus Christ. Accept one another, then, just as Christ accepted you, in order to bring praise to God."

When we take Step 2, we learn to have realistic expectations of ourselves and others. We learn not to relate to others in the same old way, expecting a different response or result than they have given us time and time again.

We begin to find the sanity we have been searching for. We remember to pray and ask God "to give us the courage to change the things we can and to accept the things we cannot change."

As our faith grows and we get to know our Higher Power better, it becomes easier for us to accept others as they really are, *not as we would have them be!*

With acceptance, however, comes responsibility. We stop placing all the blame on others for our past actions and hurts.

The next letter, *N*, stands for NEW life.

In the pit of our hurts, hang-ups, and habits, we were at our very bottom. We know the feelings expressed in 2 Corinthians 1:8–9: "We do not want you to be uninformed, brothers and sisters, about the troubles we experienced in the province of Asia. We were under great pressure, far beyond our ability to endure, so that we despaired of life itself. Indeed, we felt we had received the sentence of death. But this happened that we might not rely on ourselves but on God, who raises the dead."

Verse 10 goes on to say, "He has delivered us from such deadly peril, and he will deliver us again. On him we have set our hope that he will continue to deliver us."

The penalty for our sins was paid in full by Jesus on the cross. The hope of a new life is freedom from our bondage! "Therefore, if anyone is in Christ, the new creation has come: The old has gone, the new is here!" (2 Corinthians 5:17).

The next benefit of this step is the *I* in sanity: INTEGRITY.

We gain integrity as we begin to follow through on our promises. Others start trusting what we say. The apostle John placed great value on integrity: "It gave me great joy when some believers came and testified about your faithfulness to the truth, telling how you continue to walk in it. I have no greater joy than to hear that my children are walking in the truth." (3 John 3–4).

Remember, a half-truth is a whole lie, and a lie is the result of weakness and fear. Truth fears nothing—nothing but concealment! The truth often hurts. But it's the lie that leaves the scars.

A man or woman of integrity and courage is not afraid to tell the truth. And that courage comes from a power greater than ourselves—Jesus Christ, the way, the TRUTH, and the life.

The *T* in sanity stands for TRUST.

As we work Step 2, we begin to trust in our relationships with others and our Higher Power. "Trust in the LORD with all your heart and lean not on your own understanding; in all your ways submit to him, and he will make your paths straight" (Proverbs 3:5–6).

As we "let go and let God" and admit that our lives are unmanageable and we are powerless to do anything about it, we learn to trust ourselves and others. We begin to make real friends in recovery, in our groups, at the fellowship events, and in church. These are not the mere acquaintances and the fair-weather friends we knew while we were active in our addictions and compulsions.

In recovery you can find real friends, brothers and sisters in Christ, to walk beside you on your journey through the principles—friends whom you can trust, with whom you can share, with whom you can grow in Christ.

The last letter in our acrostic this evening is *Y*: YOUR Higher Power, Jesus Christ, loves you just the way you are! "While we were still sinners, Christ died for us" (Romans 5:8).

No matter what comes your way, together you and God can handle it! "No temptation has overtaken you except what is common to mankind. And God is faithful; he will not let you be tempted beyond what you can bear. But when you are tempted, he will also provide a way out so that you can endure it." (1 Corinthians 10:13). "The righteous cry out, and the LORD hears them; he delivers them from all their troubles. The LORD is close to the brokenhearted and saves those who are crushed in spirit" (Psalm 34:17–18).

When we accept Jesus Christ as our Higher Power and Savior, we are not only guaranteed eternal life, but we also have God's protection in time of trials. Nahum 1:7 says, "The LORD is good, a refuge in times of trouble. He cares for those who trust in him."

Wrap-Up

Recovery is a daily program, and we need a power greater than ourselves—a Higher Power who will provide us with the strength, acceptance, new life, integrity, and trust to allow us to make sane decisions based on His truth!

And if you complete the next principle, Principle 3, your future will be blessed and secure! Matthew 6:34 says, "Therefore do not worry about tomorrow, for tomorrow will worry about itself. Each day has enough trouble of its own."

Let's close in prayer.

Dear God, I have tried to "fix" and "control" my life's hurts, hang-ups, or habits all by myself. I admit that, by myself, I am powerless to change. I need to begin to believe and receive Your power to help me recover. You loved me enough to send Your Son to the cross to die for my sins. Help me be open to the hope that I can only find in Him. Please help me to start living my life one day at a time. In Jesus' name I pray, Amen.

Principle 3

Consciously choose to commit all my life and will to Christ's care and control.

Blessed are the meek, for they will inherit the earth. (Matthew 5:5)

Turn

Principle 3: Consciously choose to commit all my life and will to Christ's care and control.

Blessed are the meek, for they will inherit the earth. (Matthew 5:5)

Step 3: We made a decision to turn our lives and our wills over to the care of God.

Therefore, I urge you, brothers and sisters, in view of God's mercy, to offer your bodies as a living sacrifice, holy and pleasing to God—this is your true and proper worship. (Romans 12:1)

Introduction

Principle 3 states that we choose to commit our *lives* and *wills* to Christ's care and control. We must first commit and surrender our lives to the true Higher Power, Jesus Christ, and then we are able to turn over our wills to Him. Would you all agree with that?

When you choose to live this principle, you consciously choose to commit all your life and will to Christ's care and control. How do you do that? How do you turn your life and will over to your Higher Power, Jesus Christ?

Turn

Let's look at tonight's acrostic for the answer to that question.

Trust
Understand
Repent
New life

This step ends with new life, but you must first take three actions before that life can be yours. You must trust, understand, and repent.

First let's talk about TRUST.

Have you ever been behind a semitruck on a two-lane mountain road? Last summer Cheryl and I were taking Highway 1 toward Northern California. We were in the mountains and the scenery was beautiful. At one point, we approached a very steep incline and there must have been ten cars ahead of us. All of us were stuck behind a very slow-moving eighteen-wheeler.

The truck chugged very slowly up the hill. All of a sudden, the driver stuck his arm out of the window and motioned the cars to go around him. By his arm movement, he was telling us it was safe, there was no oncoming traffic ahead, and we could pass him. One by one, the drivers of the cars trusted their own and their families' lives to a total stranger, as they moved out and in *blind trust* went around the slow truck.

All of a sudden, it hit me! Not the truck. No, I realized that we trust our lives to complete strangers every day. We trust that oncoming cars will stop at intersections. We trust that the hamburgers we eat at fast-food restaurants won't make us sick.

Why then is it so hard for us to trust our lives to the care of God, whose eye is always upon us? I don't know about you, but I would rather walk with God in the darkest valley than walk alone, or with a stranger, in the light.

In Principle 3, you make the one-time *decision* to turn your life over to the care of God. It's your choice, not chance, that determines your destiny. And that decision only requires trust, putting your faith into action!

But what is faith? Faith is *not* a sense, sight, or reason. Faith is simply taking God at His word! And God's Word tells us in Romans 10:9: "If you declare with your mouth, 'Jesus is Lord,' and believe in your heart that God raised him from the dead, you will be saved."

For some people that's just way too simple. They want to make salvation much more difficult. But it isn't! Our salvation, thank God, depends on God's love for us, not our love for Him.

After you have decided to trust, the next step is to UNDERSTAND. Relying solely on our own understanding got most of us into recovery in the first place! After you make the decision to ask Jesus into your life, you need to begin to seek His will for your life in all your decisions. You need to get to know and understand Him and what He wants for your life.

Proverbs 3:5–6 says, "Trust in the LORD with all your heart and lean not on your own understanding; in all your ways submit to him, and he will make your paths straight."

You see, our understanding is earthbound. It's human to the core. Limited. Finite. We operate in a dimension totally unlike that of our Lord. He knows no such limitations. We see now; God sees forever!

You know something really strange? It has taken me all my life to under-stand that it is not necessary for me to understand everything.

First Corinthians 13:9–13 tells us, "For we know in part and we prophesy in part, but when completeness comes, what is in part disappears. When I was a child, I talked like a child, I thought like a child, I reasoned like a child. When I became a man, I put the ways of childhood behind me. For now we see only a reflection as in a mirror; then we shall see face to face. Now I know in part; then I shall know fully, even as I am fully known. And now these three remain: faith, hope and love. But the greatest of these is love."

Someday we will see Jesus face to face. The fog of interpretation will be lifted, and our understanding will be perfected.

Praise God that we do not need a perfect understanding of Him to ask Jesus into our lives as our Lord and Savior. Why? Because God does not lead you year by year. Not even day by day. God directs your way step by step.

The third letter in our acrostic, *R*, stands for REPENT.

Some people repent of their sins by thanking the Lord that they aren't half as bad as their neighbors. That's not true repentance! Repentance is how you begin to enjoy the freedom of your loving relationship with God. True repentance affects our whole person and changes our entire view of life. Repentance is to take God's point of view on our lives instead of our own.

To truly repent you need to do two things: First, turn away from your sins; second, turn toward God. The Bible has much to say about repentance:

"The time has come," he said. "The kingdom of God has come near. Repent and believe the good news!" (Mark 1:15)

"Therefore, you Israelites, I will judge each of you according to your own ways, declares the Sovereign LORD. Repent! Turn away from all your offenses; then sin will not be your downfall. Rid yourselves of all the offenses you have committed, and get a new heart and a new spirit. Why will you die, people of Israel?" (Ezekiel 18:30–31)

Do not conform to the pattern of this world, but be transformed by the renewing of your mind. Then you will be able to test and approve what God's will is—his good, pleasing and perfect will. (Romans 12:2)

It seems that most people repent of their sins more from a fear of punishment than from a real change of heart. But repentance is not self-loathing; it is God-loving. God isn't looking forward to punishing you! He is eagerly anticipating with open arms your turning toward Him. Then when you have chosen to turn from your sin toward Him, He will joyously give to you what the last letter in tonight's acrostic stands for: NEW life.

The new life that you will receive is the result of taking the three actions that we just covered: trusting, understanding, and repenting.

As a pastor, I have heard some pretty glum definitions of life. These are just a few:

"Life is a hereditary disease."

"Life is a sentence that we have to serve for being born."

"Life is a predicament that precedes death."

"Life's a tough proposition; and the first hundred years are the hardest."

Those are depressing words that you may feel are true if your life doesn't include Jesus Christ. After you ask Jesus into your heart, you will have a new life! You will no longer be bound to your old sinful nature. You will receive a new loving nature dwelling within you from Christ.

God has declared you "not guilty," and you no longer have to live under the power of sin! Romans 8:1–2 says it well: "Therefore, there is now no condemnation for those who are in Christ Jesus, because through Christ Jesus the law of the Spirit who gives life has set you free from the law of sin and death."

Therefore, if anyone is in Christ, the new creation has come: The old has gone, the new is here! (2 Corinthians 5:17)

In what ways does the "new life" demonstrate itself in us?

The "old you" said,	The "new you" says,
Save your life!	You must lose your life to keep it (Mark 8:35).
Get, get, get!	Give, and it will be given to you (Luke 6:38).
Lead, at all costs.	Serve (John 13:12).
Lie; the truth only complicates things.	Speak the truth in love (Ephesians 4:15).
Hate your enemy.	Love your enemy (Matthew 5:44).

Let's wrap this up now.

Wrap-Up

Again, the "turn" in Principle 3 includes three very important actions that lead to a new life in Christ: trusting, understanding, repenting.

The good news is, turning your life over to Christ is a once-in-a-lifetime commitment. Once you accept Christ in your life, it's a done deal. Ephesians 1:13 says your salvation is sealed. You can't lose it! It's guaranteed by the Holy Spirit.

The rest of the principle, however, turning your *will* over to Him, requires daily recommitment! You can begin by going to your Bible regularly, opening it prayerfully, reading it expectantly, and living it joyfully!

If you haven't asked Jesus Christ to be your Higher Power, the Lord and Savior of your life, I encourage you to do so this evening. What are you waiting for? Pray this prayer.

Dear God, I have tried to do it all by myself on my own power, and I have failed. Today I want to turn my life over to You. I ask You to be my Lord and my Savior. You are the one and only Higher Power! I ask that You help me think less about me and my will. I want to daily turn my will over to You, to daily seek Your direction and wisdom for my life. Please continue to help me overcome my hurts, hang-ups, and habits, that victory over them may help others as they see Your power at work in changing my life. Help me to do Your will always. In Jesus' name I pray, Amen.

Action

Principle 3: Consciously choose to commit all my life and will to Christ's care and control.

Blessed are the meek, for they will inherit the earth. (Matthew 5:5)

Step 3: We made a decision to turn our lives and our wills over to the care of God.

Therefore, I urge you, brothers and sisters, in view of God's mercy, to offer your bodies as a living sacrifice, holy and pleasing to God—this is your true and proper worship. (Romans 12:1)

Introduction

When we get to Principle 3, we have worked, with God's help, the first two principles to the best of our ability. We admitted our lives were out of control and unmanageable, and we came to believe that God could restore us.

But even after taking the first two steps we can still be stuck in the *cycle of failure* that keeps us bound by guilt, anger, fear, and depression.

Tonight we are going to see how to get "unstuck."

How do we get past those old familiar negative barriers of pride, fear, guilt, worry, and doubt—those barriers that keep us from taking this step? The answer is *action*!

Principle 3 is all about ACTION. It states: "Consciously choose to commit . . ." Making a choice requires action.

Almost everyone knows the difference between right and wrong, but most people don't like making decisions. We just follow the crowd because it's easier than making the decision to do what we know is right. We procrastinate making commitments that will allow change to occur from the pain of our hurts, hang-ups, and habits.

Do you know that some people think that deciding whether or not to discard their old toothbrush is a major decision? Others are so indecisive that their favorite color is plaid!

But seriously, do you know that not to decide is to decide?

Do you know putting off the decision to accept Jesus Christ as your Higher Power, Lord, and Savior really is making the decision *not to accept Him*?

Principle 3 is like opening the door: All you need is the willingness to make the decision. Christ will do the rest!

He said, "Here I am! I stand at the door and knock. If anyone hears my voice and opens the door, I will come in and eat with that person, and they with me" (Revelation 3:20).

Action

Let's look at tonight's acrostic: ACTION.

Accept

Commit

Turn it over

It's only the beginning
One day at a time
Next step

The first letter, *A*, stands for ACCEPT Jesus Christ as your Higher Power and Savior!

Make the once-in-a-lifetime *decision* to ask Jesus into your heart. Make the decision to establish that personal relationship with your Higher Power that He so desires. Now is the time to choose to commit your life. God is saying make it today! Satan says do it tomorrow.

In Romans 10:9 God's Word tells us, "If you declare with your mouth, 'Jesus is Lord,' and believe in your heart that God raised him from the dead, you will be saved."

It's only after you make this decision that you can begin to COMMIT to start asking for and following *His* will! That's the C of the word action.

I would venture that all of us here tonight have tried to run our lives on our own power and will and found it to be less than successful. In Principle 3, we change our definition of willpower. Willpower becomes the willingness to accept God's power to guide your life. We come to see that there is no room for God if we are full of ourselves.

We need to pray the prayer the psalmist prayed when he said, "Teach me to do your will, for you are my God; may your good Spirit lead me on level ground" (Psalm 143:10).

The letter *T* in action stands for TURN it over.

"Let go and let God." You have heard that phase many times in recovery. It doesn't say just let go of some things to God. It doesn't say just let go of, turn over, only the *big* things.

Proverbs 3:5–6 tells us, "Trust in the LORD with all your heart and lean not on your own understanding; in all your ways submit to him, and he will make your paths straight." "In all your ways." Not just the big things, not just the little things. Everything! You see, Jesus Christ just doesn't want a relationship with part of you. He desires a relationship with *all* of you.

What burdens are you carrying tonight that you want to turn over to Jesus? He says, "Come to me, all you who are weary and burdened, and I will give you rest. Take my yoke upon you and learn from me, for I am gentle and humble in heart, and you will find rest for your souls. For my yoke is easy and my burden is light" (Matthew 11:28–30).

The next letter in ACTION is *I*. IT'S only the beginning.

In the third principle we make the initial decision to accept Christ as our personal Savior. Then we can make the commitment to seek and follow God's will. The new life that begins with this decision is followed by a lifelong process of growing as a Christian.

Philippians 1:4–6 puts it this way: "In all my prayers for all of you, I always pray with joy because of your partnership in the gospel from the first day until now, being confident of this, that he who began a good work in you will carry it on to completion until the day of Christ Jesus."

I like to compare the third principle to buying a new house. First you make the decision to buy the new house. But that's only the beginning. There are still more steps that you need to take before you actually can move into the house. You need to go to the bank and apply for a loan. You need to get an appraisal. You need to complete the escrow. You need to contact the moving company. You need to contact the utility companies—all before you are ready to move in.

Recovery is not a three-principle program! Principle 3 is only the exciting beginning of a new life—a life we live in a new way: ONE day at a time.

The letter *O* in ACTION stands for ONE day at a time.

Our recoveries happen one day at a time. If we remain stuck in the yesterday or constantly worry about tomorrow, we will waste the precious time of the present. And it is only in the present that change and growth can occur. We can't change yesterday and we can only pray for tomorrow. Jesus gave us instructions for living this philosophy: "Therefore do not worry about tomorrow, for tomorrow will worry about itself. Each day has enough trouble of its own" (Matthew 6:34).

Believe me, if I could go back and change the past, I would do many things differently. I would choose to spare my family the pain and the hurt that my sin-addiction to alcohol caused. But I can't change even one thing that happened in my past. And neither can you.

And on the other side of the coin, I can't live somewhere way off in the future, always worrying if "this or that" is going to happen. And neither can you. I leave that up to God.

But I can and do live in today! And I can, with Jesus Christ's guidance and direction, make a difference in the way I live today. And so can you. You can make a difference one day at a time.

Wrap-Up

This finally brings us to the last letter in our acrostic. *N* stands for NEXT step.

The next step is to ask Jesus into your life to be your Higher Power. How? It's very simple.

Pastor Rick Warren has developed an easy way for you to establish a "spiritual B.A.S.E." for your life. Ask yourself the following four questions, and if you answer yes to all of them, pray the prayer that follows. That's it. That's all you have to do!

Do I . . .

- **B**elieve Jesus Christ died on the cross for me and showed He was God by coming back to life? (1 Corinthians 15:2–4)
- **A**ccept God's free forgiveness for my sins? (Romans 3:22)
- **S**witch to God's plan for my life? (Mark 1:16–18; Romans 12:2)
- **E**xpress my desire for Christ to be the director of my life? (Romans 10:9)

If you are ready to take this step, in a minute, we will pray together. If you have already taken this step, use this prayer to recommit to continue to seek and follow God's will.

Dear God, there are some here this evening that need to make the decision to commit their lives into Your hands, to ask You into their hearts as their Lord and Savior. Give them the courage to silently do so right now in this moment. It is the most important decision that they will ever make.

Pray with me. I'll say a phrase and you repeat it in your heart.

Dear God, I believe You sent Your Son, Jesus, to die for my sins so I can be forgiven. I'm sorry for my sins, and I want to live the rest of my life the way You want me to. Please put Your Spirit in my life to direct me, Amen.

If you made the decision to invite Christ into your life, let someone know. I would love to talk to you after our fellowship time.

Principle 4

———————————

Openly examine and confess my hurts, hang-ups, and habits to myself, to God, and to someone I trust.

Blessed are the pure in heart, for they will see God. (Matthew 5:8)

———————————

Sponsor

Principle 4: Openly examine and confess my hurts, hang-ups, and habits to myself, to God, and to someone I trust.

Blessed are the pure in heart, for they will see God. (Matthew 5:8)

Step 4: We made a searching and fearless moral inventory of ourselves.

Let us examine our ways and test them, and let us return to the LORD. (Lamentations 3:40)

Introduction

Last month, we talked about the importance of having a personal relationship with Jesus Christ, which you found when you made the decision to turn your life and your will over to the care of God.

Now you will see that the road to recovery is not meant to be traveled alone. You will find that you actually need three relationships. Most important is a relationship with Jesus Christ. In addition, you need the relationship of your recovery group or a church family. Last, you need the relationship of a sponsor and/or accountability partner. Identifying a sponsor and/or accountability partner is especially important before you begin Principles 4 through 6, in which you work on getting right with God, yourself, and others.

Principle 4 is all about being honest and truthful about our past! Proverbs 15:14 tells us, "The discerning heart seeks knowledge, but the mouth of a fool feeds on folly."

Our past can get pretty heavy at times, so I don't want you to handle it alone. You need a genuine mentor, coach, or, in recovery terms, a sponsor and/or an accountability partner. Some of you may still be unconvinced that you really need another person to walk alongside of you on your road to recovery, so tonight we are going to answer the five following questions:

1. Why do I need a sponsor and/or an accountability partner?
2. What are the qualities of a sponsor?
3. What does a sponsor do?
4. How do I find a sponsor and/or an accountability partner?
5. What is the difference between a sponsor and an accountability partner?

Why Do I Need a Sponsor and/or an Accountability Partner?

There are three reasons why you need a sponsor and/or an accountability partner.

Having a Sponsor or Accountability Partner Is Biblical

Ecclesiastes 4:9–12 tells us, "Two are better than one, because they have a good return for their labor: If either of them falls down, one can help the other up. But pity anyone who falls and has no one to help them up. Also, if two lie down together, they will keep warm. But how can one keep warm alone? Though one may be overpowered, two can defend themselves. A cord of three strands is not quickly broken."

Proverbs 27:17 tells us, "As iron sharpens iron, so one person sharpens another."

Having a Sponsor or Accountability Partner Is a Key Part of Your Recovery Program

Do you know that your recovery program has four key elements to success? If your program includes each of these areas, you are well on your way to the solution, to wholeness.

The first key is maintaining your honest view of reality as you work each step. I have yet to see this program fail for someone who could be completely honest with himself or herself. I have, however, seen some give up on their recoveries because they could not step out of their denial into God's truth. Having someone help to keep you honest is a real plus in successfully working the steps.

The second key element is making your attendance at your recovery group meetings a priority in your schedule. This doesn't include taking the summer off or not going to a meeting because it's raining outside. Don't get me wrong, it's great to take a vacation, but after the two weeks are up, come back to your meetings. Remember, your hurts, hang-ups, and habits don't take vacations. You need to make Friday nights here at Celebrate Recovery and other meeting nights that you attend a priority. A sponsor and/or an accountability partner can encourage you to attend your meetings.

The third element is maintaining your spiritual program with Jesus Christ through prayer, meditation, and study of His Word. We are going to focus more on this in Principle 7, but you don't have to wait until you get there to develop your relationship with Christ. Your sponsor can pray for you and help to keep you centered on God's Word.

The last key element to a successful program is getting involved in service. Once you have completed Principle 8, you will be able to serve as a sponsor. Until that time, however, there are plenty of other service opportunities to get you started.

Without exception, everyone here needs a sponsor and/or an accountability partner.

Having a Sponsor and/or an Accountability Partner Is the Best Guard Against Relapse

By providing feedback to keep you on track, a sponsor and/or an accountability partner can see your old dysfunctional, self-defeating patterns beginning to surface and point them out to you quickly. He or she can confront you with truth and love without placing shame or guilt.

Ecclesiastes 7:5 tells us that "It is better to heed the rebuke of a wise person than to listen to the song of fools." The trouble with most of us is that we would rather be ruined by praise than saved by criticism.

What Are the Qualities of a Sponsor?

The purposes of a person's heart are deep waters, but one who has insight draws them out. (Proverbs 20:5).

When you are selecting a sponsor, look for the following qualities:

1. **Does their walk match their talk? Are they living the eight principles?** I have known many people who have the 12-Step "lingo" down pat. But their lifestyle doesn't match their talk. Be certain that the person that you choose as a sponsor is someone whose life example is worthy of imitation.
2. **Do they have a growing relationship with Jesus Christ?** Do you see the character of Christ developing in them?
3. **Do they express the desire to help others on the road to recovery?** There is a difference between helping others and trying to fix others. We all need to be careful to guard the sponsorship relationship from becoming unhealthy and codependent.
4. **Do they show compassion, care, and hope but not pity?** You don't need someone to feel sorry for you, but you do need someone to be sensitive to your pain. As Pastor Rick Warren says, "People don't care about how much you know until they know about how much you care!"
5. **Are they a good listener?** Do you sense that they honestly care about what you have to say?
6. **Are they strong enough to confront your denial or procrastination?** Do they care enough about you and your recovery to challenge you?

7. **Do they offer suggestions?** Sometimes we need help in seeing options or alternatives that we are unable to find on our own. A good sponsor can take an objective view and offer suggestions. They should not give orders!

8. **Do they share their own current struggles with others?** Are they willing to open up and be vulnerable and transparent? I don't know about you, but I don't want a sponsor who says that they have worked the principles. I want a sponsor who is living and working the principles every day!

What Is the Role of a Sponsor?

1. **The most important role of a sponsor is to continually point you to Jesus as your Higher Power. They do not work the steps for you!** A good sponsor will help you create a dependence on God for your recovery and healing, not them.

2. **They can be there to discuss issues in detail that are too personal or would take too much time in a meeting.** This is especially true with Principle 4. You don't share your complete inventory in a group setting.

   "I'm the lowest form of life on the earth" is a phrase often repeated by those doing their inventory. Others deny, rationalize, and blame: "Okay, I admit I did such and such, but it's not as if I killed anybody"; "Sure, I did a, b, and c, but my spouse did d through z; compared to my spouse, I'm a saint"; "All right, I admit it, but I never would have done it if my boss wasn't such a jerk."

   The sponsor can be there to share his or her own experiences and to offer strength and hope: "You think you feel like a bum! Let me tell you how I felt when I did my inventory!"

3. **They are available in times of crisis or potential relapse.** I have always told the newcomers that I have sponsored, "Call me before you take that first drink. You can still take it after we talk, if you decide to. But please call first!" Remember Ecclesiastes 4:12: "Though one may be overpowered, two can defend themselves. A cord of three strands is not quickly broken."

4. **They serve as a sounding board by providing an objective point of view.** This is especially true in Principle 6. When you are dealing with the sensitive area of making amends and offering forgiveness, you need a good sounding board.

5. **They are there to encourage you to work the principles at your own speed.** It is not their job to work the principles for you! They can coach your progress, confront you when you're stuck, and slow you down when you're working too fast.

6. **Most important, they attempt to model the lifestyle that results from working the eight principles.** It's difficult to inspire others to accomplish what you haven't been willing to try yourself. A good sponsor lives the principles.

7. **A sponsor can resign or be fired.** Sponsorship is not a lifetime position.

How Do I Find a Sponsor and/ or an Accountability Partner?

The responsibility of finding a sponsor and/or an accountability partner is yours, but let me give you a few final guidelines to help you in your search.

1. **First and foremost, the person MUST be of the same sex as you.** NO EXCEPTIONS. I don't think I need to expand on this one.

2. **Can you relate to this person's story?** If you are choosing someone to be your sponsor, does he or she meet the qualities of a good sponsor that we just covered?

3. **Attend the Fellowship events.** Invest some time in fellowship and get to know others in your group. That's the main reason we have these fellowship events.

4. **If you ask someone to be your sponsor and/or an accountability partner, and that person says no, do not take it as a personal rejection.** Remember that their own recovery has to come first. I know a lot of you have asked your small group leader to be your sponsor. They all sponsor others, and the responsibility of leadership is great. If they turn you down, it's not personal. Their plate is simply too full! If someone turns you down, ask someone else! You can even ask for a "temporary" sponsor and/or an accountability partner. Remember, these are not lifetime commitments.

5. **Most important, ask God to lead you to the sponsor and/or an accountability partner of His choosing.** He knows you and everyone in this room. He has someone in mind already for you. All you need to do is ask!

What Is the Difference between a Sponsor and an Accountability Partner?

A sponsor is someone who has completed the four Celebrate Recovery participant's guides and has worked through the eight principles and the 12 Steps. He or she meets the seven recommendations that we talked about in the "Role of a Sponsor." The main goal of this relationship is to choose someone to guide you through the program.

An accountability partner is someone you ask to hold you accountable for certain areas of your recovery or issues, such as meeting attendance, journaling, and so forth. This person can be at the same level of recovery as you are, unlike a sponsor, who should have completed the eight principles or 12 Steps. The main goal of this relationship is to encourage one another. You can even form an accountability team of three or four.

The accountability partner or group acts as the "team," whereas the sponsor's role is that of a "coach."

You can start forming accountability teams in your small groups tonight. When you share, just ask if anyone is interested. Let God work and see what happens. I can guarantee this, though: Nothing will happen if you don't ask.

Start looking for and building your support team tonight!

Let's close in prayer.

Dear God, thank You for this group of people who are here to break out of the hurts, hang-ups, and habits that have kept them bound. Thank You for the leaders You have provided. Thank You that You love us all, no matter where we are in our recoveries. Show me the person You have prepared to be my sponsor. Help us to establish an honest and loving relationship that honors You and helps both me and my sponsor grow stronger in You. In Jesus' name I pray, Amen.

Moral

Principle 4: Openly examine and confess my hurts, hang-ups, and habits to myself, to God, and to someone I trust.

Blessed are the pure in heart, for they will see God. (Matthew 5:8)

Step 4: We made a searching and fearless moral inventory of ourselves.

Let us examine our ways and test them, and let us return to the Lord. (Lamentations 3:40)

Introduction

Tonight we are going to really dig in and begin the growth process of recovery. Now, even though Principle 4 may bring some growing pains with it, tonight we are going to look at ways to maximize the growth and minimize the pain.

I wish I could say that you can escape the pain of your past altogether by going around it or jumping over it. But the only way I know to get rid of the pain of your past is to go through it. It has been said that "we need to use our past as a springboard, not a sofa—a guidepost, not a hitching post."

I know some people who spend their lives rationalizing the past, complaining about the present, and fearing the future. They, of course, are not moving forward on the road to recovery. By coming tonight, however, you have chosen to continue going forward. And if you choose to embark on the adventure of self-discovery that begins with Principle 4 and continues through Principle 5, I can guarantee you that growth will occur.

It is here, in Principle 4, that we openly examine and confess our hurts, hang-ups, and habits to ourselves, to God, and another person we trust. We step out of the denial that has built up over the years and has kept us from really seeing the truth about our past and present situations. We look back to our past hurt to explain and understand our hang-ups and habits.

A Moral Inventory

You may be wondering, "How do I do a searching and fearless moral inventory?" Tonight's acrostic, MORAL, will explain the five things you need in order to do an honest inventory.

The word *moral* scares some people. It scared me when I first worked this step in AA. Really, the word moral simply means honest!

In this step, you need to list, or inventory, all the significant events—good and bad—in your life. You will need to be as honest as you can be to allow God to show you how you've been hurt, how you've hurt others, and how that affected you and others.

Make time
Open
Rely

Analyze

List

First you need to MAKE time. Schedule an appointment with yourself. Set aside a day or a weekend and get alone with God! God tells us in Psalm 46:10: "Be still, and know that I am God; I will be exalted among the nations, I will be exalted in the earth."

The next letter in moral, *O*, stands for OPEN.

Remember when, as a child, you would visit the doctor, and he would say, "Open wide!" in that funny sing-song voice? Well, you need to "open wide" your heart and mind to allow the feelings that the pain of the past has blocked or caused you to deny. Denial may have protected you from your feelings and repressed your pain for a while. But now it has also blocked and prevented your recovery from your hurts, hang-ups, and habits. You need to "open wide" to see the real truth.

Once you have seen the truth, you need to express it. Here's what Job had to say about being open: "Therefore I will not keep silent; I will speak out in the anguish of my spirit, I will complain in the bitterness of my soul" (Job 7:11). Perhaps the following questions will help to "wake up" your feelings and get you started on your inventory!

Ask yourself, *How have I been hurt?* The first thing that came to your mind is what you need to address first in your recovery. Addressing how we've been hurt is important because it directly affects what we believe about ourselves, others or God, and that directly impacts our habits.

Ask yourself, *What do I feel guilty about?* Do you know and understand the God-given purpose of guilt? God uses guilt to correct us through His Spirit when we are wrong. That's called conviction. And conviction hurts!

Now don't confuse conviction with condemnation. Romans 8:1 tells us, "There is now no condemnation for those who are in Christ Jesus." Once we have made the decision to ask Jesus into our hearts, once we confess our wrongs, accept Christ's perfect forgiveness, and turn from our sins, as far as God is concerned, guilt's purpose—to make us feel bad about what we did in the past—is finished. But we like to hold on to it and beat ourselves over the head—repeatedly—with it!

That's condemnation. But it's not from God, it's from ourselves. Principle 4 will help you let go of your guilt, once and for all.

The next question you need to ask is *Who do I resent?*

Resentment results from burying our hurts. If resentments are then suppressed, left to decay, they cause anger, frustration, and depression. What we don't talk out creatively, we act out destructively.

Another big question that you need to openly ask during this step is *What are my fears?*

Personally, I have a fear of going to the dentist. But even though it may hurt while I'm in the chair, when he's done driving the decay away, I feel a lot better.

Fear prevents us from expressing ourselves honestly and taking an honest moral inventory. Joshua 1:9 tells us, "Have I not commanded you? Be strong and courageous. Do not be afraid; do not be discouraged, for the LORD your God will be with you wherever you go."

Next on the list of hard questions to ask yourself: *Am I trapped in false beliefs about myself, God, or others? Am I trapped in dishonesty, lies, or self-pity?* Being honest about what we believe about ourselves, others, or God is necessary to understanding why we struggle with unhealthy habits or compulsive behaviors.

These questions are only the beginning of your inventory, but don't get discouraged. The next letter offers a reminder that you don't have to face this task alone.

The next letter is *R*, which stands for RELY.

Rely on Jesus to give you the courage and strength this step requires. Here's a suggestion: When your knees are knocking, it might help to kneel on them.

Isaiah 40:29 tells us that Jesus "gives strength to the weary and increases the power of the weak." You can do this with His help.

Before we go any further, I want to remind you that the principles and steps are in order for a reason (other than to create a nifty acrostic!). You need to complete Principle 3—turning your life and your will over to God—before you can successfully work Principle 4.

Once you know the love and power of the one and only Higher Power, Jesus Christ, there is no longer any need to fear this principle. Psalm 31:23–24 tells us: "Love the LORD, all his faithful people! The LORD preserves those who are true to him, but the proud he pays back in full. Be strong and take heart, all you who hope in the LORD." And remember, courage is not the absence of fear but the conquering of it.

Now you are ready to ANALYZE your past honestly.

To do a "searching and fearless" inventory, you must step out of your denial, because we cannot put our hurts, hang-ups, and habits behind us until we face them. You must look through your denial of the past into the truth of the present—your true feelings, motives, thoughts.

Proverbs 20:27 says, "The human spirit is the lamp of the LORD that sheds light on one's inmost being." Some of you heard the word *analyze* and got fired up, because you love to pick apart the details of a situation and look at events from all angles. Others of you have broken out into a cold sweat at the thought of analyzing anything! For those of you whose hearts are pounding and whose palms are clammy, listen closely as we talk about the *L* in moral: LIST.

Your inventory is basically a written list of the events of your past—both good and bad. (Balance is important.) Seeing your past in print brings you face to face with the reality of your character defects. Your inventory becomes a black-and-white discovery of who you truly are way down deep.

But if you just look at all the bad things of your past, you will distort your inventory and open yourself to unnecessary pain. Lamentations 3:40 tells us, "Let us examine our ways and test them." The verse doesn't say, "just examine your bad, negative ways." You need to honestly focus on the "pros" and the "cons" of your past!

I know people who have neglected to balance their inventory and have gotten stuck in their recoveries. Or even worse, they judged the program to be too hard and too painful and stopped their journey of recovery altogether—and they slipped back to their old hurts, hang-ups, and habits of the past.

An important word of caution: Do not begin this step without a sponsor or a strong accountability partner! You need someone you trust to help keep you balanced during this step, not to do the work for you. Nobody can do that except you. But you need encouragement from someone who will support your progress and share your pain. That's what this program is all about.

Wrap-Up

At the information table, you will find some blank Principle 4 worksheets. In a few weeks, we will be talking about how to put them to use in helping you work this key step.

If you are new to recovery, the good news is you don't start on this step. You start at Step 1 Principle 1. It is important to note that it is best to do your fourth step in a Step Study. If you have been in recovery for a while and you haven't yet joined a Step Study, it's time! Take that next step and dive deeper into steps and principles.

Let's pray.

Dear God, You know my past, all the good and the bad. Both the things I've done, and the things that have been done to me. In this step, I ask that You give me the strength and the courage to list those things so that I can face them and the truth, and begin to heal. Please help me reach out to others You have placed along my "road to recovery." Thank You for providing them to help me keep balanced as I do my inventory. In Christ's name I pray, Amen.

Inventory

Principle 4: Openly examine and confess my hurts, hang-ups, and habits to myself, to God, and to someone I trust.

Blessed are the pure in heart, for they will see God. (Matthew 5:8)

Step 4: We made a searching and fearless moral inventory of ourselves.

Let us examine our ways and test them, and let us return to the Lord. (Lamentations 3:40)

Introduction

Tonight we are going to look at how to start your inventory, so get ready to write. Yes, that's right. Your inventory needs to be on paper. Writing (or typing) will help you organize your thoughts and focus on recalling events that you may have repressed. Getting all of it down helps you to clearly see the connection between the hurts that lead to hang-ups that created habits. You'll discover the root issues that show up as emotional triggers, repeated patterns of behavior, and character defects. You will be amazed by the transformation it brings, and how you will grow in your relationship with Jesus Christ in the process!

Before I jump into the lesson, I just want to say, if you're a newcomer, just beginning your recovery journey, please know that you don't need to jump right in to the part of the process I'll be discussing today. Please just sit back, take it in, and when you do get to the point that you've worked through Steps 1, 2, and 3, and are ready to work on your inventory, preferably in a Step Study, hopefully tonight's lesson will have prepared you a little.

It's suggested you work on your inventory within a Step Study Group, where you work up to this step progressively, moving through Steps 1–3 before going into Step 4 inventory. This doesn't mean you can't work on your inventory alone, or any time you choose, just know that it can be a difficult step to take, and having the support and encouragement of others, hearing other's answers and sharing your own, creates a rich environment for healing, growth, restoration, and transformation.

Inventory

Now that you have the background information and you've built your accountability team, it's time to start writing your inventory. This lesson will provide you with the tools you need. Getting all of it down helps you to clearly see the connection between the hurts that lead to hang-ups that created habits. You'll discover the root issues that show up as emotional triggers, repeated patterns of behavior, and character defects. You will be amazed by the transformation it brings, and how you will grow in your relationship with Jesus Christ in the process!

How do I start my inventory?

The Celebrate Recovery Inventory is divided into five sections. It will help you keep focused on reality and recall events that you may have repressed. Remember, you are not going through this alone. You are developing your support team to guide you, but even more important, you are growing in your relationship with Jesus Christ!

It will take you more than one page to write out your inventory. You have permission to copy the "Celebrate Recovery Principle 4 Inventory Worksheet" on pages 277.

Column 1: "Who hurt me?"

In this column, **you list the person or institution who hurt you**. So even though this column is called The Person it can also be institutions or places. For example, you may have resentments, fears, or negative emotions toward an organization like the church, the government, or the medical establishment. Or you may have been dealing with a chronic illness that has built up resentment. While working on this list, go back as far as you can into early childhood. Sometimes, people feel guilty listing their parents or other caregivers, but we've all been raised by imperfect people. We list them to explain and understand our history, not to assign blame. Again, list people, institutions, or places. If you get overwhelmed, back up and take it one event at a time. Pick one or two events that had the most impact on you and your life and start there. Then move on to one or two more. Pray and ask God who or what from your life needs to go in Column 1. He is faithful and will show you. Lamentations 3:22–23 tells us, "Because of the LORD's great love we are not consumed, for his compassions never fail. They are new every morning; great is your faithfulness." We are not alone in this process!

Column 2: "What happened?"

In this column, you are going to **list what happened** when the person or institution hurt you. It is important to be specific about these actions. For example, you might list a parent who always told you to stop crying or told you your feelings didn't matter. Friends may have dismissed your feelings as you went through a divorce. These reflections can be painful, but God is with us every step of the way.

Isaiah 41:10 says, "So do not fear, for I am with you; do not be dismayed, for I am your God. I will strengthen you and help you; I will uphold you with my righteous right hand." It is imperative to have a sponsor and/or accountability partner supporting you as you work on this inventory. They will be there to support you as you walk through the pain, some or all of this group can be accountability partners. If you do not have one, keep looking! Your step study group is also working through the same process You can begin to build relationships with them. They will be there to support you as you walk through the pain.

Column 3: "How did you feel?"

In this column, you will **list how did this action make you feel**. It is important to acknowledge our emotions. These emotions affect what we believe, which in turn. directly affects our behaviors, or habits. Many of us were taught to repress our emotions. If we cannot express how we feel, or how we were hurt, then we cannot heal. Denying our pain and emotions does not make them go away. They store up in our body and make us hurt until we feel them. Try to list two or three emotions in this column. Since so many of us were taught to disconnect from our emotions from an early age, this can be very difficult. It can help to have an emotions list on hand as you work on your inventory.

Trust in him at all times, you people; pour out our hearts to him, for God is our refuge. (Psalm 62:8)

Column 4: "What was the damage"

In this column, you are going to **list what was the damage**. This includes any beliefs you might have developed as a result. Remember, how you've been hurt directly affects what you think or believe about yourself, others, or God. These beliefs are our hang-ups. For example, a belief system could be that your emotions make you a burden, or that you are unworthy of love. How did your worldview change? Did you develop mistrust for a group of people based on this particular event? Or is there a pattern of broken relationships, slander, loss of physical safety, financial loss or damaged intimacy from abusive relationships?

No matter how you have been hurt, no matter how lost you may feel, God wants to comfort you and restore you. Remember Ezekiel 34:16: "I will search for the lost and bring back the strays. I will bind up the injured and strengthen the weak, but the sleek and the strong I will destroy. I will shepherd the flock with justice."

Column 5: "What was/What is my part?"

Now it's time to see what part you have played. So far, in Columns 1-4 you have explored how you have been hurt and the impact that pain has had on your life. This is the column where we stop looking outward and we start looking inward. There are two pitfalls to avoid here, one, blaming everyone else for your behaviors and habits and taking no responsibility for your actions, and two, believing that none of the first four columns have had any impact on your choices or formed your coping mechanisms.

Ask yourself, **"What was/what is my part?"** For example, do you try to control others in an attempt to feel safe? Or do you drink, shop, or go online too much in an attempt to escape pain in your life? Also ask yourself, "Did I have a part in the action that hurt me?" If so, write out what your part was.

List all the people whom you have hurt and how you have hurt them. "Search me, God, and know my heart; test me and know my anxious thoughts. See if there is any offensive way in me, and lead me in the way everlasting" (Psalm 139:23–24).

Please note: If you have been in an abusive relationship, especially as a small child, you can find great freedom in this part of the inventory. You see that you had **NO** part, **NO** responsibility for the cause of the resentment. By simply writing the words "none" or "not guilty" in column 5, you can begin to be free from the misplaced shame and guilt you have carried with you.

Celebrate Recovery has rewritten Step 4 for those who have been sexually or physically abused: Made a searching and fearless moral inventory of ourselves, realizing all wrongs can be forgiven. Renounce the lie that the abuse was our fault.

Wrap-Up

There are five tools to help you prepare your inventory:

1. Memorize Isaiah 1:18: " 'Come now, let us settle the matter,' says the Lord. 'Though your sins are like scarlet, they shall be as white as snow; though they are red as crimson, they shall be like wool.' "
2. Read the "balancing the scale verses" on page 60 of Volume 2!
3. Keep your inventory balanced. List both the good and the bad! This is very important! As God reveals the good things that you have done in the past, or are doing in the present, list them on the reverse side of your copies of the "Celebrate Recovery Principle 4 Inventory Worksheet."
4. Continue to develop your support team.
5. Pray continuously.

Don't wait to start your inventory. Don't let any obstacle stand in your way. If you don't have a sponsor or accountability partner yet, talk to someone tonight! If you need a participant's guide, pick one up at the information table. Set a time and place and get busy! You *can* do it!

Spiritual Inventory Part I

Principle 4: Openly examine and confess my hurts, hang-ups, and habits to myself, to God, and to someone I trust.

Blessed are the pure in heart, for they will see God. (Matthew 5:8)

Step 4: We made a searching and fearless moral inventory of ourselves.

Let us examine our ways and test them, and let us return to the LORD. (Lamentations 3:40)

Introduction

Tonight we begin the first of two lessons in which we will look at our spiritual inventory, using the "Spiritual Evaluation" Pastor Rick Warren developed for this step.[1]

Principle 4 begins the process of openly examining and confessing your faults to yourself, to God, and to another person you trust. Most of us don't like to look within ourselves for the same reason we don't like to open a letter that we know has bad news. But remember what we talked about in Lesson 9: You need to keep your evaluation, your inventory, balanced. It needs to include both the good and the bad within you. Let's look at what a spiritual inventory, or evaluation, is all about!

God's Word tells us, "Search me, God, and know my heart; test me and know my anxious thoughts. See if there is any offensive way in me, and lead me in the way everlasting" (Psalm 139:23–24).

Do you know everyone has three different "characters"?

1. The character we exhibit.
2. The character we think we have.
3. The character we truly have.

We will work on four areas of our character shortcomings tonight and four more at our next session. This exercise will help you get started on your inventory as you search your heart!

Relationships with Others

In Matthew 6:12–13 Jesus tells us to pray, "And forgive us our debts, as we also have forgiven our debtors. And lead us not into temptation, but deliver us from the evil one."

Ask yourself the following questions regarding your relationships with others:

- **Who has hurt you?**
- **Against whom have you been holding a grudge?** It doesn't take a doctor to tell you that

---

1. The eight areas of the spiritual inventory were written by Pastor Rick Warren. With his permission, I have added my teaching notes and comments.

it is better to remove a grudge than to nurse it. No matter how long you nurse a grudge, it won't get better. Writing the grudge down on your inventory is the first step in getting rid of it.

- **Against whom are you seeking revenge?** Did you know that seeking revenge is like biting a dog just because the dog bit you? It really doesn't help you or the dog!
- **Are you jealous of someone?** In Song of Songs 8:6 jealousy is said to be as unyielding as the grave. It burns like blazing fire!

NOTE: The people that you name in these areas will go in column 1 of your "Celebrate Recovery Principle 4 Inventory Worksheet" in Volume 2.

- **Who have you hurt?** How did you hurt them? You may have hurt them unintentionally. Maybe it was intentional.
- **Have you tried to justify your bad attitude by saying it is "their fault"?**
- **Who have you been critical of or gossiped about?** It isn't that difficult to make a mountain out of a molehill. Just add a little dirt on it. That's what gossip is—just a little dirt! I find it amazing that a tongue four inches long can destroy a man six feet tall. That's why James 1:26 tells us to "keep a tight rein on [our] tongues."

NOTE: The people that you name in these areas will go in column 5 of your "Celebrate Recovery Principle 4 Inventory Worksheet."

Next, let's look at what's important to you.

Priorities in Your Life

We do what is important to us. Others see our priorities by our actions, not our words. Personally, I'd rather see a sermon than hear one any day.

What are the priorities in your life?

Matthew 6:33 tells us what will happen if we make God our number one priority: "But seek first his kingdom and his righteousness, and all these things will be given to you as well."

- **After making the decision to turn your life and your will over to God, in what areas of your life are you still not putting God first?** What closet are you not letting Him enter and clean out?
- **What in your past is interfering with your doing God's will? Your ambition? Your pleasures?** Is it driven by serving God or is it driven by envy? If your pleasure has been found in the world, Proverbs 21:17 warns, "Whoever loves pleasure will become poor, whoever loves wine and olive oil will never be rich." Is your pleasure now found in Jesus Christ? Psalm 16:11 tells us, "You make known to me the path of life; you will fill me with joy in your presence, with eternal pleasures at your right hand."
- **What have been your priorities in your job? Friendships? Personal goals?** Were they just self-centered, self-serving?
- **Who did your priorities affect?**
- **What was good about your priorities?**
- **What was wrong about them?** The next area of our spiritual inventory is to examine our attitudes.

Your Attitude

Ephesians 4:31 says, "Get rid of all bitterness, rage and anger, brawling and slander, along with every form of malice."

- **Do you always try to have an "attitude of gratitude" or do you find yourself always complaining about your circumstances?** When you feel dog tired at night, do you ever think that it might be because you growled all day?
- **In what areas of your life are you ungrateful?** If we can't be grateful for the bad things in our lives that we have received, we can at least be thankful for what we have escaped. And the one thing we can all be grateful for is found in 1 Corinthians 15:57: "But thanks be to God! He gives us the victory through our Lord Jesus Christ."
- **Have you gotten angry and easily blown up at people?**

- **Have you been sarcastic?** Do you know that sarcasm can be a form of verbal abuse?
- **What in your past is still causing you fear or anxiety?** As we have said before, your fear imprisons you; your faith liberates you. Fear paralyzes; faith empowers! Fear disheartens; faith encourages! Fear sickens; faith heals! Faith in Jesus Christ will allow you to face your past fears, and with faith you can be free of fear's chains. First John 4:18 says, "There is no fear in love. But perfect love drives out fear, because fear has to do with punishment. The one who fears is not made perfect in love."

The last area we are going to talk about tonight is your integrity.

Your Integrity

Colossians 3:9 tells us, "Do not lie to each other, since you have taken off your old self with its practices."

- **In what past dealing were you dishonest?** An honest man alters his ideas to fit the truth. A dishonest man alters the truth to fit his ideas.
- **Have you stolen things?** I told you that your inventory wasn't going to be easy.
- **Have you exaggerated yourself to make yourself look better?** Did you know that there are no degrees of "honest"? Either you are or you aren't!
- **In what areas of your past have you used false humility?** Did you know that humility is never gained by seeking it? To think we have it is sure proof that we don't.
- **Have you pretended to live one way in front of your Christian friends and another way at home or at work?** Are you a "Sunday Christian" or a seven-day, full-time follower of Jesus Christ? Do you try to practice the eight principles seven days a week or just here at Celebrate Recovery on Friday nights?

Wrap-Up

Well, that's enough to work on for one week, but next week we'll dig in again and look at part two of our spiritual inventory. We'll explore our old ways of thinking—our minds; the ways we have treated or mistreated God's temple—our bodies; how we did or didn't walk by faith in the past; our important past relations with our family and church.

As you start to work on your spiritual inventory, remember two things. First in Isaiah 1:18 it says, " 'Come now, let us settle the matter,' says the LORD. 'Though your sins are like scarlet, they shall be as white as snow; though they are red as crimson, they shall be like wool.' " Second—I can't say it enough—keep your inventory balanced. List the positive new relationships that you have, the areas of your life that you have been able to turn over to God, how your attitude has improved since you have been in recovery, the ways you have been able to step out of your denial into God's truth.

Let's close in prayer.

Father God, thank You for each person here tonight. Thank You for giving them the courage to begin this difficult step of making an inventory. Give them the desire and strength they need to proceed. Encourage them and light their way with Your truth. In the strong name of Jesus I pray, Amen.

Spiritual Inventory Part 2

Principle 4: Openly examine and confess my hurts, hang-ups, and habits to myself, to God, and to someone I trust.

Blessed are the pure in heart, for they will see God. (Matthew 5:8)

Step 4: We made a searching and fearless moral inventory of ourselves.

Let us examine our ways and test them, and let us return to the LORD. (Lamentations 3:40)

Introduction

Tonight we are looking at the second part of our spiritual inventory, where we pray, "Search me, God, and know my heart; test me and know my anxious thoughts. See if there is any offensive way in me, and lead me in the way everlasting" (Psalm 139:23–24).

Last week, we discussed in part one of our spiritual inventories four areas of our lives. We asked ourselves some hard questions.

We looked at our relationships to others, our priorities, our attitudes, and our integrity. We talked about how our past actions in each of these areas had a negative or a positive effect on our lives and the lives of others.

Tonight, we are going to finish our spiritual inventory. We will look for some of our additional hurts, hang-ups, or habits that can prevent God from working effectively in our lives and our recoveries.

Evaluating each area will help you complete your inventory.

Your Mind

Did you know that the most difficult thing to open is a closed mind? Romans 12:2 gives us clear direction regarding our minds: "Do not conform to the pattern of this world, but be transformed by the renewing of your mind. Then you will be able to test and approve what God's will is—his good, pleasing and perfect will."

Some questions to ask yourself in this area:

- **How have you guarded your mind in the past? What did you deny?** Once again you need to see and examine how your coping skills may have protected you from pain and hurt in the past. It may have done so, however, by preventing you from living in and dealing with reality.
- **Do you know that two thoughts cannot occupy your mind at the same time?** It is your choice as to whether your thoughts will be constructive or destructive, positive or negative.
- **In what ways has your emotional and mental health been harmed by others?** Has someone ever used shame or guilt to manipulate or control you?
- **Have you filled your mind with hurtful and unhealthy movies, Internet sites, television programs, magazines, or books?** Your ears and your eyes are doors and

windows to your soul. So, remember "garbage in, garbage out." Straight living cannot come out of crooked thinking. It just is not going to happen. Remember Proverbs 15:14: "The discerning heart seeks knowledge, but the mouth of a fool feeds on folly."

- **Have you failed to concentrate on the positive truths of the Bible?** I believe that three of the greatest sins today are indifference to, neglect of, and disrespect for the Word of God. Have you set aside a daily quiet time to get into God's instruction manual for your life?

Next, let's look at how we have treated our bodies.

Your Body

Do you not know that your bodies are temples of the Holy Spirit, who is in you, whom you have received from God? You are not your own; you were bought at a price. Therefore honor God with your bodies. (1 Corinthians 6:19–20)

- **In what ways have you mistreated your body?**
- **Have you abused alcohol, drugs, food, or sex?**

This was, and still is, a tough one for me. In the depth of my alcoholism my weight dropped down to 160 pounds (my normal weight is 220 pounds). I almost died. I kept getting my suit pants taken in, and finally, the tailor explained to me that he couldn't take them in any more—the back pockets were touching. I asked God to help me get my strength and weight back. He truly blessed me. Boy, did He bless me! Now, it's time for moderation in my eating.

It is through our bodies or flesh that Satan works, but thank God that the believer's body is the temple of the Holy Spirit. God freely gives us the grace of His Spirit. He values us so much that He chose to place His Spirit within us. We need to have as much respect for ourselves as our Creator does for us.

- **In what ways has your body been harmed by others?**
- **What activities or habits caused harm to your physical health?** Remember, it was the God of creation who made you. Look at Psalm139:13–14: "For you created my inmost being; you knit me together in my mother's womb. I praise you because I am fearfully

and wonderfully made; your works are wonderful, I know that full well." Many people say that they have the right to do whatever they want to their own bodies. Although they think that this is freedom, they really become enslaved to their own desires, which ultimately cause them great harm.

Your Family

Sometimes our family can be our biggest source of hurt. Whether you have a good relationship with your family, or no relationship, the good news is, if you're a Christian you are a part of God's family! And that's the best family to be in! "See what great love the Father has lavished on us, that we should be called children of God! And that is what we are! The reason the world does not know us is that it did not know him" (1 John 3:1).

- **In the past, has anyone in your family mistreated you?** Have you been physically or emotionally mistreated by someone in your family. Emotional abuse doesn't have to take the form of raging, yelling, or screaming. Emotional neglect, parentification (meaning a child takes on the responsibilities of a parent), using guilt or shame to manipulate, or methodically tearing down someone's self-esteem are all forms of emotional abuse.
- **Have you mistreated anyone in your family? How?** Perhaps you have physically or emotionally mistreated your family. Emotional abuse doesn't have to take the form of raging, yelling, or screaming. Tearing down a child's or spouse's self-esteem and being emotionally unavailable to them are both ways you may have harmed your loved ones.
- **Against whom in your family do you have a resentment?** This can be a difficult area in which to admit your true feelings. It's easier to admit the resentments you have against a stranger or someone at work than someone in your own family. Denial can be a pretty thick fog to break through here. But you need to do it if you are going to successfully complete your inventory.
- **To whom do you owe amends?** You identify them now and work on becoming willing to deal with amends in Principle 6. All you are really looking for is your part in a damaged relationship.
- **What is the family secret that you have been denying?** What is the "pink elephant" in the middle of your family's living room that no one talks about? That's the family secret!

Your Church

And let us consider how we may spur one another on toward love and good deeds, not giving up meeting together, as some are in the habit of doing, but encouraging one another—and all the more as you see the Day approaching. (Hebrews 10:24–25)

- **Have you been hurt by the Church?**
- **Have you been faithful to your church in the past?** Your church is like a bank: The more you put into it, the more interest you gain in it.
- **Have you been critical instead of active?** If you don't like something in your church, get involved so you can help change it or at least understand it better. Turn your grumbling into service!
- **Have you discouraged your family's support of their church?** If you aren't ready to get involved in your church, that's your decision. But don't stop the rest of your family from experiencing the joys and support of a church family!

Wrap-Up

We've made it all the way through the eight different areas to help you begin and complete your inventory.

Once again, listen to Isaiah 1:18. Memorize it! God says, " 'Come now, let us settle the matter,' says the Lord. 'Though your sins are like scarlet, they shall be as white as snow; though they are red as crimson, they shall be like wool.' "

A couple of reminders as we close:

- Use the "Balancing the Scales" verses found in Volume 2.
- Keep your inventory balanced. List strengths and weaknesses.
- Find an accountability partner or a sponsor. I cannot say this enough: The road to recovery is not a journey to be made alone!

God bless you as you courageously face and own your past. He will see you through!

Confess

Principle 4: Openly examine and confess my hurts, hang-ups, and habits to myself, to God, and to someone I trust.

Blessed are the pure in heart, for they will see God. (Matthew 5:8)

Step 5: We admitted to God, to ourselves, and to another human being the exact nature of our wrongs.

Therefore confess your sins to each other and pray for each other so that you may be healed. (James 5:16)

Introduction

The following illustration is part of a message I heard at Willow Creek Church, and it is undoubtedly the best illustration that I have found to represent this principle.

Does the name Jessica McClure trip any memory bells in your mind? She was the eighteen-month-old girl from Midland, Texas, who fell in a deep, abandoned well-pipe several years ago. About four hundred people took part in her fifty-eight-hour rescue attempt, which was spurred on by her cries of anguish that could be clearly heard at ground level through the pipe.

Now, I found it fascinating that, at one point, a critical decision was made. The rescuers decided that the rescue would have two phases: Phase one was to simply get somebody down there, next to her, as soon as possible; phase two was actually extracting her from the well.

Phase one was driven by the knowledge that people tend to do and think strange things when they are trapped alone in a dark scary place for long periods of time. They get disorientated and their fears get blown out of proportion. Their minds play tricks on them. Sometimes they start doing self-destructive things. Sometimes they just give up! So the rescue experts decided that they needed to get a person down there to be with her as soon as possible. Then they would turn their attention on how they were going to get her out of the well. The plan worked, and eventually Jessica was rescued.

Now, how does the rescue of Jessica McClure relate to Step 5?

When people like us get serious about recovery, about spiritual growth, when we go on the 12-Step spiritual adventure, when we take that first step, we admit that we have some problems that make our lives unmanageable. When we turn to God and say, "God, I need help with those problems," then we might feel as though we are free falling. In a sense we are. We are out of control in a way. We can no longer live the way we are so used to living. The old ways just don't work anymore.

So, during the last couple of months, if you worked Step 4 honestly and thoroughly, you might be feeling as if you are trapped at the bottom of a deep, dark well. If you stay there long enough you can become disoriented and wonder why you took this recovery journey to begin with. You might feel like you want to bail out at this point.

You might start making statements like these: "You know that I am a royally messed up man." "The truth about me is that I'm a royally messed up woman." "No one's collection of sins and character defects is as bad as mine." "If anyone ever found out the truth about me, they would never have anything to do with me for the rest of their life."

Some of you get to that point and you say, "Why don't I just bail out of this program? Why don't I just go back to projecting an image of adequacy to everybody and not deal with all this unsettling truth about myself?"

It's at this critical point in the process that we need to get another human being to come alongside of us in that well as soon as possible. You need to get someone next to you before you give up and get back into denial. In a way, the fifth step says that you can only grow so far alone; then you reach the point that continued growth and healing is going to require assistance from someone else.

We are right at that critical juncture tonight. We are at the point where we are being asked to come clean by telling another human being the truth about who we really are. But how?

Confess

The first step is to CONFESS my wrongs. Tonight's acrostic will show you just how to do that.

Confess your shortcomings, resentments, and sins
Obey God's direction
No more guilt
Face the truth
Ease the pain
Stop the blame
Start accepting God

The *C* in confess is CONFESS your shortcomings, resentments, and sins. God wants us to come clean. He already knows all of our resentments, shortcomings and sins. Confession is just us telling Him we know them too.

For the person who confesses, shame is over and realities have begun. Proverbs 28:13 tells us, "Whoever conceals their sins does not prosper, but the one who confesses and renounces them finds mercy." Confession is necessary for fellowship. Our sins have built a barrier between us and God.

The *O* in confess stands for OBEY God's direction.

Principle 4 sums up how to obey God's direction in confessing our hurts, hang-ups, and habits. First, we confessed (admitted) our hurts, hang-ups, and habits to God. "It is written, 'As surely as I live,' says the Lord, 'every knee will bow before me; every tongue will acknowledge God.'" So then, each of us will give an account of ourselves to God."(Romans 14:11–12).

Then we do what we are instructed to do in James 5:16, and share them with someone we trust: "Therefore confess your sins to each other and pray for each other so that you may be healed. The prayer of a righteous person is powerful and effective."

The next letter is *N*: No more guilt.

This principle can restore our confidence, our relationships, and allow us to move on from our "rear-view mirror" way of living that kept us looking back and second-guessing ourselves and others.

In Romans 8:1 we are assured that "There is no condemnation now for those who are in Christ Jesus." The verdict is in, "For all have sinned and fall short of the glory of God, and all are justified freely by his grace through the redemption that came by Christ Jesus" (Romans 3:23–24).

So that's the "C-O-N" of confess. The "con" is over! We have followed God's directions on how to confess our hurts, hang-ups, and habits.

After we "fess" up, we will have four positive changes in our lives. The first is that we will be able to FACE the truth. It has been said that "man occasionally stumbles over the truth, but most of the time he will pick himself up and continue on." Recovery doesn't work like that. Recovery *requires* honesty! After we complete this principle we can allow the light of God's truth to heal our hurts, hang-ups, and habits. We stop denying our true feelings. "Create in me a pure heart, O God, and renew a steadfast spirit within me. Do not cast me from your presence or take your Holy Spirit from me. Restore to me the joy of your salvation and grant me a willing spirit, to sustain me" (Psalm 51:10–12).

Have you ever noticed that a person who speaks the truth is always at ease? The next positive change that confession brings is to EASE the pain.

We are only as sick as our secrets! When we share our deepest secrets, we begin to divide the pain and the shame. A healthy self-worth develops that is no longer based on the world's standards but on the truth of Jesus Christ!

Pain is inevitable for all of us, but misery is optional. Psalm 32:3–5 says, "When I kept silent, my bones wasted away through my groaning all day long. For day and night your hand was heavy on me; my strength was sapped as in the heat of summer. Then I acknowledged my sin to you and did not cover up my iniquity. I said, "I will confess my transgressions to the LORD." And you forgave the guilt of my sin."

The first *S* in confess reminds us that we can now STOP the blame.

It has been said that people who can smile when something goes wrong probably just thought of somebody they can blame it on. But the truth is, we cannot find peace and serenity if we continue to blame ourselves or others. Our secrets have isolated us from each other long enough! They have prevented intimacy in all of our important relationships.

Jesus tells us in Matthew 7:3–5: "Why do you look at the speck of sawdust in your brother's eye and pay no attention to the plank in your own eye? How can you say to your brother, 'Let me take the speck out of your eye,' when all the time there is a plank in your own eye? You hypocrite, first take the plank out of your own eye, and then you will see clearly to remove the speck from your brother's eye."

Finally, the last *S* shows us that it is time to START accepting God's forgiveness. Once we accept God's forgiveness we are able to look others in the eye. We see ourselves and our actions in a new light. We are ready to find the humility to exchange our shortcomings in Principle 5.

"Therefore, if anyone is in Christ, the new creation has come: The old has gone, the new is here! All this is from God, who reconciled us to himself through Christ and gave us the ministry of reconciliation: that God was reconciling the world to himself in Christ, not counting people's sins against them. And he has committed to us the message of reconciliation" (2 Corinthians 5:17–19).

If you asked me to sum up the benefits of Principle 4 in one sentence, it would be this: In confession we open our lives to the healing, reconciling, restoring, uplifting grace of Jesus Christ who loves us in spite of ourselves.

First John 1:9 reminds us that "If we confess our sins, he is faithful and just and will forgive us our sins and purify us from all unrighteousness."

Wrap-Up

Maybe you came tonight a little fearful of having to think about sharing your inventory. I hope you have been encouraged, and I trust you have been able to see the benefits of this task before you. Next time we will discuss the how-tos of finding a person with whom you can share your inventory. Let's close in prayer.

Dear God, thank You for Your promise that if we confess, You will hear us and cleanse us, easing our pain and guilt. Thank You that You always do what is right. In Jesus' name, Amen.

Admit

Principle 4: Openly examine and confess my hurts, hang-ups, and habits to myself, to God, and to someone I trust.

Blessed are the pure in heart, for they will see God. (Matthew 5:8)

Step 5: We admitted to God, to ourselves, and to another human being the exact nature of our wrongs.

Therefore confess your sins to each other and pray for each other so that you may be healed. (James 5:16)

Introduction

This week we are going to focus on confessing (admitting) our hurts, hang-ups, and habits and the secrets of our past to another person.

Why Admit My Wrongs?

This part of Principle 4 is often difficult for people. I am often asked, "Why do I have to admit my wrongs to another?"

Many of us have been keeping secrets almost all of our lives. Every day those secrets take a toll on us. The toll we pay is emotional and physical pain, and keeps us in bondage to our habits. Admitting—out loud—those secrets strips them of their power. They lose much of their hold on us when they are spoken.

Still, we are afraid to reveal our secrets to another person, even someone we trust. We somehow feel as if we have everything to lose and nothing to gain. I want you to hear the truth tonight. Do you know what we really have to lose by telling our secrets and sins to another?

1. *We lose our sense of isolation.* Somebody is going to walk alongside us in our pain. Our sense of aloneness will begin to vanish.

2. *We will begin to lose our unwillingness to forgive.* When people accept and forgive us, we start to see that we can forgive others.

3. *We will lose our inflated, false pride.* As we see and accept who we are, we begin to gain true humility, which involves seeing ourselves as we really are and seeing God as He really is.

4. *We will lose our sense of denial.* Being truthful with another person will tear away our denial.

Now that you know what you have to *lose* when you admit your wrongs to another, let me tell you three benefits you will *gain*.

1. *We gain healing that the Bible promises.* Look at James 5:16 again: "Con-fess your sins to each other and pray for each other so that you may be healed." The key word here

is *healed.* The verse doesn't say, "Confess your sins to one another and you will be forgiven." God *forgave* you when you confessed your sins to *Him.* Now He says you will begin the healing process when you confess your sins to *another.*

2. *We gain freedom.* Our secrets have kept us in chains—bound, frozen, unable to move forward in any of our relationships with God and others. Admitting our sins snaps the chains so God's healing power can start. "Then they cried to the LORD in their trouble, and he saved them from their distress. He brought them out of darkness, the utter darkness, and broke away their chains" (Psalm 107:13–14).

   Unconfessed sin, however, will fester. In Psalm 32:3–4 David tells us what happened to him when he tried to hide his sins: "When I kept silent, my bones wasted away through my groaning all day long. For day and night your hand was heavy on me; my strength was sapped as in the heat of summer." Remember, "Openness is to wholeness as secrets are to sickness." My grandpa used to say, "If you want to clear the stream, you need to get the hog out of the spring." Admit and turn from your sins. Remember that the only sin God can't forgive is the one that is not confessed.

3. *We gain support.* When you share your inventory with another person, you get support! The person can keep you focused and provide feedback. When your old friend "denial" surfaces and you hear Satan's list of excuses—"It's really not that bad"; "They deserved it"; "It really wasn't my fault"—your support person can be there to challenge you with the truth. But most of all, you need another person simply to listen to you and hear what you have to say.

How Do I Choose Someone?

You get to choose the person who you share your inventory with, so choose carefully! You don't want someone to say, "You did what?" or "You shouldn't have done that." You don't need a judge and jury. We already talked about the verdict. Remember Romans 3:23–24: "For all have sinned and fall short of the glory of God, and all are justified freely by his grace through the redemption that came by Christ Jesus." and 1 John 1:9: "If we confess our sins, he is faithful and just and will forgive us our sins and purify us from all unrighteousness."

You just need someone to listen. I find that it works best to choose someone who is a growing Christian and is familiar with the Celebrate Recovery principles or the 12 Steps.

1. *Choose someone of the same sex as you, whom you trust and respect.* Enough said!
2. *Ask your sponsor or accountability partner or someone you trust.* They will have a sense of empathy, and if the person can share personal experiences, you will have a healthy exchange.
3. *Set an appointment with the person, a time without interruptions!* Get away from the telephones, kids, all interruptions for at least two hours. I have heard of some inventories that have taken eight hours to share. That's perhaps a little dramatic.

Guidelines for Your Meeting

1. Start with prayer. Ask for courage, humility, and honesty. Here is a sample prayer for you to consider:

   God, I ask that You fill me with Your peace and strength during my sharing of my inventory. Thank You for sending Your Son to pay the price for me, so my sins can be forgiven. During this meeting help me to be humble and completely honest. Help me to share all of the wounds from my past as well as the results of my own behaviors, so I can begin to find healing. Thank You for providing me with this program and _____ (the name of the person with whom you are sharing your inventory). Thank You for allowing the chains of my past to be snapped. In my Savior's name I pray, Amen.

2. Read the Principle 4 verses found on page 89 in Volume 3, *Getting Right with God, Yourself, and Others.*
3. Keep your sharing balanced—weaknesses and strengths!
4. End in prayer. Thank God for the tools He has given to you and for the complete forgiveness found in Christ!

Principle 5

Voluntarily submit to every change God wants to make in my life and humbly ask Him to remove my character defects.

Blessed are those who hunger and thirst for righteousness, for they will be filled. (Matthew 5:6)

Ready

Principle 5: Voluntarily submit to every change God wants to make in my life and humbly ask Him to remove my character defects.

Blessed are those who hunger and thirst for righteousness, for they will be filled. (Matthew 5:6)

Step 6: We were entirely ready to have God remove all these defects of character.

Humble yourselves before the Lord, and he will lift you up. (James 4:10)

Introduction

Congratulations! If you are ready for Principle 5, you have already taken some major steps on the road to recovery. You admitted you have hurts, hang-ups, or habits and were powerless over it; you came to believe that God could and would help you; you sought Him and turned your life and your will over to His care and direction; you wrote a spiritual inventory and shared that with God and another person. You've been busy! That's a lot of work—hard work!

Maybe you're thinking that it's about time to take a breather and relax for a while. Think again!

In some recovery material, Step 6 (Principle 5) has been referred to as the step "that separates the men from the boys"! I would also like to add, "separates the women from the girls"! So tonight we are going to answer the question, "What does it mean to be entirely READY?"

Ready

One of the reasons that Principle 5 "separates the men from the boys"—or the women from the girls—is because it states that we are ready to "voluntarily submit to every change God wants to make in my life."

Most of us, if not all of us, would be very willing to have *certain* hang-ups, or character defects go away. The sooner the better! But let's face it, some defects are hard to give up.

I'm an alcoholic, but there came a time in my life, a moment of clarity, when I know I had hit bottom and was ready to stop drinking. But was I ready to stop lying? Stop being greedy? Ready to let go of resentments? I had been doing these things for a long time. Like weeds in a garden they had taken root!

Remember we developed our hang-ups, our character defects, and our habits out of the pain in our past. In this principle, you and God will work on healing them together.

Tonight's acrostic will show you how to get READY to allow Him to do that.

Release control
Easy does it
Accept the change
Do replace your character defects
Yield to the growth

The first letter tonight stands for RELEASE control. That reminds me of a story I heard.

A man bumped into an old friend in a bar. He said, "I thought you gave up drinking. What's the matter, no self-control?" The friend replied, "Sure I've got plenty of self-control. I'm just too strong-willed to use it!"

God is very courteous and patient. In Principle 3, He didn't impose His will on you. He waited for you to invite Him in!

Now in Principle 5, you need to be "entirely ready," willing to let God into every area of your life. He won't come in and clean up an area unless you are willing to ask Him in.

It has been said that "willingness is the key that goes into the lock and opens the door that allows God to begin to remove your character defects." I love the way the psalmist invites God to work in his life: "Teach me to do your will, for you are my God; may your good Spirit lead me on level ground" (Psalm 143:10).

Simply put, the *R*—release control—is "Let go; let God!"

The *E* in ready stands for EASY does it. These principles and steps are not quick fixes! You need to allow time for God to work in your life.

This principle goes further than just helping you stop certain habits or behaviors. Remember, your habit or behavior is the *symptom, or result,* of your hurts, and hang-ups.

Let me explain. Our habits or behaviors are like a weed in a garden: They will keep reappearing unless they are pulled out by the roots. And the roots of our habits and behaviors are our hurts and hang-ups. We need to heal the pain in our lives, and address what we believe about ourselves, others and God.

In my case, the major sin in my life was abusing alcohol. The defect of character was my lack of any positive self-image. So, when I worked Principle 5, I went after the defect—my lack of a positive self-image—that caused me to abuse alcohol. That takes time, but God will do it. He promised! "The LORD is my strength and my shield; my heart trusts in him, and he helps me. My heart leaps for joy, and with my song I praise him" (Psalm 28:7).

The next letter is *A*: ACCEPT the change.

Seeing the need for change and allowing the change to occur are two different things, and the space between recognition and willingness can be filled with fear. Besides that, fear can trigger our old dependency on self-control. But this principle will not work if we are still trapped by our self-will. We need to be ready to accept God's help throughout the transition. The Bible makes this very clear in 1 Peter 1:13–14: "Therefore, with minds that are alert and fully sober, set your hope on the grace to be brought to you when Jesus Christ is revealed at his coming. As obedient children, do not conform to the evil desires you had when you lived in ignorance."

As I said, all the steps you have taken on the road to recovery have helped you build the foundation for the "ultimate surrender" that is found in Principle 5.

James 4:10 says, "Humble yourselves before the Lord, and he will lift you up." All we need is the willingness to let God lead on us on our road to recovery.

Let's move on to the *D* in ready, which is extremely important: DO replace your character defects.

You spent a lot of time with your old hang-ups, compulsions, obsessions, and habits. When God removes one, you need to replace it with something positive, such as recovery meetings, church activities, 12th-Step service, and volunteering! If you don't, you open yourself for a negative character defect to return.

Listen to Matthew 12:43–45: "When an impure spirit comes out of a person, it goes through arid places seeking rest and does not find it. Then it says, 'I will return to the house I left.' When it arrives, it finds the house unoccupied, swept clean and put in order. Then it goes and takes with it seven other spirits more wicked than itself, and they go in and live there. And the final condition of that person is worse than the first. That is how it will be with this wicked generation."

I said that one of my major defects of character was a negative self-image, a nonexistent self-esteem, to be more exact. I wasted a lot of time in bars, attempting to drown it. When I started working the 12 Steps, I found I had lots of time on my hands. I tried to fill it by doing positive things that would build my self-esteem, rather than tear it down.

In addition to working my program and attending meeting after meeting, I fellowshipped and worked with "healthy" people. I volunteered. As the months passed, I got more involved at church too. That's when God called me to start to build Celebrate Recovery. I started going to seminary.

You don't have to start a ministry, but you do have to replace your negative character defect with something positive. There are many, many opportunities to serve and get involved in at church.

The last letter in ready is the *Y*: YIELD to the growth.

At first, your old self-doubts and low self-image may tell you that you are not worthy of the growth and progress you are making in the program. Don't listen! Yield to the growth. It is the Holy Spirit's work within you.

"No one who is born of God will continue to sin, because God's seed remains in them; they cannot go on sinning, because they have been born of God" (1 John 3:9).

Wrap-Up

The question is, "Are you entirely ready to voluntarily submit to any and all changes God wants to make in your life?"

If you are, then read the Principle 5a verses found in Volume 3 on pages 95–96, and pray the following prayer:

Dear God, thank You for taking me this far in my recovery journey. Now I pray for Your help in making me be entirely ready to change all my hang-ups and habits. Give me the strength to deal with all that I have turned over to You. Allow me to accept all the changes that You want to make in me. Help me be the person that You want me to be. In Your Son's name I pray, Amen.

Victory

Principle 5: Voluntarily submit to every change God wants to make in my life and humbly ask Him to remove my character defects.

Blessed are those who hunger and thirst for righteousness, for they will be filled. (Matthew 5:6)

Step 6: We were entirely ready to have God remove all these defects of character.

Humble yourselves before the Lord, and he will lift you up. (James 4:10)

Step 7: We humbly asked Him to remove all our shortcomings.

If we confess our sins, he is faithful and just and will forgive us our sins and purify us from all unrighteousness. (1 John 1:9)

Introduction

Tonight we are going to look at an overview of Principle 5. We are going to answer the question, *How can you have victory over your defects of character?*

Victory

We are going to use the acrostic VICTORY.

Voluntarily submit
Identify character defects
Change your mind
Turn over character defects
One day at a time
Recovery is a process
You must choose to change

The *V* is VOLUNTARILY submit to every change God wants me to make in my life and humbly ask Him to remove my shortcomings. The Bible says that we are to make an offering of our very selves to God. "Therefore, I urge you, brothers and sisters, in view of God's mercy, to offer your bodies as a living sacrifice, holy and pleasing to God—this is your true and proper worship. Do not conform to the pattern of this world, but be transformed by the renewing of your mind. Then you will be able to test and approve what God's will is—his good, pleasing and perfect will" (Romans 12:1–2).

When you accepted Principle 3, you made the most important decision of your life by choosing to turn your life over to God's will. That decision got you right with God; you accepted and determined to follow His Son Jesus Christ as your Lord and Savior.

Then you began to work on you. You made a fearless and moral inventory of yourself. The first step in any victory is to recognize the enemy. My inventory showed me that I was my greatest enemy.

You came clean by admitting and confessing to yourself, to God, and to another person your wrongs and your sins. For probably the first time in your life, you were able to take off the muddy glasses of denial and look at reality with a clear and clean focus.

Now you are considering what Step 6 says: that you are "entirely ready to have God remove all these defects of character." You're at the place in your recovery where you say, "I don't want to live this way anymore. I want to get rid of my hurts, hang-ups, and habits. But how do I do it?"

The good news is that *you* don't do it!

Step 6 doesn't read, "You are entirely ready to have you remove all these defects of character," does it? No, it says, "[You are] entirely ready to have *God* remove all these defects of character."

So how do you begin the process to have God make the positive changes in your life that you and He both desire?

You start by doing the *I* in victory: IDENTIFY which character defects you want to work on first. Go back to the wrongs, shortcomings, and sins you discovered in your inventory. Falling down doesn't make you a failure, staying down does! God doesn't want us just to admit our wrongs, He wants to make us right! He wants to give us a future and a hope! God doesn't just want to forgive us, He wants to change us! Ask God to first remove those character defects that are causing you the most pain. Be specific! "In their hearts humans plan their course, but the Lord establishes their steps" (Proverbs 16:9).

Let's move to the *C*, which stands for CHANGE your mind.

Second Corinthians 5:17 tells us that when you become a Christian, you are a new creation, a brand new person inside. The old nature is gone. The changes that are going to take place are the result of a team effort. Your responsibility is to take the action to follow God's direction for change. You have to let God transform (change) you by renewing your mind.

Let's look at Romans 12:2: "Do not conform to the pattern of this world, but be transformed by the renewing of your mind. Then you will be able to test and approve what God's will is—his good, pleasing and perfect will."

To transform something means to change its condition, its nature, its function, and its identity. God wants to change more than just our behaviors. He wants to change the way we think. Simply changing behaviors is like trimming the weeds in a garden instead of removing them. Weeds always grow back unless they are pulled out by the roots. We need to let God transform our minds!

How? By the *T* in victory: TURNING your character defects over to Jesus Christ. Relying on your own willpower, your own self-will, has blocked your recovery. Your past efforts to change your hurts, hang-ups, and habits by yourself were unsuccessful. But if you "humble yourselves before the Lord, and he will lift you up" (James 4:10).

Humility is not a bad word, and being humble doesn't mean you're weak. Humility is like underwear: We should have it, but we shouldn't let it show. Humility is to make the right estimate of one's self or to see ourselves as God sees us.

You can't proceed in your recovery until you turn your defects of character over to Jesus. Let go! Let God!

The next letter is *O*: ONE day at a time.

Your character defects were not developed overnight, so don't expect them to be instantly removed. Recovery happens one day at a time! Your lifelong hurts, hang-ups, and habits need to be worked on in twenty-four-hour increments. You've heard the old cliché: "Life by the yard is hard; life by the inch is a cinch." Jesus said the same thing: "Therefore do not worry about tomorrow, for tomorrow will worry about itself. Each day has enough trouble of its own" (Matthew 6:34).

When I start to regret the past or fear the future, I look to Exodus 3:14 where God tells us that His name is "I AM."

I'm not sure who gets the credit for the following illustration, but it's right on. God tells me that when I live in the past with its mistakes and regrets, life is hard. I can take God back there to heal me, to forgive me, to forgive my sins. But God does not say, "My name is 'I was.' " God says, "My name is 'I AM.' "

When I try to live in the future, with its unknown problems and fears, life is hard. I know God will be with me when that day comes. But God does not say, "My name is 'I will be.' " He says, "My name is I AM."

When I live in today, this moment, one day at a time, life is not hard. God says, "I am here." "Come to me, all you who are weary and burdened, and I will give you rest" (Matthew 11:28).

Let's look at the letter *R*: RECOVERY is a process, "one day at a time" after "one day at a time."

Once you ask God to remove your character defects, you begin a journey that will lead you to new freedom from your past. Don't look for perfection, instead rejoice in steady progress. What you need to seek is "patient improvement." Hear these words of encouragement from God's Word: " In all my prayers for all of you, I always pray with joy because of your partnership in the gospel from the first day until now, being confident of this, that he who began a good work in you will carry it on to completion until the day of Christ Jesus" (Philippians 1:4–6).

The last letter in victory is *Y*: YOU must choose to change.

As long as you place self-reliance first, a true reliance on Jesus Christ is impossible. You must voluntarily submit to every change God wants you to make in your life and humbly ask Him to remove your shortcomings. God is waiting to turn your weaknesses into strengths. All you need to do is *humbly ask*!

"But he gives us more grace. That is why Scripture says: "God opposes the proud but shows favor to the humble." Submit yourselves, then, to God. Resist the devil, and he will flee from you. Come near to God and he will come near to you. Wash your hands, you sinners, and purify your hearts, you double-minded" (James 4:6–8).

Wrap-Up

To make changes in our lives, all I had to do and all you need to do is to be entirely ready to let God be the life-changer. We are not the "how" and "when" committee. We are the preparation committee: All we have to be is *ready*!

Tonight, Jesus is asking you, "Do you want to be healed? Do you want to change?" You must choose to change. That's what Principle 5 is all about! Let's close with prayer.

Dear God, show me Your will in working on my shortcomings. Help me not to resist the changes that You have planned for me. I need You to "direct my steps." Help me stay in today, not get dragged back into the past or lost in the future. I ask You to give me the power and the wisdom to make the very best I can out of today. In Christ's name I pray, Amen.

Principle 6

Evaluate all my relationships. Offer forgiveness to those who have hurt me and make amends for harm I've done to others, except when to do so would harm them or others.

Blessed are the merciful, for they will be shown mercy. (Matthew 5:7)

Blessed are the peacemakers, for they will be called children of God. (Matthew 5:9)

Amends

Principle 6: Evaluate all my relationships. Offer forgiveness to those who have hurt me and make amends for harm I've done to others, except when to do so would harm them or others.

Blessed are the merciful, for they will be shown mercy. (Matthew 5:7)

Blessed are the peacemakers, for they will be called children of God. (Matthew 5:9)

Step 8: We made a list of all persons we had harmed and became willing to make amends to them all.

Do to others as you would have them do to you. (Luke 6:31)

Introduction

This week, we are going to focus on Principle 6. In fact, we are going to spend the next two months on Principle 6. That's how important it is to our recovery.

Tonight, we are going to give an overview of Principle 6, which is all about making amends. "Forgive me as I learn to forgive" sums it up pretty well.

We started doing repair work on the *personal* side of our lives earlier in our recovery by admitting our powerlessness, turning our lives and wills over to God's care, doing our moral inventory, sharing our sins or wrongs with another, and admitting our shortcomings and asking God to remove them. But now we begin to do some repair work on the *relational* side of our lives. Making your amends is the beginning of the end of your isolation from God and others.

Still, some of us balk at making amends. We think, "If God has forgiven me, isn't that enough? Why should I drag up the past? After all, making amends doesn't sound natural."

The answer to that objection is simple: Making amends is not about your *past* so much as it is about your *future*. Before you can have the healthy relationships that you desire, you need to clean out the guilt, shame, and pain that has caused many of your past relationships to fail.

So, in the words of Step 8, it is time to make "a list of all persons that we [have] harmed and [become] willing to make amends to them all." At this point, you are only looking for the willingness. Step 8 only requires that we identify those to whom we need to make amends or offer forgiveness.

Luke 6:31 reminds us to treat others the way that we want to be treated. For some of you, that may be very difficult. You have been hurt very badly or abused. Many of you had nothing to do with the wrong committed against you.

Often I have counseled people on Principle 6 and on the critical importance of forgiveness, only to have them say, "Never will I forgive! Not after what was done to me!" In these cases, the wrong against the individual was often child molestation, sexual abuse, or adultery. Such sins are deep violations that leave painful wounds.

Forgiving the perpetrator of such wrongs, even after the one harmed has dealt with the emotional pain, seems impossible. We are going to deal specifically with this issue in the lesson on the three types of forgiveness.

For now, listen to the way Celebrate Recovery rewords this step for those in the sexual/ physical abuse groups:

Make a list of all persons who have harmed us and become willing to seek God's help in forgiving our perpetrators, as well as forgiving ourselves. Realize we've also harmed others and become willing to make amends to them.

Let's look at the second part of Principle 6: ". . . make amends for harm I've done to others, except when to do so would harm them or others."

Listen as I read Matthew 5:23–24: "Therefore, if you are offering your gift at the altar and there remember that your brother or sister has something against you, leave your gift there in front of the altar. First go and be reconciled to them; then come and offer your gift."

The first part of Principle 6 deals with being willing to consider forgiveness. The second part of Principle 6 calls us to action as we make our amends and offer our forgiveness. Going back to the garden metaphor, we need to pull out the dead weeds in our past broken relationships so that we can clear a place where our new relationships can be successfully planted or restored. That's why Principle 6 is so important.

Amends

Let's look at tonight's acrostic and answer the question, *How do I make AMENDS?*

Admit the hurt and the harm
Make a list
Encourage one another
Not for them
Do it at the right time
Start living the promises of recovery

The *A* is ADMIT the hurt and the harm. Principle 4 showed us how important it is to open up to God and to others. Your feelings have been bottled up far, far too long, and that has interfered with all your important relationships. In this step of your recovery you need to once again face the hurts, resentments, and wrongs that others have caused you or that you have caused to others. Holding on to resentments not only blocks your recovery, it blocks God's forgiveness in your life.

Luke 6:37 tells us, "Do not judge, and you will not be judged. Do not condemn, and you will not be condemned. Forgive, and you will be forgiven."

The next letter in amends is *M*: MAKE a list.

In Volume 3 you will find the "Amends" list worksheet. You can find the "Celebrate Recovery Inventory" worksheets on pages 59 and 60 in Volume 2. You can use these sheets to help you make your amends list.

In column 1, on your inventory, you will find the list of people that you need to forgive. These are the people who have hurt you. In column 5, you will find the list of people to whom you owe amends. These are the ones whom you have hurt.

During the next two months, add to the lists as God reveals to you other names to include. Remember, all you are doing at this point is writing them down.

If it has been a while since you did your inventory, God may have revealed others to you that you need to add to your list. That's why it's important to start off with the "Amends" worksheet.

When you are making your list, don't worry about the "how-tos" in making your amends. Don't ask questions like How could I ever ask my dad for forgiveness? *How could I ever forgive my brother for what he did?* Go ahead and put the person on your list anyway. "Do to others as you would have them do to you" (Luke 6:31).

The *E* in amends stands for ENCOURAGE one another.

It has been said that encouragement is oxygen to the soul. Before you make your amends or offer your forgiveness to others, meet with your accountability partner or sponsor, someone to encourage you and to provide a good "sounding board." That person's objective opinion is valuable to ensure that you make amends and offer forgiveness with the right motives.

Hebrews 10:24 says, "And let us consider how we may spur one another on toward love and good deeds." If you are asked to be an encourager, an accountability partner, or a sponsor, be honored. And remember, you can't hold a torch to light another's path without brightening your own.

The *N* in amends is the reason for making the amends: NOT for them.

You need to approach those to whom you are offering your forgiveness or amends humbly, honestly, sincerely, and willingly. Don't offer excuses or attempt to justify your actions; focus only on your part.

In five words, here's the secret to making successful amends: *Do not expect anything back!* You are making your amends, not for a reward, but for freedom from your hurts, hang-ups, and habits.

Principle 6 says that I am responsible to "make amends for harm I've done to others." Jesus said, "But love your enemies, do good to them, and lend to them without expecting to get anything back. Then your reward will be great, and you will be children of the Most High, because he is kind to the ungrateful and wicked. Be merciful, just as your Father is merciful." (Luke 6:35–36). God loves us generously and graciously, even when we are at our worst. God is kind; we need to be kind!

Do you know that you can become addicted to your bitterness, hatred, and revenge, just as you can become addicted to alcohol, drugs, and relationships? A life characterized by bitterness, resentment, and anger will kill you emotionally and shrivel your soul. They will produce the "Three Ds":

Depression

Despair

Discouragement

An unforgiving heart will cause you more pain and destruction than it will ever cause the person who hurt you.

Let's move on to the *D* in amends: DO it at the right time.

This principle not only requires courage, good judgment, and willingness, but a careful sense of *timing!*

Psalms 27:14 tells us, "Wait for the LORD; be strong and take heart and wait for the LORD." There is a right time and a wrong time to offer forgiveness or to make amends.

Before making amends, you need to pray, asking Jesus Christ for His guidance, His direction, and His perfect timing.

Principle 6 goes on to say, ". . . except when to do so would harm them or others."

Listen to Philippians 2:3–4: "In humility value others above yourselves, not looking to your own interests but each of you to the interests of the others."

Don't wait until you *feel* like making your amends or offering your forgiveness; living this principle takes an act of the will! Or perhaps I should say a *crisis* of the will. Making your amends is an act of obedience to Scripture and of personal survival.

The last letter in amends is *S*: START living the promises of recovery.

As we complete this principle, we will discover God's gift of true freedom from our past. We will begin to find the peace and serenity that we have long been seeking. We will become ready to embrace God's purpose for our lives.

God promises, "I will repay you for the years the locusts have eaten" (Joel 2:25).

Wrap-Up

Principle 6 offers you freedom—freedom from the chains of resentment, anger, and hurt; freedom, through your amends for the harm you caused others, to look them in the eye, knowing that you are working with God in cleaning up your side of the street.

In your small groups, I encourage those of you who have completed Principle 6 to share the freedom and the blessings that you have received.

Let's pray.

Dear God, I pray for willingness—willingness to evaluate all my past and current relationships. Please show me the people who I have hurt, and help me become willing to offer my amends to them. Also, God, give me Your strength to become willing to offer forgiveness to those who have hurt me. I pray for Your perfect timing for taking the action that Principle 6 calls for. I ask all these things in Your Son's name, Amen.

Forgiveness

Principle 6: Evaluate all my relationships. Offer forgiveness to those who have hurt me and make amends for harm I've done to others, except when to do so would harm them or others.

Blessed are the merciful, for they will be shown mercy. (Matthew 5:7)

Blessed are the peacemakers, for they will be called children of God. (Matthew 5:9)

Step 8: We made a list of all persons we had harmed and became willing to make amends to them all.

Do to others as you would have them do to you. (Luke 6:31)

Step 9: We made direct amends to such people whenever possible, except when to do so would injure them or others.

"Therefore, if you are offering your gift at the altar and there remember that your brother or sister has something against you, leave your gift there in front of the altar. First go and be reconciled to them; then come and offer your gift." (Matthew 5:23–24)

Introduction

Tonight we are going to continue to work on evaluating all of our relationships. We will work on forgiving those who have hurt us and, when possible, make amends for the harm we've done to others, without expecting anything in return.

We have discussed how to make your amends, but tonight I would like to talk about something that can block, stall, or even destroy your recovery: the inability to accept and offer *forgiveness*.

I think we all agree that forgiveness is a beautiful idea until we have to practice it.

A guy once told me, "John, you won't catch me getting ulcers. I just take things as they come. I don't ever hold a grudge, not even against people who have done things to me that I'll never forgive." Right!

I saw this sign on a company bulletin board: "To err is human; to forgive is not company policy."

There are a lot of jokes about forgiveness, but forgiveness is not something that those of us in recovery can take lightly, because forgiveness is clearly God's prescription for the broken. No matter how great the offense or abuses, along the path to healing lies forgiveness.

We all know that one of the roots of compulsive behavior is pain—buried pain.

Facing your past and forgiving yourself and those who have hurt you, and making amends for the pain that you have caused others, is the only lasting solution.

Forgiveness breaks the cycle! It doesn't settle all the questions of blame, justice, or fairness, but it does allow relationships to heal and possibly start over.

So tonight let's talk about the three kinds of forgiveness.

Forgiveness

In order to be completely free from your resentments, anger, fears, shame, and guilt, you need to give and accept *forgiveness* in all areas of your life. If you do not, your recovery will be stalled and thus incomplete.

The first and most important forgiveness is extended from God to us. Have you accepted

God's forgiveness? Have you accepted Jesus' work on the cross? By His death on the cross, all our sins were canceled, paid in full; a free gift for those who believe in Him as the true and only Higher Power, Savior, and Lord.

Jesus exclaimed from the cross, "It is finished" (John 19:30). No matter how grievously we may have injured others or ourselves, the grace of God is always sufficient! His forgiveness is always complete!

Romans 3:22–26 says, "This righteousness is given through faith in Jesus Christ to all who believe. There is no difference between Jew and Gentile, for all have sinned and fall short of the glory of God, and all are justified freely by his grace through the redemption that came by Christ Jesus. God presented Christ as a sacrifice of atonement, through the shedding of his blood—to be received by faith. He did this to demonstrate his righteousness, because in his forbearance he had left the sins committed beforehand unpunished—he did it to demonstrate his righteousness at the present time, so as to be just and the one who justifies those who have faith in Jesus."

Remember, if God wasn't willing to forgive sin, heaven would be empty.

The second kind of forgiveness is extended from us to others. Have you forgiven others who have hurt you? This type of forgiveness is a process. You need to be willing to be willing, but to be truly free, you must let go of the pain of the past harm and abuse caused by others.

Forgiveness is all about letting go. Remember playing tug-of-war as a kid? As long as the people on each end of the rope are tugging, you have a war. You "let go of your end of the rope" when you forgive others. No matter how hard they may tug on their end, if you have released your end, the war is over. It is finished! But until you release it, you are a prisoner of war!

Think about who your anger is hurting most. I'll give you a hint. It's you! Forgiveness enables you to become fully freed from your anger and allows you to move forward positively in those relationships.

The Bible has a lot to say about forgiveness. Romans 12:17–18 says, "Do not repay anyone evil for evil. Be careful to do what is right in the eyes of everyone. If it is possible, as far as it depends on you, live at peace with everyone."

Causing an injury puts you *below* your enemy. Revenging an injury makes you *even* with him. Forgiving him sets you one *above* him. But more importantly, it sets you free!

Offering forgiveness to others can look one of three ways:

1. Forgiving others in our hearts and minds. This is a forgiveness that takes place in our hearts, when verbally communicating our forgiveness is not safe or possible.

2. Verbally offering our forgiveness to others. Pray and ask God to guide you to which is best for your situation.

3. Writing a letter to someone who is unsafe (you may choose to send or not send the letter) or to someone who may have passed away.

If you have been the victim of sexual abuse, physical abuse, or childhood emotional abuse or neglect, I am truly sorry for the pain you have suffered. I hurt with you. But you will not find the peace and freedom from your perpetrators until you are able to forgive them. Remember, forgiving them in no way excuses them for the harm they caused you, but it will release you from the power they have had over you. I have rewritten Steps 8 and 9 of the 12 Steps for you.

Step 8: Make a list of all persons who have harmed us and become willing to seek God's help in forgiving our perpetrators, as well as forgiving ourselves. Realize we've also harmed others and become willing to make amends to them.

Step 9: Extend forgiveness to ourselves and to others who have perpetrated against us, realizing this is an attitude of the heart, not always confrontation. Make direct amends, asking forgiveness from those people we have harmed, except when to do so would injure them or others.

To recap, we need to accept God's forgiveness by accepting what Jesus did for us on the cross, and we need to forgive and ask forgiveness of others. The last kind of forgiveness is perhaps the most difficult for us to extend.

We need to forgive ourselves. Have you forgiven yourself? You can forgive others, you can accept God's forgiveness, but you may feel the guilt and shame of your past is just too much to forgive.

This is what God wants to do with the darkness of your past: " 'Come now, let us settle the matter,' says the LORD. 'Though your sins are like scarlet, they shall be as white as snow; though they are red as crimson, they shall be like wool' " (Isaiah 1:18).

No matter how unloved or worthless you may feel, God loves you! Your feelings about yourself do not change His love for you one bit.

Let me ask you a question: If God Himself can forgive you, how can you withhold forgiveness from yourself? In fact, I believe that we must forgive ourselves before we can honestly forgive others. The first name on your amends list needs to be God, the second needs to be yours. Why?

The answer is found in Matthew 22:36, where Jesus was asked, " 'Which is the greatest commandment in the Law?' Jesus replied: 'Love the Lord your God with all your heart and with all your soul and with all your mind.' This is the first and greatest commandment. And the second is like it: 'Love your neighbor as yourself.' All the Law and the Prophets hang on these two commandments."

Now how can you love or forgive your neighbor, if you can't love or forgive yourself? If you have not forgiven yourself, your forgiveness to others may be superficial, incomplete, and done for the wrong motives.

Self-forgiveness is not a matter of assigning the blame to someone else and letting yourself off the hook. It's not a license for irresponsibility. It is simply an acknowledgment that you are human like everybody else and that you've reached the stage in your recovery at which you are able to give yourself greater respect.

Wrap-Up

As you take the necessary steps of forgiveness, you will discover that you are letting go of the guilt and shame. You'll be able to say, "I'm not perfect, but God and I are working on me. I still fall down, but with my Savior's help, I can get up, brush myself off, and try again.

We can say, "I forgive myself because God has already forgiven me, and with His help, I can forgive others."

When you forgive yourself, you don't change the past, but you sure do change the future!

Grace

Principle 6: Evaluate all my relationships. Offer forgiveness to those who have hurt me and make amends for harm I've done to others, except when to do so would harm them or others.

Blessed are the merciful, for they will be shown mercy. (Matthew 5:7)

Blessed are the peacemakers, for they will be called children of God. (Matthew 5:9)

Step 9: Made direct amends to such people whenever possible, except when to do so would injure them or others.

"Therefore, if you are offering your gift at the altar and there remember that your brother or sister has something against you, leave your gift there in front of the altar. First go and be reconciled to them; then come and offer your gift." (Matthew 5:23–24)

Introduction

Tonight, we are going to finish discussing Principle 6. We have talked about how to evaluate all our relationships, offer forgiveness to those who have hurt us, and make amends for the harm that we have done to others, when possible, without expecting anything back.

As we grow as Christians and as we grow in our recovery, we want to follow the guidance and directions of Jesus Christ. As we get to know Him better, we want to model His teachings and model His ways. We want to become more like Him. Honestly, if we are going to implement Principle 6 to the best of our ability, we need to learn to model God's grace. But how?

Grace

The key verses of Celebrate Recovery are 2 Corinthians 12:9–10: "But he said to me, 'My grace is sufficient for you, for my power is made perfect in weakness.' Therefore I will boast all the more gladly about my weaknesses, so that Christ's power may rest on me. That is why, for Christ's sake, I delight in weaknesses, in insults, in hardships, in persecutions, in difficulties. For when I am weak, then I am strong.

Celebrate Recovery is built on and centered in Christ's grace and love for each of us.

Let's look at tonight's acrostic: GRACE.

God's gift
Received by our faith
Accepted by God's love
Christ paid the price
Everlasting gift

The *G* in grace is GOD'S gift.

Grace is a gift. Grace cannot be bought. It is freely given by God to you and me. When we offer (give) our amends and expect nothing back, that's a gift from us to those whom we have hurt.

Romans 3:23–24 tells us, "For all have sinned and fall short of the glory of God, and all are justified freely by his grace through the redemption that came by Christ Jesus."

First Peter 1:13 says, "Therefore, with minds that are alert and fully sober, set your hope on the grace to be brought to you when Jesus Christ is revealed at his coming."

If my relationship with God was dependent on my being perfect, I would have trouble relating to God most of the time. Thank God that my relationship with Him is built on His grace and love for me. He gives the strength to make the amends and offer the forgiveness that Principle 6 requires.

And how do we receive God's gift of grace? That's the *R* in grace: RECEIVED by our faith.

No matter how hard we may work, we cannot earn our way into heaven. Only by professing our faith in Jesus Christ as our Lord and Savior can we experience His grace and have eternal life.

Ephesians 2:8–9 says, "For it is by grace you have been saved, through faith—and this is not from yourselves, it is the gift of God—not by works, so that no one can boast."

Philippians 3:8–9 states, "What is more, I consider everything a loss because of the surpassing worth of knowing Christ Jesus my Lord, for whose sake I have lost all things. I consider them garbage, that I may gain Christ and be found in him, not having a righteousness of my own that comes from the law, but that which is through faith in Christ—the righteousness that comes from God on the basis of faith."

You and I tend to be more interested in what we *do*. God is more interested in what we *are*.

Romans 5:2 says of Jesus, "Through whom we have gained access by faith into this grace in which we now stand. And we boast in the hope of the glory of God."

Just a word of warning: Our walk needs to match our talk. Our beliefs and values are seen by others in our actions. And it is through our faith in Christ that we can find the strength and courage needed for us to take the action Principle 6 requires: making our amends and offering our forgiveness.

The next letter in grace is *A*. We are ACCEPTED by God's love.

God loved you and me while we were still out there sinning. Romans 5:8 says, "God demonstrates his own love for us in this: While we were still sinners, Christ died for us."

We can, in turn, love others because God first loved us. We can also forgive others because God first forgave us. Colossians 3:13 says, "Bear with each other and forgive one another if any of you has a grievance against someone. Forgive as the Lord forgave you."

Ephesians 2:4–5 reminds us, "But because of his great love for us, God, who is rich in mercy, made us alive with Christ even when we were dead in transgressions—it is by grace you have been saved."

I don't know about you, but I know that I do not deserve God's love. But the good news is He accepts me in spite of myself! He sees all my failures and loves me anyway. And the same goes for you.

Hebrews 4:16 tells us, "Let us then approach God's throne of grace with confidence, so that we may receive mercy and find grace to help us in our time of need."

Let's move on to the C in grace: CHRIST paid the price.

Jesus died on the cross so that all our sins, all our wrongs, are forgiven. He paid the price, sacrificed Himself for you and me so that we may be with Him forever.

When we accept Christ's work on the cross, we are made a new creation. We can then rely on God's strength and power to enable us to forgive those who have hurt us. We can set aside our selfishness and speak the truth in love. We focus only on our part in making amends or offering our forgiveness.

Ephesians 1:7 says, "In him we have redemption through his blood, the forgiveness of sins, in accordance with the riches of God's grace."

The last letter in grace is *E*: God's grace is an EVERLASTING gift.

Once you have accepted Jesus Christ as your Savior and Lord, God's gift of grace is forever. Let me read a quote from the Big Book of AA, pages 83–84: "We will know a new freedom and a new happiness. . . . We will comprehend the word serenity and we will know peace. . . . We will suddenly realize that God is doing for us what we could not do for ourselves."

And here's a quote from the Bible: "For I am convinced that neither death nor life, neither angels nor demons, neither the present nor the future, nor any powers, neither height nor depth, nor anything else in all creation, will be able to separate us from the love of God that is in Christ Jesus our Lord." (Romans 8:38–39).

Also, 2 Thessalonians 2:16–17 states, "May our Lord Jesus Christ himself and God our Father, who loved us and by his grace gave us eternal encouragement and good hope, encourage your hearts and strengthen you in every good deed and word."

My life verse is 1 Peter 2:9–10, where God says, "But you are a chosen people, a royal priesthood, a holy nation, God's special possession, that you may declare the praises of him who called you out of darkness into his wonderful light. Once you were not a people, but now you are the people of God; once you had not received mercy, but now you have received mercy."

I stand before you as a product of God's grace. Everyone here this evening who has let Christ into his or her life is also a product of God's grace. As we model this grace, we will be able to do the work that Principle 6 requires.

Let's close tonight with Colossians 1:6: "The gospel is bearing fruit and growing throughout the whole world—just as it has been doing among you since the day you heard it and truly understood God's grace."

Principle 7

Reserve a daily time with God for self-examination, Bible reading, and prayer in order to know God and His will for my life and to gain the power to follow His will.

Crossroads

Principle 7: Reserve a daily time with God for self-examination, Bible reading, and prayer in order to know God and His will for my life and to gain the power to follow His will.

Step 10: We continued to take personal inventory and when we were wrong, promptly admitted it.

So, if you think you are standing firm, be careful that you don't fall!
(1 Corinthians 10:12)

Introduction

You have arrived at a very important junction. You have traveled a long road, which required facing your denial; surrendering your life to Jesus Christ; taking an honest look at your life; listing, confessing, and sharing all your wrongdoing; being humble enough to allow God to make major changes in you; becoming willing to forgive or make amends; offering your forgiveness to those that have hurt you; making amends for all the harm that you have caused to others . . . .

WOW! That's quite a journey! Not too long ago, most of us would have said that it was an impossible journey, that we could never have changed or grown so much, that we could never have done the work that the first six principles ask of us.

And we would be right. We could never have made it through by ourselves on our own power. In fact, the only reason we have made it this far is because we made a decision way back in Principle 3 to turn our lives and wills over to the care of God.

Jesus explains it this way in John 8:32: "You will know the truth, and the truth will set you free." Then in John 14:6 He defines Truth by saying, "I am the way and the truth and the life. No one comes to the Father except through me." We have been set free from our addictions and our obsessive/compulsive behaviors because of the "Truth" we have asked into our hearts, Jesus Christ.

Because of this life-changing decision you made, Jesus has come in—at your invitation—and rebuilt the foundation of your life! You will undoubtedly see major changes, if you haven't already!

Principle 7 and Step 10 are a crossroads of your recovery. It is not a place to stop and rest on past accomplishments. We need to thank God for getting us this far on our road to recovery, praise Him for the many victories over our hurts, hang-ups, and habits we have seen in working the first nine steps, but we also need to continue working the last three steps with the same devotion and enthusiasm that got us to this point in our recoveries.

First Corinthians 10:12 puts it this way: "So, if you think you are standing firm, be careful that you don't fall!"

Most recovery material refers to Steps 10 through 12 (Principles 7 and 8) as the "maintenance steps." I disagree with the use of the word maintenance.

I believe that it is in these steps and principles that your recovery, your new way of living, really takes off, really bears the fruit of all the changes that God and you have been working on together.

It is in Principles 7 and 8 where you and I will live out our recoveries for the remainder of our time here on this earth—one day at a time! That's much, much more than "maintenance," folks!

Step 10

As we begin to work Step 10[1], we will see that it is made up of three key parts. Of course, we need an acrostic. Tonight the word is TEN.

Take time to do a daily inventory
Evaluate the good and the bad
Need to admit our wrongs promptly

The *T* answers the "what" question: TAKE time to do a daily inventory. To inventory something is simply to count it. Businesses take inventory all the time. Principle 7 reminds us to "reserve a daily time with God for self-examination, Bible reading, and prayer." This gives us quiet time to count the good and bad things we did during a particular period of time. Lamentations 3:40 exhorts us to "examine our ways and test them, and . . . return to the LORD."

We need to ask ourselves these questions:

- What good did I do today?
- In what areas did I blow it today?
- Did I do or say anything that hurt anyone today?
- Do I owe anyone amends?
- What did I learn from my actions today?

I do this on a daily basis. I reflect on my day to see if I harmed someone, acted or reacted out of fear or selfishness, or went out of my way to show kindness.

As we stressed in Principle 4, our daily inventories need to be balanced. We need to look at the things we did right as well as the areas in which we missed the mark and blew it! Believe it or not, by the time we get to Principle 7, we actually start doing a lot of things right. But if we are not careful, we can slowly slip back into our old habits, hang-ups, and dysfunctions, so we need to take regular, ongoing inventories.

The *E* in our acrostic answers the "why" question: EVALUATE the good and the bad.

---

1. Please note that though Step 10 and Principle 7 differ somewhat in their focus, both point toward the same result: the character and image of Christ in our daily life. This lesson will emphasize the step more than the principle, but in no way do we intend to discount the many benefits of daily living Principle 7.

The step doesn't say, ". . . *if* we're wrong." That's what I *wish* it said. "*If* I'm ever wrong" . . . "*if* perhaps I blew it" . . . No. The step says *when* I'm wrong.

Sometimes, I really do not want to work this step. It forces me to admit that, on a daily basis, I'm going to be wrong and I'm going to make mistakes. I struggled with this for years in my early recovery, until one day I saw a sign that was hanging in a meeting room in downtown Los Angeles. The sign read: "Would you rather be right . . . or well?"

Would *you* rather be right or well?

First John 1:8–10 says: "If we claim to be without sin, we deceive ourselves and the truth is not in us. If we confess our sins, he is faithful and just and will forgive us our sins and purify us from all unrighteousness. If we claim we have not sinned, we make him out to be a liar and his word is not in us."

In John 3:21 Jesus tells us, "Whoever lives by the truth comes into the light." Step 10 brings us, on a daily basis, into the light.

Once we see the light, we have a choice. We can ignore it or we can act on it. If we act, we are living the last part of Step 10 and answer the "then what" question. We NEED to admit our wrongs promptly.

For years I couldn't admit it when I was wrong. My wife can vouch for that! I couldn't admit my mistakes. My refusal to offer amends blocked all my relationships, especially with my family. As I grew and matured in the Word and recovery, I discovered that I had to *own* my mistakes and take responsibility for my actions. I couldn't do that if I didn't take time daily to allow God to show me where I missed the mark.

There's another word that I wish had been left out of Step 10, the word *promptly*. It's easier for me to admit the mistakes I made ten years ago than the mistakes I just made today. But Step 10 says promptly! As soon as I realize that I blew it I need to promptly admit it!

In Matthew 5:23–24, Jesus tells us, "Therefore, if you are offering your gift at the altar and there remember that your brother or sister has something against you, leave your gift there in front of the altar. First go and be reconciled to them; then come and offer your gift."

In other words, admit your wrongs . . . promptly!

Wrap-Up

One way to easily keep track of your good and bad behavior is to keep a journal. Volume 4 has space on pages 129–135 for you to practice using a journal for one week. Now, your journal is not for you to record the calories that you had for lunch today or your carpool schedule for school. Your journal is a tool for you to review and write down the good and the bad things you did today.

Look for negative patterns, issues that you are continually writing down and having to promptly make amends for—again and again. Share them with your sponsor or accountability partner, and set up an action plan for you, with God's help, to overcome them.

Try to keep your journal for seven days. Start out by writing down one thing that you are thankful for from your experiences from the day. That will get you writing.

If you haven't used a journal so far in your recovery, I believe you will find this recovery tool a great help! I encourage you to make journaling a daily part of your program.

Next week we will talk about the how-tos of Step 10 and ways of avoiding constantly needing to offer your amends.

Daily Inventory

Principle 7: Reserve a daily time with God for self-examination, Bible reading, and prayer in order to know God and His will for my life and to gain the power to follow His will.

Step 10: We continued to take personal inventory and when we were wrong, promptly admitted it.

So, if you think you are standing firm, be careful that you don't fall!
(1 Corinthians 10:12)

Introduction

Tonight we want to focus on the how-tos of Step 10. But first, I would like to see how you did with your seven days of Step 10 journaling. I know for many of you it was the first experience in writing down your thoughts on a daily basis. I thought it would be interesting to randomly call on some of you to come up here and read them for the whole group. Just kidding!

But, it is important to recap our day in written form—the good and the bad, the successes and the times when we blew it. Here's why:

1. When you write down areas in which you owe amends, it will help you to see if patterns are developing, so that you can identify them and work on them with the help of Jesus Christ and your sponsor.
2. You can keep the amends you owe to a very "short list." As soon as you write down an issue you can make a plan to PROMPTLY offer your amends. After you make the amends you can cross it off in your journal.

Inventory

Some of you may have had trouble getting started writing in your journal. Let me give you three hints that will help you get started putting the ink on the paper.

1. Start off by writing down just one thing that happened that particular day for which you are thankful. Just one thing can get you started, and it will also help you sleep better that night.
2. Ask your accountability partner/sponsor to hold you accountable for writing in your journal each night.
3. This is the one that really works for me! Memorize Galatians 5:22–23, the "fruit of the Spirit": "The fruit of the Spirit is love, joy, peace, forbearance, kindness, goodness, faithfulness, gentleness and self-control."

Daily ask yourself any of these questions to prompt your writing, starting each question with the word "today":

- How did I show *love* to others? Did I act in an unloving way toward anyone?
- Did others see in me the *joy* of having a personal relationship with the Lord? If not, why not?
- How was my serenity, my *peace*? Did anything happen that caused me to lose it? What was my part in it?
- Was I *patient* (forbearing)? What caused me to lose my patience? Do I owe anyone amends?
- Would anyone say that I was *kind/good*? In what ways did I act unkind?
- How was my *faithfulness*? Did I keep my word with everyone?
- How was my *gentleness* and *self-control*? Did I lose my temper, speak a harsh or unkind word to someone?

As we work Step 10 and Principle 7, we begin the journey of applying what we have discovered in the first nine steps. We humbly live daily—in reality, not denial. We have done our best to amend our past. Through God's guidance, we can make choices about the emotions that affect our thinking and actions. We start to take action—positive action—instead of constant *reaction.*

In Principle 7 we desire to grow daily in our new relationship with Jesus Christ and others. Instead of attempting to be in control of every situation and every person we come in contact with, or spinning out of control ourselves, we are starting to exhibit self-control, the way God wants us to be. Remember "self under control" is what we are seeking. Self under *God's* control is what we are striving for.

God has provided us with a daily checklist for our new lifestyle. It's called the "Great Commandment," and it is found in Matthew 22:37–40 where Jesus said, " 'Love the Lord your God with all your heart . . . soul and . . . mind.' This is the first and greatest commandment. And the second is like it: 'Love your neighbor as yourself.' All the Law and the Prophets hang on these two commandments."

When you do your daily personal inventory, ask yourself, "Today, did my actions show what the second greatest commandment tells me to do? Did I love my neighbor (others) as myself?"

As we live the two commandments by putting the principles and steps into action in our lives, we will become more like Christ. We will become doers of God's Word, not hearers only. James 1:22 says, "Do not merely listen to the word, and so deceive yourselves. Do what it says." Our actions need to be consistent with our talk. You may be the only Bible someone ever reads.

That's being a real "Living Bible." That's how the apostle Paul lived. He says in 1 Thessalonians 1:4–5, "For we know, brothers and sisters loved by God, that he has chosen you, because our gospel came to you not simply with words but also with power, with the Holy Spirit and deep conviction. You know how we lived among you for your sake." Others should see God's truth shown in our lives.

Step 10 does not say how often to take an inventory, but I would like to offer three suggestions that can help us keep on the right road, God's road to recovery.

Do an Ongoing Inventory

We can keep an ongoing inventory throughout the day. The best time to admit we are wrong is the exact time that we are made aware of it. Why wait? Let me give you an example.

Yesterday afternoon, I snapped at my son. I was immediately faced with a choice. I could admit that I was wrong ("I shouldn't have snapped at Johnny; all he wanted to do was play catch") and make amends with him ("Johnny, I'm sorry for speaking so sharply; I was wrong"), or I could wait until later and risk rationalizing it away ("He saw I was busy; he had no right to ask me to play at that time").

You don't have to wait until you go home, cook dinner, watch TV, and then start your journal. If you do an ongoing inventory during the day, you can keep your amends list very short!

Do a Daily Inventory

At the end of each day, we look over our daily activities, the good and the bad. We need to search where we might have harmed someone or where we acted out of anger or fear. But once again, remember to keep your daily inventory balanced. Be sure to include the things that you did right throughout the day. The best way to do this is to journal.

I spend about fifteen minutes just before I go to sleep, journaling my day's events, asking God to show me the wrongs that I have committed. Then, as promptly as I can the next morning, I admit them and make my amends.

Do a Periodic Inventory

I take a periodic inventory about every three months. I get away on a "mini retreat"! I would encourage you to try it. Bring your daily journal with you, and pray as you read through the last ninety days of your journal entries. Ask God to show you areas in your life that you can improve on in the next ninety days and *celebrate the victories* that you have made.

By taking an ongoing, a daily, and a periodic inventory we can work Step 10 to the best of our abilities. With God's help we can keep our side of the street clean.

Here are a few key verses to learn and follow for Step 10.

The hearts of the wise make their mouths prudent, and their lips promote instruction. (Proverbs 16:23)

Do not let any unwholesome talk come out of your mouths, but only what is helpful for building others up according to their needs, that it may benefit those who listen. (Ephesians 4:29)

The wise in heart are called discerning, and gracious words promote instruction. (Proverbs 16:21)

Anxiety weighs down the heart, but a kind word cheers it up! (Proverbs 12:25)

If I speak in the tongues of men or of angels, but do not have love, I am only a resounding gong or a clanging cymbal. (1 Corinthians 13:1)

Step 10 Daily Action Plan

1. Continue to take a daily inventory, and when you are wrong, promptly make your amends.
2. Summarize the events of your day in your journal.
3. Read and memorize one of the Principle 7a verses on page 143 of Volume 4.
4. Work all steps and principles to the best of your ability.

The key verse for this lesson is Mark 14:38: "Watch and pray so that you will not fall into temptation. The spirit is willing, but the flesh is weak." Let's close in prayer.

Dear God, thank You for today. Thank You for giving me the tools to work my program and live my life differently, centered in Your will. Lord, help me to make my amends promptly and ask for forgiveness. In all my relationships today help me to do my part in making them healthy and growing. In Jesus' name I pray, Amen.

Relapse

Principle 7: Reserve a daily time with God for self-examination, Bible reading, and prayer in order to know God and His will for my life and to gain the power to follow His will.

Step 11: Sought through prayer and meditation to improve our conscious contact with God, praying only for knowledge of His will for us and power to carry that out.

Let the message of Christ dwell among you richly. (Colossians 3:16)

Introduction

(Note: At Saddleback Church, we start with Lesson 1 in January. Therefore, we are teaching Principle 7 in November. That's why this lesson begins with a reference to Christmas.)

Tonight, we are going to start working on Principle 7. We are going to look specifically at how to maintain the momentum of your recovery during the approaching holidays!

Holidays can be tough, especially if you are alone, or if you are still hoping your family will live up to your expectations. This is a key time of the year to guard against slipping back to your old hurts, hang-ups, or habits. A key time to guard against relapse!

Therefore, tonight we are going to talk about how you can prevent RELAPSE. You don't have to start your Christmas shopping yet, but it's not too early to start working on a relapse-prevention program.

Preventing Relapse

Tonight's acrostic is RELAPSE:

Reserve a daily quiet time
Evaluate
Listen to Jesus
Alone and quiet time
Plug in to God's power
Slow down
Enjoy your growth

The first letter in relapse stands for Principle 7 itself: RESERVE a daily quiet time with God for self-examination, Bible reading, and prayer in order to know God and His will for my life and gain the power to follow His will.

As I said, during the holidays, it's easy to slip back into our old hurts, hang-ups, and habits. The alcoholic goes back to drinking, the overeater gains back the weight, the gambler goes back to "lost wages" (Las Vegas), the workaholic fills up his schedule, the codependent goes back to an unhealthy relationship. The list goes on and on.

The first step in preventing a relapse is to admit that you will be tempted, that you are not above temptation. Jesus wasn't, why should you be?

We find the account of Jesus' temptation in Matthew 4:1–11:

> Then Jesus was led by the Spirit into the wilderness to be tempted by the devil. After fasting forty days and forty nights, he was hungry. The tempter came to him and said, "If you are the Son of God, tell these stones to become bread."
>
> Jesus answered, "It is written: 'Man shall not live on bread alone, but on every word that comes from the mouth of God.' "
>
> Then the devil took him to the holy city and had him stand on the highest point of the temple. "If you are the Son of God," he said, "throw yourself down. For it is written: 'He will command his angels concerning you, and they will lift you up in their hands, so that you will not strike your foot against a stone.' "
>
> Jesus answered him, "It is also written: 'Do not put the Lord your God to the test.' " Again, the devil took him to a very high mountain and showed him all the kingdoms of the world and their splendor. "All this I will give you," he said, "if you will bow down and worship me." Jesus said to him, "Away from me, Satan! For it is written: 'Worship the Lord your God, and serve him only.' "
>
> Then the devil left him, and angels came and attended him.

The test was over; the devil left. Jesus was tempted. He never sinned, but He was tempted.

Mark 14:38 tells us: "Watch and pray so that you will not fall into temptation. The spirit is willing, but the flesh is weak."

Remember, being tempted isn't a sin. It's falling into the action of the temptation that gets us into trouble. You know it's odd, temptations are different from opportunities. Temptations will always give you a second chance!

Temptation is not a sin; it is a call to battle. When we are tempted to fall back into our old hurts, hang-ups, and habits we need to say to Satan as Jesus did in Matthew 4:10: "Jesus said to him, 'Away from me, Satan! For it is written: "Worship the Lord your God, and serve him only." ' "

The next word in our acrostic reminds us of Step 10: EVALUATE.

Let me just recap what we have talked about in the last two lessons. Your evaluation needs to include your physical, emotional, relational, and spiritual health.

As Pastor Rick Warren says, don't forget the value of doing a "H-E-A-R-T" check. Ask yourself daily if you are

Hurting

Exhausted

Angry

Resentful

Tense

If you answer yes to any of the above, just use the tools you have learned in recovery to help get you back on track. We find specific instructions for this step in Psalm 16:7–10: "I will praise the LORD, who counsels me; even at night my heart instructs me. I keep my eyes always on the LORD. With him at my right hand, I will not be shaken. Therefore my heart is glad and my tongue rejoices; my body also will rest secure, because you will not abandon me to the realm of the dead, nor will you let your faithful one see decay."

Daily practice of Step 10 maintains your honesty and humility.

The *L* is LISTEN to your Higher Power, Jesus Christ.

We need to take a time-out from the world's busyness long enough to listen to our bodies, our minds, and our souls. We need to slow down enough to hear the Lord's directions. "The LORD is my shepherd, I lack nothing. He makes me lie down in green pastures, he leads me beside quiet waters, he refreshes my soul. He guides me along the right paths for his name's sake." (Psalm 23:1–3).

Let's look at the letter *A*, which stands for ALONE and quiet time.

The first part of Step 11 says: "We sought through prayer and meditation to improve our conscious contact with God."

In Principle 3, we made a decision to turn our lives and our wills over to God's care; in Principle 4, we confessed our sins to Him; and in Principle 5, we humbly asked Him to remove our shortcomings.

Now, in Principle 7 in order to keep your recovery growing, you need to have a daily quiet time with Jesus. Even He spent time alone with His Father; you need to do the same. Set a daily appointment time to be alone with God, so that you can learn to listen carefully, learn how to hear God!

In Psalm 46:10 God tells us to "He says, "Be still, and know that I am God; I will be exalted among the nations, I will be exalted in the earth."

Step 11 uses the word *meditation*. Meditation may be new to you, and you may feel uncomfortable. The definition of *meditation* is simply "slowing down long enough to hear God." With practice, you will begin to realize the value of spending time alone with God.

The Enemy will use whatever he can to disrupt your quiet time with God. He will allow you to fill your schedule with so many good things that you burn out or do not have the time to keep your appointment with God. The Enemy loves it when he keeps us from growing and from working on the most important relationship in our lives—our relationship with Jesus.

Psalm 1:1–3 tells us: "Blessed is the one who does not walk in step with the wicked or stand in the way that sinners take or sit in the company of mockers, but whose delight is in the law of the LORD, and who meditates on his law day and night. That person is like a tree planted by streams of water, which yields its fruit in season and whose leaf does not wither—whatever they do prospers."

The next letter is *P*: PLUG in to God's power through prayer.

I can't tell you the number of people who, in counseling, have asked me, "Why did God allow that to happen to me?"

I reply, "Did you pray and seek His will and guidance before you made the decision to get married, before you made the decision to change jobs?" or whatever their issue might be.

You see, if we don't daily seek His will for our lives, how can we blame Him when things go wrong?

Some people think their job is to give God instructions. They have it backward. Our job is to daily seek His will for our lives. You see, God's guidance and direction can only start when our demands stop.

Don't misunderstand me here. I'm only suggesting that we must stop *demanding* things of God, not stop asking things of Him. Specific prayer requests are another way to be plugged in to God's power.

In Philippians 4:6–7, Paul tells us to pray about everything asking for God's perfect will in all our decisions: "Do not be anxious about anything, but in every situation, by prayer and petition, with thanksgiving, present your requests to God. And the peace of God, which transcends all understanding, will guard your hearts and your minds in Christ Jesus."

The verse says *His* answers, *His* perfect will—not mine or yours. Ours are imperfect and most often self-centered. We often use prayer as a labor-saving device, but I need to remind myself daily that God will not do for me what I can do for myself. Neither will God do for you what you can do for yourself.

Let's look at the S in our acrostic: SLOW down long enough to hear God's answer.

After you spend time praying to God, you need to slow down long enough to hear His answers and direction. We can become impatient. We want God's answer now! But, we need to remember our timing can be flawed and God's timing is always perfect!

"There is a time for everything, and a season for every activity under the heavens" (Ecclesiastes 3:1). Psalms 130:5 tells us: "I wait for the LORD, my whole being waits, and in his word I put my hope."

Finally, the last letter in relapse is *E*: ENJOY your growth.

You need to enjoy your victories. Rejoice in and celebrate the small successes along your road to recovery! First Thessalonians 5:16–18 tells us to "Rejoice always, pray continually, give thanks in all circumstances; for this is God's will for you in Christ Jesus." And don't forget to share your victories, no matter how small, with others in your group. Your growth will give others hope!

With daily practice of these principles and with Christ's loving presence in your life, you will be able to maintain and continue to grow in recovery!

Wrap-Up

Honestly, sometimes I wish I could take a vacation from my recovery, especially during the holidays. I'm sure you all have felt that way at one time or another. But let me assure you that relapse is real. It does happen! And it can be very costly. I urge you to take the actions that we talked about tonight to prevent relapse.

Let's get practical. Here are some things to do to prevent relapse during the holidays:

1. Pray and read your Bible daily. Establish a specific time of day to have your "quiet time."
2. Make attending your recovery meeting a priority. Stay close to your support team. If you find yourself saying, "I'm too busy to go to Celebrate Recovery tonight," make time. Flee from whatever you are doing and come share your recovery.
3. Spend time with your family if they are safe. If they are not, spend time with your church family. We are going to have Celebrate Recovery every Friday night throughout the holidays. You do not have to be alone this holiday season.
4. Get involved in service. Volunteer! You don't have to wait until you get to Principle 8 to start serving.

These are just a few ideas and suggestions. Share tonight in your small groups on ways that you, with God's help, can prevent relapse in your recovery.

Gratitude

_____

Principle 7: Reserve a daily time with God for self-examination, Bible reading, and prayer in order to know God and His will for my life and to gain the power to follow His will.

Step 11: We sought through prayer and meditation to improve our conscious contact with God, praying only for knowledge of His will for us and power to carry that out.

Let the message of Christ dwell among you richly. (Colossians 3:16)

_____

Introduction

Tonight we are going to focus our attention outward rather than inward. We have taken many steps on our road to recovery. Our first step was to admit that we were (and are) powerless. Our second step led us to choose, once and for all, a power by which to live. We took our third and most important step when we chose to turn our lives and wills over to the only true Higher Power, Jesus Christ.

As we continue our journey, we grow in our conscious contact with God and He begins to unfold in our lives. And, as we begin to grow in our understanding of Him, we begin to live out the decision we made in Principle 3. We keep walking now, in peace, as we maintain inventories on a regular basis and as we continue to deepen our relationship with Christ. The way we do this according to Principle 7, is to "reserve a daily time with God." During this time we focus on Him by praying and meditating.

Prayer is talking to God. Meditation is listening to God on a daily basis. When I meditate I don't get into some yoga-type position or murmur, "om, om, om." I simply focus on and think about God or a certain Scripture verse or maybe even just one or two words. This morning I spent ten or fifteen minutes just trying to focus on one word: *gratitude*.

I need to meditate every morning, but I don't. Some mornings my mind wanders and I find it very difficult to concentrate. Those old familiar friends will come back. You know, that old familiar committee of past dysfunction. The committee will try to do everything it can to interrupt my quiet time with God. Through daily working the principles to the best of my ability, however, I've learned to shut them up most of the time.

I've learned to listen to God, who tells me that I have great worth. And He will say the same to you—if you will listen.

When I start my day with Principle 7 and end it by doing my daily inventory, I have a pretty good day—a reasonably happy day. This is one way I choose to live "one day at a time" and one way I can prevent relapse.

Another way to prevent relapse, especially during the holidays, is by maintaining an attitude of gratitude.

Gratitude

This week, the week before we celebrate Thanksgiving, I suggest that your prayers be focused on your gratitude in four areas of your life: toward God, others, your recovery, and your church. I'm going to ask you to write them down on your "gratitude list." This is an interactive lesson.

Teacher's note: Make copies and hand out the "Gratitude List" found in Appendix 10. After you present each of the four areas on the list, pause and give the participants a couple of minutes to complete each of the sections.

We are going to take some time now for you to build your gratitude list for this Thanksgiving. First, for what are you thankful to *God*? Offer prayers of gratitude to your Creator.

In Philippians 4:4–6, we're told, "Rejoice in the Lord always. I will say it again: Rejoice! Let your gentleness be evident to all. The Lord is near. Do not be anxious about anything, but in every situation, by prayer and petition, with thanksgiving, present your requests to God." Psalm 107:1 encourages us to "Give thanks to the LORD, for he is good; his love endures forever." What wonderful deeds they are! What are at least two areas of your life in which you can see God's work and that you are thankful for this holiday season?

You can reflect on the last eleven months or on what God has done for you this week or even today. Then take a moment to list just a few of the special things for which you are thankful to your Higher Power.

The next area is to list the individuals whom God has placed in your life to walk alongside you on your road of recovery. We need to be thankful for *others*.

"Let the peace of Christ rule in your hearts, since as members of one body you were called to peace. And be thankful. Let the message of Christ dwell among you richly as you teach and admonish one another with all wisdom through psalms, hymns, and songs from the Spirit, singing to God with gratitude in your hearts." (Colossians 3:15–16).

Who are you thankful for? Why? Take a moment to list them.

The third area we can be thankful for is our *recovery*.

"Therefore, since we are surrounded by such a great cloud of witnesses, let us throw off everything that hinders and the sin that so easily entangles. And let us run with perseverance the race marked out for us, fixing our eyes on Jesus, the pioneer and perfecter of faith. For the joy set before him he endured the cross, scorning its shame, and sat down at the right hand of the throne of God. Consider him who endured such opposition from sinners, so that you will not grow weary and lose heart" (Hebrews 12:1–3)"

What are two recent growth areas of your recovery for which you are thankful? Again, list them now.

"Enter his gates with thanksgiving and his courts with praise; give thanks to him and praise his name. For the LORD is good and his love endures forever; his faithfulness continues through all generations." (Psalm 100:4–5).

What are two things for which you are thankful to your church?

Wrap-Up

Take your "gratitude list" home with you tonight and put it in a place where you will see it often. It will remind you that you have made progress in your recovery and that you are not alone, that Jesus Christ is always with you.

Using your gratitude list, going to your recovery meetings and making them a priority, and getting involved in service in your church are the best ways I know to prevent relapse during the holidays.

Let's close in prayer.

Dear God, help me set aside all the hassles and noise of the world to focus and listen just to You for the next few minutes. Help me get to know You better. Help me to better understand Your plan, Your purpose for my life. Father, help me live within today, seeking Your will and living this day as You would have me.

It is my prayer to have others see me as Yours; not just in my words but more importantly, in my actions. Thank You for Your love, Your grace, Your perfect forgiveness. Thank You for all those You have placed in my life, for my program, my recovery, and my church family. Your will be done, not mine. In Your Son's name I pray, Amen.

Principle 8

Yield myself to God to be used to bring this Good News to others, both by my example and by my words.

Blessed are those who are persecuted because of righteousness, for theirs is the kingdom of heaven. (Matthew 5:10)

Give

Principle 8: Yield myself to God to be used to bring this Good News to others, both by my example and by my words.

Blessed are those who are persecuted because of righteousness, for theirs is the kingdom of heaven. (Matthew 5:10)

Step 12: Having had a spiritual experience as the result of these steps, we try to carry this message to others and to practice these principles in all our affairs.

Brothers and sisters, if someone is caught in a sin, you who live by the Spirit should restore that person gently. But watch yourselves, or you also may be tempted. (Galatians 6:1)

Introduction

I think that if God had to choose his favorite principle, He would choose Principle 8: "Yield myself to God to be used to bring this Good News to others, both by my example and by my words."

Why do I think Principle 8 is God's favorite? Because it is putting our faith into action. God's Word tells us in James 2:17, "Faith by itself, if it is not accompanied by action, is dead." Active faith is important to God!

Don't get me wrong, works are not going to save you. Only faith in Jesus Christ as your Lord and Savior can do that. It is through our actions, however, that we demonstrate to God and others the commitment we have to our faith in Jesus Christ.

So tonight, we are going to begin to work on Principle 8. The corresponding step is Step 12, the "carrying the message" step, the "giving back" step.

What is "giving back" all about? What does it truly mean to give?

To answer that question, I did a word study on the meaning of *give* or *giving*. In the New Testament, the word give has seventeen different Greek words with seventeen different meanings. So tonight, I thought you would find it interesting for me to do a thirty-minute lecture on each of the uses of the word *give*. Just kidding!

Perhaps we'll take a more practical look at the meaning of the word give as it relates to Principle 8, since that's what this principle is really all about.

Principle 8 does not tell us to give in unhealthy ways, ways that would hurt us or cause us to relapse into our codependent behaviors. No, Principle 8 is talking about healthy, non-codependent giving of oneself without the slightest trace of expecting to receive back. Remember, no person has ever been honored for what they have received. Honor has always been a reward for what someone gave.

First Peter 3:15 sums up Principle 8: "But in your hearts revere Christ as Lord. Always be prepared to give an answer to everyone who asks you to give the reason for the hope that you have. But do this with gentleness and respect."

In Principle 8, we *yield* ourselves to be used by God to bring this good news to others, both by our example and our words.

Give

It is in Principle 8 we learn what it means to truly GIVE.

God first
I becomes we
Victories shared
Example of your actions

The *G* stands for GOD first.

When you place God first in your life, you realize that everything you have is a gift from Him. You realize that your recovery is not dependent or based on material things, it is built upon your faith and your desire to follow Jesus Christ's direction.

Romans 8:32 says "He who did not spare his own Son, but gave him up for us all—how will he not also, along with him, graciously give us all things?"

We are never more like God than when we give—not just money or things but our very selves. That's what Jesus did for us. He gave us the greatest gift of all—Himself.

The second letter in give is *I*. When we give, the I becomes we.

None of the steps or principles begin with the word *I*. The very first word in Step 1 is *we*. In fact, the word *we* appears in the 12 Steps fourteen times. The word *I* never appears even once in any of the 12 Steps. The road to recovery is not meant to be traveled alone. This is not a program to be worked in isolation.

Jesus said, " 'Love the Lord your God with all your heart and with all your soul and with all your mind.' This is the first and greatest commandment. And the second is like it: 'Love your neighbor as yourself' " (Matthew 22:37–39).

When you have reached this step in your recovery and someone asks you to be a sponsor or to be an accountability partner, do it! The rewards are great, and being a sponsor or an accountability partner is one way to carry the message!

Ecclesiastes 4:9–12 makes this concept of giving very clear: "Two are better than one, because they have a good return for their labor: If either of them falls down, one can help the other up. But pity anyone who falls and has no one to help them up. Also, if two lie down together, they will keep warm. But how can one keep warm alone? Though one may be overpowered, two can defend themselves. A cord of three strands is not quickly broken."

The third letter stands for VICTORIES shared.

God never, never, never, ever wastes a hurt! He can take our hurts and use them to help others. Principle 8 gives us the opportunity to share our experiences, victories, and hopes with one another.

Deuteronomy 11:2 tells us to remember what we've learned about the Lord through our experiences with Him. We start off by saying, "This is how it was for me; this is the *experience* of what happened to me. This is how I gained the *strength* to begin my recovery, and there's *hope* for you."

Second Corinthians 1:3–4 encourages us to "Praise be to the God and Father of our Lord Jesus Christ, the Father of compassion and the God of all comfort, who comforts us in all our troubles, so that we can comfort those in any trouble with the comfort we ourselves receive from God."

All the pain, all the hurt that my twenty years of abusing alcohol caused, all the destruction that I caused to myself and those I loved, finally made sense when I got to Principle 8. I finally understood Romans 8:28: "And we know that in all things God works for the good of those who love him, who have been called according to his purpose."

He called me according to His plans, and because I answered God's call, I can stand here as an example that God works all things for good according to His purpose.

To God be the glory!

I want to spend the rest of my life doing recovery work. You know, though, it's not really work. It's service, a service of joy.

This thought leads us to the last letter in give: EXAMPLE of your actions. You all know that your actions speak louder than your words. Good intentions die unless they are executed.

In James 1:22 we are exhorted to be doers of the word. But, in order to be of help to another, we are to bring the Good News to others.

That's what Step 12 says. It doesn't say to bring a little good news or to bring good news only to others who are in recovery.

You have all heard the term "Sunday Christians." Let us not become just "Friday night recovery buffs."

Works—actions, not words—are proof of your love for God and another person. Faith without works is like a car without gasoline. First John 3:18 says, "Dear children, let us not love with words or speech but with actions and in truth."

Giving and serving is a thermometer of your love. You can give without loving. That's what we sometimes do in a codependent relationship. Or we give because we feel we have to. You can give without loving, but you can't love without giving.

Wrap-Up

The Lord spreads His message through the Principles and the 12 Steps. We are the instruments for delivering the Good News. The way we live will show others our commitment to our program, to our Lord, and to them!

I would like to leave you with Luke 8:16: "No one lights a lamp and hides it in a clay jar or puts it under a bed. Instead, they put it on a stand, so that those who come in can see the light."

We're not hiding things; we're bringing everything out into the open. So be careful that you don't become misers . . . generosity begets generosity. Bring the Good News with joy!

Yes

Principle 8: Yield myself to God to be used to bring this Good News to others, both by my example and by my words.

Blessed are those who are persecuted because of righteousness, for theirs is the kingdom of heaven. (Matthew 5:10)

Step 12: Having had a spiritual experience as the result of these steps, we try to carry this message to others and to practice these principles in all our affairs.

Brothers and sisters, if someone is caught in a sin, you who live by the Spirit should restore that person gently. But watch yourselves, or you also may be tempted. (Galatians 6:1)

Introduction

Modern technology is something else! Take an old, beat-up Diet Coke can—dirty, dented, holes in it. A few years ago, it would have been thrown in the garbage and deemed useless, of no value. Today it can be recycled, melted down, purified, and made into a new can—shiny and clean—that can be used again.

We're going to talk about recycling tonight—recycling your pain by allowing God's fire and light to shine on it, to melt down your old hurts, hang-ups, and habits so they can be used again in a positive way. They can be recycled to show others how you worked the principles and steps with Jesus' healing into the solution and how you have come through the darkness of your pain into Christ's glorious freedom and light.

Society tells us that pain is useless. In fact, people are coming to believe that *people* in pain are useless! At Celebrate Recovery, we know that pain has value, as do the people who experience it. So while the world says no, tonight we say yes!

Yes

Tonight's acrostic couldn't be any more positive! It is the word YES.

Yield myself to God
Example is what is important
Serve others as Jesus Christ did

The *Y* is Principle 8 itself: YIELD myself to God to be used to bring this Good News to others, both by my example and by my words.

To truly practice this principle, we must give God the latitude He needs to use us as He sees fit. We do that by presenting everything we have—our time, talents, and treasures—to Him. We hold loosely all that we call our own, recognizing that all of it comes from His hand. When we have yielded to Him, God can use us as His instruments to carry the message to others in word and action.

Galatians 6:1–2 tells us: "Brothers and sisters, if someone is caught in a sin, you who live by the Spirit should restore that person gently. But watch yourselves, or you also may be tempted. Carry each other's burdens, and in this way you will fulfill the law of Christ."

People take your example far more seriously than they take your advice.

That leads us to the *E* in yes: EXAMPLE is what is important!

Your walk needs to match your talk. We all know that talk is cheap, because the supply always exceeds the demand.

If you want someone to see what Christ will do for them, let them see what Christ has done for you.

Here is a question to ask yourself when you get to this principle: Does my lifestyle reflect what I believe? In other words, does it show others the patterns of the world—selfishness, pride, and lust—or does it reflect the love, humility, and service of Jesus Christ?

"The goal of this command is love, which comes from a pure heart and a good conscience and a sincere faith" (1 Timothy 1:5).

This year, we have all been blessed by some outstanding and courageous testimonies at Celebrate Recovery. I would like all those who gave their testimonies this year to stand. These people believe in Principle 8! They believe in it enough to share not only in the safety of their small groups but also with the whole recovery family. They believe in Jesus Christ enough to share their lives with others. They stood up here and shared their weaknesses and strengths with others who are suffering from similar pain, hurts, hang-ups, and habits. They gave others a piece of their heart—not a piece of their mind.

Our goal again for next year is to have two testimonies each month as we work on each step. So, if you have been in recovery for a while and haven't shared your story as yet, get busy, write it out, and get it to me. We need to hear and you need to share your miracle in the coming year.

The last letter in yes is *S*: SERVE others as Jesus Christ did.

When you have reached Principle 8, you are ready to pick up the "Lord's towel," the one with which He washed the disciples' feet in the upper room the night before He was crucified.

Jesus said, "Now that I, your Lord and Teacher, have washed your feet, you also should wash one another's feet. I have set you an example that you should do as I have done for you" (John 13:14–15).

You don't all have to give your testimonies to three hundred people to do service. All service ranks the same with God. You can say "y-e-s" to Principle 8 in many ways!

1. *Be an accountability partner.* Find someone in your small group who agrees to encourage and support you as you work through the principles. You agree to do the same for that person. You hold one another accountable for working an honest program.

2. *Be a sponsor.* Sponsors are people who have worked the steps. Their job is to guide newcomers on their journey through the steps, to give a gentle nudge when they are procrastinating or to slow them down when they are rushing through a step. Sponsors do so by sharing their personal journey on their road to recovery.

3. *Become a greeter.* Greeters get to Celebrate Recovery at 6:45 p.m. They welcome and provide directions for newcomers. They provide the newcomer with the important first impression of Celebrate Recovery!

4. *Help with the fellowship events.* You need to arrive by 6:00 p.m. to help set up. If you can't get here early, stay a few minutes after to help clean up. You can bake a cake.

5. *Help with the Bar-B-Que.* We'll be starting in the spring. We need help with set-up, clean-up, and everything in between.

6. *Invite someone to church.* Ask someone from your secular groups or a neighbor, a friend, or a coworker!

The world is full of two kinds of people—givers and takers. The takers eat well and the givers sleep well. Be a giver. There are many, many more areas to serve! Make suggestions! Get involved!

Principle 8 comes down to this: Do what you can, with what you have, where you are.

Wrap-Up

The road to recovery leads to service. When you reach Principle 8, the road splits. Some of you will choose to serve at Celebrate Recovery. Others will choose to serve in other areas of the church. The fact is, we need both.

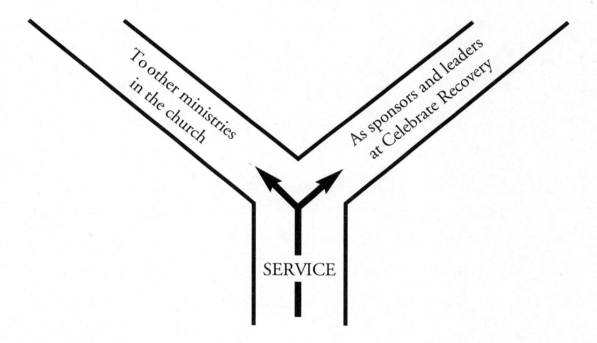

We need you to share your experiences, strengths, and hopes with newcomers here on Friday nights. You do that as leaders, sponsors, and accountability partners. But the church also needs your service. As you serve outside of Celebrate Recovery, you can share with others and get them into recovery when they are ready to work on their hurts, hang-ups, and habits.

Every morning, before I get out of bed I pray this Principle 8 prayer:

Dear Jesus, as it would please You, bring me someone today whom I can serve. Amen.

Will you pray it this week?

Seven Reasons We Get Stuck

Introduction

Tonight, I want to call a time-out. Let's take a week to have you discuss and evaluate where you are on your individual roads to recovery. I believe it is valuable for us all to take a breath, pause, and review our program. We need to stop for a moment and thank God as we look back on our progress and our growth. We need to make sure we are still moving forward through the principles, that we are not hung up on a particular one.

Some of you may have just begun the journey through the principles. Others are somewhere in the middle. It really doesn't matter which one you're on. Anyone can get off track and stuck.

Seven Reasons

Tonight we are going to talk about the seven reasons we get "stuck" in our recoveries!

1. You Have Not Completely Worked the Previous Principle

Perhaps you are trying to move through the principles too quickly. Slow down! Give God time to work! Just moving forward isn't always progress. Did your brakes ever go out when you were driving down a hill? You may be going fast, but it's not progress. It's panic! Remember, this program is a process. It's not a race to see who finishes first.

Galatians 5:25 says, "Since we live by the Spirit, let us keep in step with the Spirit."

Take your time with each principle. Work it to the best of your ability. Remember, many people get lost while trying to find an easier route for the straight and narrow.

2. You Have Not Completely Surrendered Your Will and Your Life to the Lord

Remember, there are two parts to Principle 3. The first is to ask Jesus Christ into your heart as your Higher Power, your Lord and Savior. The second is to seek to follow His will for your life in all your decisions. Perhaps you are trusting Jesus with the "big" things, but you still think you can handle the "small" things.

Proverbs 3:5–6 tells us, "Trust in the LORD with all your heart and lean not on your own understanding; in all your ways submit to him, and he will make your paths straight."

What part of your life are you still holding on to? What areas of your life are you withholding from God? What don't you trust Him with?

3. You Have Not Accepted Jesus' Work on the Cross for Your Forgiveness

You may have forgiven others, but you think your sin is too big to be forgiven.

First John 1:9 tells us, "If we confess our sins, he is faithful and just and will forgive us our sins and purify us from all unrighteousness." Every wrong! Not just some of our wrongs, but all of them! Believe me, your sin isn't that special, isn't that different.

"For he chose us in him before the creation of the world to be holy and blameless in his sight. In love he predestined us for adoption to sonship through Jesus Christ, in accordance with his pleasure and will—to the praise of his glorious grace, which he has freely given us in the One he loves. In him we have redemption through his blood, the forgiveness of sins, in accordance with the riches of God's grace" (Ephesians 1:4–7).

I think the real question here is "Have you forgiven yourself?" That's where I see most people getting stuck in their recoveries.

This is what God wants you to do with the darkness of your past: " 'Come now, let us settle the matter,' says the LORD. 'Though your sins are like scarlet, they shall be as white as snow; though they are red as crimson, they shall be like wool' " (Isaiah 1:18).

Remember, "Therefore, there is now no condemnation for those who are in Christ Jesus, because through Christ Jesus the law of the Spirit who gives life has set you free from the law of sin and death" (Romans 8:1–2).

4. You Have Not Forgiven Others Who Have Harmed You

You must let go of the pain of past harm and abuse. Until you are able to release it and forgive it, it will continue to hold you as its prisoner.

It has been said that forgiveness is the key that unlocks the door of resentments and removes the handcuffs of hate. It is the power that breaks the chains of bitterness and the shackles of selfishness.

"Be kind and compassionate to one another, forgiving each other, just as in Christ God forgave you" (Ephesians 4:32).

Do you know that you may need to ask forgiveness for blaming God?

There is God's will, the Devil's will, and your free will all at work on the earth. Remember, the harm others did to you was from their free will, not God's will.

5. You Are Afraid of the Risk in Making the Necessary Change

It may be fair to say that some people here tonight put off change and procrastinate as long as they can. There can be several reasons for delaying positive change.

You may be paralyzed by the fear of failure.

Remember, falling down doesn't make you a failure. It's staying down that makes you one. This is where your faith and trust in Jesus Christ comes into play.

You may fear intimacy because of the fear of rejection or being hurt again.

This is why it is so important to move slowly in a new relationship, taking time to seek God's will, develop realistic expectations, and establish proper boundaries.

You may resist change (growth) because of the fear of the unknown.

My life is a mess, my relationships are a mess, but at least I know what to expect. All together now—"A mess!" If you really try working the steps and principles on that hurt, hang-up, or habit, your life will change.

Some people change jobs, mates, and friends, but never think of changing themselves. What does God's Word tell us?

"So do not fear, for I am with you; do not be dismayed, for I am your God. I will strengthen you and help you; I will uphold you with my righteous right hand" (Isaiah 41:10). So we say with confidence, "The Lord is my helper; I will not be afraid. What can mere mortals do to me?" (Hebrews 13:6).

6. You Are Not Willing to "Own" Your Responsibility

None of us is responsible for all the things that have happened to us. But we are responsible for the way we react to them. Let me give you some examples.

In the case of abuse, in no way is the victim at fault or responsible for the abuse.

Step 8 in our sexual/physical abuse 12 Steps reads as follows:

Made a list of all persons who have harmed us and became willing to seek God's help in forgiving our perpetrators as well as forgiving ourselves. Realize that we have also harmed others and become willing to make amends to them.

My kids are not responsible for being children of an alcoholic, but they are responsible for their own actions and recovery. You need to take the responsibility for your part in a broken relationship, a damaged friendship, or with a distant child or parent.

Search me, God, and know my heart; test me and know my anxious thoughts" (Psalm 139:23).

We increase our ability, stability, and responsibility when we increase our accountability to God.

7. You Have Not Developed an Effective Support Team

Do you have a sponsor or an accountability partner? Do you have the phone numbers of others in your small group? Have you volunteered for a 12-Step commitment to your support group?

There are a lot of opportunities to get involved at Celebrate Recovery:

- Cafe team
- Greeters
- Sponsors
- Accountability partners
- Much more . . .

All you have to do is ask!

Walk with the wise and become wise, for a companion of fools suffers harm. (Proverbs 13:20)

Carry each other's burdens, and in this way you will fulfill the law of Christ. (Galatians 6:2)

Remember, the roots of happiness grow deepest in the soil of service.

Wrap-Up

Now you know the seven areas in which we can get bogged down, stuck in our recoveries. How do I know? Because somewhere along my own personal road to recovery, I visited them all.

Take time this week and reflect on your progress, your growth. If you are stuck, talk to your accountability partner, your sponsor, or your small group leader. Find out which of the seven reasons you are hung up on, and together, implement a plan of action and move ahead on your journey.

Keep Celebrate Recovery's Daily Action Plan for Serenity (printed here as well as on page 176 in Volume 4) where you can see it and review it daily.

Celebrate Recovery's Daily Action Plan for Serenity

1. Daily, continue to take an inventory. When you are wrong, promptly admit it.

2. Daily, study God's Word and pray asking God to guide you and help you apply His teaching and will in your life.

3. Daily, work and live the Principles to the best of your ability, always looking for new opportunities to help and serve others—not just at your recovery meetings but in all areas of your life.

The Journey Continues

If you've been in Celebrate Recovery for a while, you have probably done more than one Step Study. Remember, in Step studies we go through the first four Celebrate Recovery volumes. These guides have been used since 1994 by more than 3.5 million people as they have traveled the road to recovery. Chances are, you have gone through the four Volumes multiple times.

Because of this, we are so excited to bring you a **brand new, revolutionary** Step Study curriculum! For the first time in any recovery program, Christ-centered or secular, Celebrate Recovery is introducing new tools to help take your recovery further. These new tools, called *The Journey Continues*, build on the existing Celebrate Recovery material. In fact, the original Celebrate Recovery participant's guides (Volumes 1–4) are now called *The Journey Begins*. Nothing has changed in these original guides, and they should still be used for people who are entering their first step study.

The Journey Continues, Volumes 5–8, are designed for people who have done at least one Step Study, completed *The Journey Begins* (Volumes 1–4), and preferably taken some time to apply the principles and truths they have learned to their lives. (We recommend a period of at least six months to allow participants to really practice their recovery.) *The Journey Continues* contains twenty-five lessons designed to help participants dig deeper into their recoveries and take them further in their walk with God. There are new acrostics, new questions, and of course, hundreds of Bible verses. (**At the end of this section, on pages 221–226, a replica of Lesson 2, "Power," from Volume 5, *Moving Forward in God's Grace*, is included so that you can experience for yourself both the similarities and differences of this new curriculum.**)

Who Is *The Journey Continues* For?

- Anyone who has completed at least one *The Journey Begins* Step Study.
- Anyone who has applied the Principles to their lives. We strongly suggest a period of at least six months after completing *The Journey Begins*.
- Anyone who is ready to take his or her recovery to the next level.

- Anyone who has discovered any new hurts, hang-ups, and habits since completing one or more *The Journey Begins* Step Study.
- And especially anyone who has completed a *The Journey Begins* group but has taken some time away from recovery.

Who Is The Journey Continues Not For?

- Anyone who has not completed a *The Journey Begins* Step Study.
- Anyone who has not had time to apply the Christ-centered steps and principles to their lives.
- Newcomers. They should start with a *The Journey Begins* step study.

Now that you know a little about *The Journey Continues*, let's look at how to implement the new material in your Celebrate Recovery ministry.

Implementation

In order to successfully run *The Journey Continues* step studies, a few things will need to be in place. First, you will have to make sure you are offering *The Journey Begins* step studies on an ongoing basis. We suggest a ratio of 1:1, meaning that for every *The Journey Continues* group you offer, you will need to offer one *The Journey Begins* group. For some ministries this won't be possible, so just make sure that your ministry doesn't stop offering *The Journey Begins* groups in an effort to start *The Journey Continues* groups.

Also, the lessons contained in *The Journey Continues* are not meant to be taught during your General (large group) Meeting Night. The lessons found in the *Celebrate Recovery Leader's Guide* are not to be replaced by the lessons in *The Journey Continues*. Remember, the General Meeting Night is all about the newcomer, and the newcomer hasn't heard the original lessons yet. **Do not substitute any part of the lessons found in the leader's guide with the acrostics found in *The Journey Continues*!** Each lesson of *The Journey Continues* has additional content to explain the new concepts and help participants apply them to their lives.

As in *The Journey Begins* and in the Open Share Groups, *The Journey Continues* groups are gender specific, and the five small group guidelines are used every time. Also, as in *The Journey Begins* groups, they are mixed recovery issues. No outside materials are to be used.

Everyone knows it's more exciting to start something new than it is to maintain something. But newcomers and people who have not yet completed a *The Journey Begins* group need to start at the beginning. As soon as people hear of *The Journey Continues*, they are going to want to do the "advanced" material. That's why it's so important that we don't refer to *The Journey Continues* as advanced. It builds on *The Journey Begins*.

The best way to think of this is math (stay with me). In mathematics, no one starts with calculus; instead, students learn addition, then subtraction, multiplication, and move on to division. Each skill builds on the last. In order to progress to the next level, students must be able to at least understand and apply the previous one. *The Journey Continues* works the same way. In order to move on to *The Journey Continues*, participants should complete at least one *The Journey Begins* group and be given some time to apply the principles to their lives.

Unlike math, however, no test will be given! In fact, there may be some folks who will be tempted to judge who is and isn't ready to move into a *The Journey Continues* group. Resist this temptation! Avoid making "rules" or having a gatekeeper who makes these kinds of decisions. Instead communicate who *The Journey Continues* groups are for and what participants should do before they join one. Ask sponsors and leaders to back you up on this, and train them to inform people of the requirements.

At the first meeting of a *The Journey Continues* group, the leader should remind everyone of the requirements and make sure everyone understands them. However, the group leader is not required to check or know that the participants have completed a *The Journey Begins* group or taken the time to apply the principles to their lives. It is not the group leader's responsibility to judge. However, *The Journey Continues* is a deeper study; therefore, deeper commitment should be expected. Leaders should communicate that all answers need to be written in advance (just as in *The Journey Begins*) and that more participation and involvement will be expected from the participants of these groups.

All groups should have a trained leader and co-leader. Because the format and function of *The Journey Continues* groups are the same as *The Journey Begins*, there is no need for intense leadership training. However, all leaders should take the time to familiarize themselves with the material in advance. Please apply the leadership training for step studies found in the *Advanced Leadership Training Guide* (ALT) to *The Journey Continues* groups as well.

Although these groups are designed to dig deeper into recovery issues, they do not need to be run any differently than *The Journey Begins* groups. One possible pitfall may be that because some groups will have done *The Journey Begins* and then go right in to *The Journey Continues*, there may be some temptation to skip the guidelines and allow the group to be more casual. Make sure that this does not happen! As groups get closer, it can be even more crucial to ensure the guidelines are being followed. Don't let familiarity create problems in the groups.

Participants will be asked to complete a new moral inventory. This will be done in Volume 6, *Asking God to Grow My Character*, and though the same inventory worksheets will be used, there is a brand new tool as well. Called "Pro's from My Inventory," it has been added to help participants keep specific track of all of the good things they are doing and that have been done to them. After all, these participants have been in recovery for a while now, so they can expect to be seeing more growth and victory. Encourage participants to use this new tool to help them see all of the changes Christ has made in them through Celebrate Recovery!

The two major focuses of *The Journey Continues* are spiritual growth and service. In almost every lesson participants will be asked who they are serving and how are they growing. It is important that Ministry Leaders provide ample service opportunities and encourage participants to get involved.

For more information on *The Journey Continues*:

- Please visit www.celebraterecovery.com/thejourneycontinues.
- Come to a Celebrate Recovery one-day seminar or summit.
- Download the free Celebrate Recovery app.
- Tap "State Reps" to find someone you can talk to in your area for any questions.
- Review a replica of one of the twenty-five new lessons on the following pages.

Power

Principle 1: Realize I'm not God. I admit that I am powerless to control my tendency to do the wrong thing and that my life is unmanageable.

Blessed are the poor in spirit, for theirs is the kingdom of heaven. (Matthew 5:3)

Step 1: We admitted we were powerless over our addictions and compulsive behaviors, that our lives had become unmanageable.

I know that good itself does not dwell in me, that is, in my sinful nature. For I have the desire to do what is good, but I cannot carry it out. (Romans 7:18)

Please begin your time together by reading "Casting Anxiety, Day 12" from the *Celebrate Recovery Daily Devotional*.

In Lesson 2 of *The Journey Begins*, we looked at the "serenity robbers" we would give up when we admitted we were powerless. By admitting our powerlessness, we find that there is a true Higher Power, whose name is Jesus, who can and will restore us to sanity. And He can do so much more!

You are either going to serve God or self. You can't do both! Matthew 6:24 says, "No one can serve two masters. Either you will hate the one and love the other, or you will be devoted to the one and despise the other. You cannot serve both God and money." Another term for serving "ourselves" is serving the "flesh." *Flesh* is the Bible's word for our unperfected human nature, our sin nature.

If you leave the "h" off the end of *flesh* and reverse the remaining letters, you spell the word *self*. Flesh is the self-life. It is what we are when we are left to our own devices. When our "self" is out of control, all attempts at control—of self or others—fail. In fact, our attempt to control ourselves and others is what got us into trouble in the first place. To have long-lasting peace in your life, God needs to be the one in control.

Because you now have a relationship with Jesus, you now have the POWER to overcome any hurt, hang-up, or habit. Let's look at what that power can do in your life.

POWER

P—Peace of mind can be found

Instead of having our minds racing, trying to keep all of the plates spinning, we can now enjoy the peace of mind that God offers. Then we can turn from trying to do things on our own power and rely on His instead.

And the peace of God, which transcends all understanding, will guard your hearts and your minds in Christ Jesus. (Philippians 4:7)

Now may the Lord of peace himself give you peace at all times and in every way. The Lord be with all of you. (2 Thessalonians 3:16)

O—Overcoming temptation is possible

Once it may have felt that temptation was impossible to resist. Now that we have God's power, we have the ability to look for ways to escape temptation before giving in.

No temptation has overtaken you except what is common to mankind. And God is faithful; he will not let you be tempted beyond what you can bear. But when you are tempted, he will also provide a way out so that you can endure it. (1 Corinthians 10:13)

So I say, walk by the Spirit, and you will not gratify the desires of the flesh. (Galatians 5:16)

W—Worrying can stop

Worry happens when we face a problem bigger than ourselves. When we know that we can't solve a problem with our own power, or when we fear that we will be overcome by something we can't handle, we worry. However, when we trust God and plug into His power through prayer, we find we can stop worrying because nothing is too big for God to handle.

Therefore do not worry about tomorrow, for tomorrow will worry about itself. Each day has enough trouble of its own. (Matthew 6:34)

Those who know your name trust in you, for you, LORD, have never forsaken those who seek you. (Psalm 9:10)

E—Every character defect can be healed

There's no issue that God can't heal. Even after completing a step study, we may be holding onto things we have been unwilling to face. We may have some hurts we are afraid to hand over to God, or a secondary recovery issue that we have not dealt with. We now have the power to face them because of God's power. There isn't a character defect or issue in the world that God can't heal!

He heals the brokenhearted and binds up their wounds. (Psalm 147:3)

R—Real relationships can be formed

Denial and the refusal to admit we have had problems caused us to lose or damage many of our relationships in the past. Coming out of denial, and admitting we are powerless, gives us the ability to stop trying to act like we have it all together and form true trust and intimacy with others.

For just as each of us has one body with many members, and these members do not all have the same function, so in Christ we, though many, form one body, and each member belongs to all the others. (Romans 12:4–5)

And let us consider how we may spur one another on toward love and good deeds, not giving up meeting together, as some are in the habit of doing, but encouraging one another—and all the more as you see the Day approaching. (Hebrews 10:24–25)

Questions for Reflection and Discussion

1. Have you fully admitted your powerlessness over your life's hurts, hang-ups, and habits? If not, what's holding you back?

2. How have you experienced "the peace of God, which transcends all understanding"? Share details.

3. How are you plugging into God's power when you are stressed?

4. Share a time when you have felt God's power help you overcome a temptation. Be specific.

5. Sharing a victory over temptation with a newcomer is so important! Who do you know that would be encouraged by hearing that story?

6. What are you worried about today? How can you turn that worry over to God?

7. Now that you've been in recovery for a while, what character defects are you planning on focusing on during *The Journey Continues*?

8. Have you been holding back a particular hurt, hang-up, or habit that you are now ready to face? If so, what is it?

9. Question 6 of the POWERLESS lesson in Volume 1, *The Journey Begins* asks, "How has your denial isolated you from your important relationships?" Have you seen any change in those relationships since your involvement in Celebrate Recovery? If so, what has happened? If not, why not?

10. What healthy, real relationships have you formed in Celebrate Recovery, and how have they helped your recovery journey?

Prayer

Dear God, please continue to give me the power to overcome my hurts, hang-ups, and habits. I know I need to stop pretending I have it all under control, and that I need to rely on Your power. Help me overcome temptations and worry, and allow me to lean on the people You have placed in my life. Amen.

Closing Thoughts

The grace of our Lord was poured out on me abundantly, along with the faith and love that are in Christ Jesus. Here is a trustworthy saying that deserves full acceptance: Christ Jesus came into the world to save sinners—of whom I am the worst. But for that very reason I was shown mercy so that in me, the worst of sinners, Christ Jesus might display his immense patience as an example for those who would believe in him and receive eternal life. Now to the King eternal, immortal, invisible, the only God, be honor and glory for ever and ever. Amen. (1 Timothy 1:14–17)

We have come to the end of this leader's guide, and you are now ready to begin the most exciting part—the actual stepping out and starting one of the most important and significant ministries in your church.

Romans 12:10–13 is my prayer for you and your new recovery program:

Be devoted to one another in love. Honor one another above yourselves. Never be lacking in zeal, but keep your spiritual fervor, serving the Lord. Be joyful in hope, patient in affliction, faithful in prayer. Share with the Lord's people who are in need. Practice hospitality.

Please visit our website, www.celebraterecovery.com, for ongoing and updated information. I am looking forward to learning about all the lives that will be changed and families reunited because of your decision to start Celebrate Recovery.

In His steps,
John Baker

Appendices

Appendix 1

Celebrate Recovery® Leadership Covenant

I have read and agree to follow the *Celebrate Recovery Leader's Guide.*

- I will attend monthly Celebrate Recovery leaders' meetings.
- I will uphold Celebrate Recovery's five small group guidelines in my small group meetings.
- I will pray for each person in my group.
- I will pray for the unity, health, and growth of the church.
- I will squelch gossip and resolve conflict with the truth by applying Matthew 18:15–17.
- I will continue working on my personal recovery and support team.
- I will develop another person to be my coleader.

Signed

_____Leader _____ Ministry Leader

Date _____

Appendix 2

Sample Celebrate Recovery® Leader Information Sheet

Name:_____Date:_____

Address:_____

City:_____ Zip:_____

Phone: _____ Email:_____

I agree to develop my testimony: Yes_____ No_____ If yes, when_____

Open share group I attend:_____

I have been in recovery since:_____

Attended CR since:_____ My sobriety date is: _____

Date completed CR step study:_____

I have had a Celebrate Recovery leader's interview: **Yes** or **No** (circle)

I have completed CR information meeting/orientation: **Yes** or **No** (circle)

I have completed open share group training: **Yes** or **No** (circle)

I have completed step study training: **Yes** or **No** (circle)

I have completed sponsor training: **Yes** or **No** (circle)

I have completed testimony writing workshop: **Yes** or **No** (circle)

I have served in the following areas of ministry or CR service:

The following area of ministry brings me the most joy in my life:

I am interested in getting involved in service at CR because:

Recovery references (please list at least two):

Names of my step study leaders:

Sample Celebrate Recovery© Leader's Interview Questions

- How are you continuing to grow in your own recovery?
- In what areas do you need further training and growth?
- Who will you ask for accountability or mentoring?
- Do you struggle with being vulnerable? Why or why not?
- What impact has vulnerability made on your group?
- How do you think God sees you?
- Do you ever feel unworthy OR prideful? Why?
- How do you feel about accepting responsibility?
- How will your relationship with God help you carry out these responsibilities?
- What areas are easy for you to serve in and which ones are difficult?
- What would "stepping out of your comfort zone" be for you?
- Do you feel confident in your abilities to uphold the small group guidelines in your group? Why or why not?
- What has been your experience with loving confrontation?
- What will you do to get to know the needs of your group?
- What can you do to encourage your group?

Appendix 3

Writing a Celebrate Recovery Testimony

Our greatest resources in Celebrate Recovery are our one true Higher Power Jesus Christ, the indwelling Holy Spirit, and the Scriptures. All Celebrate Recovery curriculum and meetings depend upon these vital resources. Beyond these, the next most powerful resource available to us is a personal testimony of recovery. The importance of the testimony is seen in the prominent role it plays in the annual schedule of large group meetings. Twenty-two of the fifty-two meetings feature a recovery testimony. Because testimonies are so important, there are guidelines for preparing and presenting a recovery testimony. Many will enter your large group meetings with life-and-death issues. Often they are looking for an excuse to leave and not return. This is not the time to have someone "shoot from the hip." You need to be sure that those who attend hear a Christ-centered recovery testimony that is based on real experiences and filled with hope.

One **requirement** of Celebrate Recovery is that all recovery testimonies be written, reviewed, and edited before being read in the large group time or in other venues. They should be submitted to the ministry leader for review at least two weeks before the presentation. Some of the most frequently asked questions at Celebrate Recovery events or by those visiting our local ministry include:

- Why is it necessary to have testimonies written and reviewed?
- What are the reasons for reading a testimony from a script?
- Isn't it boring to hear testimonies read?

The last question is the easiest to answer. The excitement and appeal of a Celebrate Recovery testimony is in hearing how God has powerfully rescued and transformed one of His children. It's never boring when God's power is showcased through the victory He has given someone in their life!

Why Is It Necessary to Have Testimonies Written and Reviewed?

1. It helps the presenter prepare with confidence

You will find that many of your Celebrate Recovery attendees doubt both the value of their story to others and their ability to communicate their story. Having them write their testimony provides an opportunity for ministry leaders to mentor, guide, and encourage those who are reluctant to share. As you work with individuals through the review process, you have the opportunity to build their confidence.

2. It avoids triggers

One of the most important promises you make to those who attend your Celebrate Recovery is that it's a safe place. Part of keeping Celebrate Recovery a safe place is ensuring that what is shared in a testimony does not trigger unhealthy responses. Writing out a testimony that is reviewed ensures there will be no graphic descriptions and/or inappropriate language in what is shared. What can be appropriately shared in an open share group that is gender- and issue-specific might not be appropriate to voice in the large group meeting.

3. It prevents unnecessary offense

Many who enter your program may have had a negative experience with church earlier in life. Resentment voiced toward particular denominations or groups could deeply offend other participants if these are mentioned by name. By reviewing a testimony, you can help people share their experience without attaching negative labels to secular recovery groups, specific churches, or denominations.

4. It eliminates "churchy" language

The audience in your large group meeting will include individuals who have little or no experience with the church. They may not know what "redemption" means, but they can understand that Jesus has the power to set them free from their addictions, their harmful habits, and their shame and guilt.

5. **It ensures that the testimony focuses on recovery principles and experiences.**

Recovery testimonies are most powerful when they focus on the hope that God can deliver us from specific hurts, hang-ups, and habits during our lives on the earth. Testimonies need to offer evidence that the principles and steps taught in Celebrate Recovery really work.

6. **It provides a working text for preparing short testimonies for other venues.**

One of the most powerful tools you can employ in expanding the impact of Celebrate Recovery within your own church membership is to have Celebrate Recovery testimonies read on Sunday mornings or in other weekend services. In these situations, testimonies may need to be shorter in length. Working from a script of the long testimony makes this much easier. Preparing to share in a worship service where children and youth are present also means adapting the testimony to be appropriate for such an audience.

What Are the Reasons for Reading a Testimony from a Script?

1. **It places the focus on what God has done.**

Some people may be tempted to try to be clever or entertaining. The objective of the testimony is to clearly communicate how God sets us free from our hurts, hang-ups, and habits. Simply reading the testimony ensures the good communication of the story. "Playing to the audience" could divert presenters, to the point that they fail to finish their account of recovery.

2. **It ensures that what has been approved is what is shared.**

All the advantages of leadership reviews of testimonies will be lost if the presenter is not directed to read what has been approved.

3. **It feels safer and is consistent for all, as everyone reads their testimony. No one needs to be a public speaker.**

Many individuals with powerful testimonies may not share if they believe they have to have a talent for public speaking. Some of the most powerful testimonies come from the most fearful individuals. Without a script to read from they would never be able to share these vital stories of God's transforming power.

4. **It frees the emotions of the participant.**

Time and again, individuals are understandably overcome by emotion in telling their stories. With a script they can let the tears flow for a few moments and then get back on track.

5. **It ensures the length of the testimony enables the Large Group Meeting to end on time.**

Even the most skilled and experienced communicator can lose track of time.Reading from a script helps them finish within the allotted time.

Many who hear the recommendation that testimonies be written, reviewed, edited, and read may feel that this quenches the Holy Spirit during the presentation. However, we believe that the guidance of the Holy Spirit can be just as powerful during the process of preparation as He can during the presentation itself.

Appendix 4

Sample Testimonies

We've included sample testimonies from one man, one woman, and a married couple. Please note, these are not to be read in your Large Group as a testimony.

These are only provided for you to see examples of written and edited testimonies.

John's Testimony

My name is John, and I am a grateful believer in Jesus Christ who struggles with codependency. My earliest memories are probably kindergarten and the beginning of grade school. I was a pretty happy and extroverted little fella. I was very active, full of joy and energy, secure and comfortable in my own skin. We were Mom, Dad, my older brother (by three years), and then twin sisters a year younger—all together in Duluth, Minnesota. My parents were saved and belonged to an exciting new independent Pentecostal church. They were young and zealous, and had young and zealous friends, and a young and zealous pastor. My father worked at a men's clothing store and my mom stayed home with us kids. Some of the families from our young and zealous church got together and decided to buy some property just outside the city limits in a lovely, private wooded area. They all wanted to build some homes together, form a Christian neighborhood, with Christian kids riding their Christian bikes on a Christian road, with Christian dogs chasing Christian cats . . .

Our family quickly signed on to that project and soon we were living in a freshly built log home on Morning Star Drive. I guess I was in the second grade or so when, one by one, each of us four clueless siblings were called upstairs into our parents' bedroom for news of the divorce. This is how Mom wanted to break it to us. This is one of my few branded-in memories. I remember the unfinished texture of the wooden baluster on the balcony, my hand sort of trailing behind me on the railing trying to somehow slow my progress to my father and mother's room.

My older brother came out sobbing, and I just kept walking toward their room, straining to look through their cracked door. There was something evil crouched beyond that door: depression, pain . . . unwelcome, unasked-for change.

It was so quiet after the divorce announcement. My parents used to fight a lot before the announcement, but now my dad hadn't the spirit for fighting; he gave up. Again, the realization of past yelling matches came after the hush fell on that big log home. My father, one of the heroes, if there are any in this testimony, was so infinitely sad. My mom knew the pain she was causing—I do believe that—but at the same time, I have come to understand that she didn't. She was not making decisions based on the truth. She was lying to herself, and to us, about how much fun her new life would be, our new life, would be. It was a fresh start, a new and exciting adventure. Her world was a cleverly constructed fantasy of greener grass. She packed us up and moved us away from my father to a farm where a new family was waiting. I remember her turning her head to us in the passenger and back seats while driving and repeating over and over, "Isn't this exciting?" At the first meeting of the soon-to-be stepfamily, I remember lots of dogs and the smell of a dairy farm. I was game; it DID look exciting. My sisters took things in stride as well, but my older brother did not. I adapted to this new life. I did whatever I was told; I was compliant; I had fun; I rode motorcycles; I pitched in with the haying; I picked rocks in the fields; I camped out with my stepbrother; I shot a pistol, rode the three-wheeler, grabbed an electric fence on a dare to see who could hold on the longest. I did it. I conformed.

My brother did not.

In the midst of my mother's chaotic relationship with this new husband, my brother went a little crazy. Our oldest stepbrother was a bullying beast of a teenager who had his father's temper. He was full of hate, full of rage, and I stayed out of his way, laughed at his dirty jokes, did what I was told. My brother did not laugh, did not do what he was told, did not stay out of anyone's way.

One night, out in the barn, my older brother had enough of our "bully stepbrother" and tried to crush his head with a lead pipe. He whiffed badly. I watched as my brother paid a terrible price for standing up to a bully. It was a terrifying experience, which led to me and my brother both moving back to our dad's. My brother and I carried on a new existence at my father's home in that huge, empty log tomb. Dad was not coping well and we weren't enough to keep him going. He had seen his church collapse a few months earlier in a scandal. His church, his marriage, and his life had been taken from him; the rug had been pulled out; that was his new reality and ours. Somewhere in the transition from grade school to middle school, depression took me like anesthesia. I remember it coming on, then I remember coming out of it. I ate a lot,

I know that. I was like a Hoover vacuum on a very low setting. Whatever food was near me got sucked in, slowly but surely. I stared at whatever TV had to offer for hours after school, when other kids were outside playing. I began to skip school, constantly faking migraines. My mother was divorced again and off the farm. I didn't care, I was depressed. She had repented of her foolishness, and my brother and I were going to live with her and my sisters again in a nice little duplex. I didn't care, I was depressed. I was back with mom, my sisters, and my brother, and I was put in counseling. Now, I did care about that. I hated that. Maybe my hating counseling shocked me out of my depression. Counseling scared me straight.

When I did awaken from my depressed stupor, I found myself in the body of this scared, fat, introverted older kid. Mom was on welfare trying to get an education, so I wore a lot of second-hand clothing. Bullies were a terror to me. I was much larger than most kids my age, but I was afraid of everyone. I was what others said I was. There was no doubt in my mind. I just wanted to disappear. That's how I coped. I began to deal with problems through invisibility. A very big boy willing every part of his being to disappear into thin air best describes me at this time of my life. I was living a life of "quiet desperation." I was tortured and tormented by my classmates, physically and emotionally abused, and I felt like I deserved it.

I was helpless, powerless, and daily frozen with fear, being constantly silenced by crippling insecurity. This overwhelming insecurity at times reclaims its hold on me. A strange residual social fear lingers, but I have learned to trust that it remains for God's purposes. I choose to embrace this weakness and say with Paul: "His power is perfected in my weakness. When I am weak, I am truly strong." One day it all began to change. It started when I stood up to a guy in my class who wanted to take my seat, and what do you know, he backed down. I started lifting weights, then I went by myself and tried out for the football team, and I made it. Then I went to the church youth group, started cracking jokes, started talking to girls. By my junior year of high school, I was starting for the varsity football team and ENJOYING school for the first time in my life.

My grades stunk, but I was happy and independent. I had been getting more and more involved in the youth group, and I began developing a vibrant relationship with God. I had prayed for salvation at five years of age with my father, but now I was beginning to understand and answer a clear call to His service.

At fifteen, I seriously committed myself to Jesus Christ. I made a vow to live for Him for the rest of my life. I graduated from high school and eventually moved with my mom to the Twin Cities where I was back to being a "nobody." I had been lightly recruited by a couple local colleges for football and had received a small scholarship at a Christian university in Missouri, but that insecurity came back stronger than ever, convincing me all efforts to succeed were hopeless. I began a slow and steady roll back into depression. I was not in church, not in school. I was back to a day-to-day existence without meaning, without purpose, working the graveyard shift at a local gas station. My mom had many relationships over the years following the farm with one deadbeat after the other; but in St. Paul, Minnesota, she picked up their king in a bar one summer evening.

He told her that he was the son of a wealthy CEO, and that he would pay her back if she would spring for a weekend of partying in Duluth. He had no intention of paying for anything; he wasn't the son of a CEO; he was a con man running up her credit cards, depleting her savings, until finally he showed his true colors. One evening he took the rented Cadillac my mother had charged for their lavish weekend fantasy and disappeared. After my mom called the police a few days following his departure, I found him late one night passed out on the seat of the stolen Caddy.

I wanted to save my mom from these guys every time. She was always able to sell me on them, and then when she turned against them, I was right there with her, comforting her, consoling. I was blinded to her responsibility in these situations. I wanted to be somebody's favorite—to save someone—and she was beginning to rely on my shoulder to cry on. No matter what she had done to me, or to the family over the years, I loved her, I still believed in her, she relied on me, and that was what I desperately clung to. So, I called the police on the loser in the Caddy, and I was the hero, until my mom decided to bail the con man out of jail. When she walked through the door with him, I almost fell out of my chair. The king was back. I gave my mom an ultimatum. I was amazed and hysterical with anger when she gave me her answer. No. This man would stay, and I would go. Back to my dad's I went. Soon after moving back to my father's, I had an opportunity to move north and play football at a community college. It was at this remote, "nowhere" school that I learned about the wonderful numbing effects of alcohol. It was easy to let it all go there in Virginia, Minnesota. I was alone, I was depressed, and I was a waste. My life consisted of football, a meager schedule of classes, alcohol whenever and however I could get it, and a girlfriend hand-picked to put up with my moodiness and drinking.

I had plugged into a local church the moment I arrived, but it couldn't hold me; I just was too wrapped up in my pain, in coping. The discovery of alcohol was a revelation. It made me more depressed, but in a bittersweet, self-pitying, brooding sense. I dropped out of college after my first year and ended up rooming with my best friend from high school back in Duluth. I began working another graveyard shift cleaning the floors at a grocery store. I was sleeping through the days, stockpiling alcohol on the shelf, working a dead-end job that I could barely hold, picking fights. Now I was becoming the bully. I would drink at home, and then go out drinking, drive home drunk, and drink. There was nothing else in my future. This was my life, for the rest of my life.

One night I was alone, and I was sober, or I was drunk, or someplace in between. I do remember the shotgun in my hands. I had my grandfather's double-barreled shotgun across my lap. I tried to put it to my head, but fear swept over me. Was I so pathetic that I couldn't even kill myself? I began playing games with loading it and trying to peek down the barrel to see if I could get up the courage to take this seriously. I wept and screamed on the floor of my room for God to save me, but I was alone. He must have had enough and abandoned me; I couldn't blame Him. I wanted Him to leave me alone; I didn't deserve love. I was going to die, and I was going to be as insignificant in death as I was in life. I was finally ready. Calm and determined, sniffing away the last of the tears, I said my last half-hearted prayer, "Lord, if You're there, it's time to let me know, or I'm finished." Another ridiculous ultimatum.

But, in that little upstairs apartment, God answered me. The room glossed over, and I was in a cave. Ribs became part of the infrastructure of the room, and I was inside something. It was a vision. The only one I have ever had. And it wasn't angels and harps. It was me clearly in the inner guts of a fish. I grabbed hold of that vision with two desperate hands, finding and opening my old Bible from youth group. I had no idea where the story of Jonah was. It was a book in itself. The story was familiar, but what did that have to do with me? Then I saw it, the prayer in the second chapter. Jonah's prayer is what was in me. My spirit had been speaking this in groans, in the throes of anguish. "In my distress I called to the LORD, and he answered me. From deep in the realm of the dead I called for help, and you listened to my cry. . . . I said, 'I have been banished from your sight. . . .' The engulfing waters threatened me, the deep surrounded me. . . . To the roots of the mountains I sank down; the earth beneath barred me in forever. But you, Lord my God, brought my life up from the pit. When my life was ebbing away, I remembered you, Lord, and my prayer rose to you. . . . What I have vowed I will make good. I will say, 'Salvation comes from the LORD' " (Jonah 2:1–9).

I dedicated myself to the Lord that moment, telling Him that what I had vowed as a committed Christian in my youth, I would make good. I signed up for the fall to go to the Christian university in Missouri where I had initially, upon graduation, received a seed scholarship for football. I had no idea where the funds would come from, but it was clear that was the place

God wanted me. It was where He had wanted me all along. I had been running from a call. Like Jonah.

I was accepted to the school and the money somehow was there for me to attend. Life was so sweet these three years of school. I was away at school, playing football. I had Christ-centered classes, and Christian friends, so why was I still struggling to maintain my sobriety? There were rules against drinking. I had even signed a covenant that I would abstain from alcohol.

But that didn't mean opportunities didn't present themselves; it didn't mean opportunities weren't created. My last binge ended late one night after staring into the disappointed eyes of the most beautiful woman God has ever breathed life into. My girlfriend had been able to melt away some of the walls that were again forming around me—we even began talking about marriage, about kids, about everything—but we hadn't talked about this drinking stuff before.

Another stamped-in, burned-in memory is when I stopped by her off-campus apartment after having a few drinks, and then a few more drinks with some friends who lived in the same apartment complex. My girlfriend didn't say so, but it was all over her face when she saw me. She was disappointed. I don't think she ever really thought twice about us—we were in love and flying recklessly and blissfully toward our future—but in that instant, I saw a loss of respect . . . even some doubt. She loved me for the right reasons—for the Christian man I wanted to be— and this wasn't it. It was in this moment, confronted with this past-and-once-again-present coping strategy, that the double-standard I was keeping between my Christian ascent and my worldly descent came to a head. I was either going to become the man God had created and called or go back to despair, loneliness, death, and hell. I chose life, and have never, in over a decade of sobriety, ever regretted my decision. My girlfriend and I got married, and I received a degree in criminal justice, but ended up enjoying a counseling group I was placed in during my practicum so much that I began to explore counseling and social work as a career.

Together we moved to my wife's home state of Delaware where I began working for the state's Division of Family Services as a family crisis therapist. During my five years in that office, I toiled through a master's program in social work and began group and individual work at a private counseling agency on the side to earn hours for my clinical licensing. I loved the work, I loved counseling, and I loved group process.

What I didn't realize is that in working two to three jobs ministering to others, I was neglecting my ministry at home to my family. Three jobs at times kept me away constantly, and I was even volunteering any leftover hours at the church. It was exhausting—and a trying time for my marriage. I tried to convince my wife, unsuccessfully, that this work was my mission field. I was giving my all in answer to "the call." But my absence was wearing on her, on us. We had two girls, and I didn't see much of them. My explanation to them, to myself, and to God was that I was needed out there; people needed me; they needed saving! She had her parents to lean on, my kids had their grandparents. Those I helped didn't have anyone but me. Isn't being a Christian about helping the helpless AT ANY COST? What I didn't fully realize is that through college, working toward a degree, playing football, and now with my career goals, my master's degree, my striving for success in counseling others, I was succumbing to the pressure of trying to earn back my value. The value I had lost by being a fat, spineless nobody without any answers. My professional life was a tenuous balance of keeping everyone happy with me, spinning anything negative, running from conflict, blaming others, justifying my very existence, running, running to keep that distance . . . keeping the helpless loser I once was far behind me. One day, God called me to a fast. A one-week fast. I managed to doubt it and fight it for a good month, but I finally relented. When the fast was over, I was incredibly disappointed. No lightning bolts, no giant handwriting on the wall.

What a rip-off! Oh well. It was done and I had been obedient. A few weeks later, my brother-in-law, a youth pastor working in a little church in West Virginia, called and asked if I would travel to West Virginia to talk to his church's men's ministry about outreach. His pastor had felt God leading the church to do more for those outside their four walls. I said I would be glad to do it, and soon found myself talking to a small group of men in Clarksburg, West Virginia about Celebrate Recovery, and some other outreach programs I was heading up in our church in Delaware.

A week later, I was being asked to consider interviewing in this same church to do outreach ministry full-time. God was orchestrating a miraculous life-change, and soon I was chugging through the mountains in a U-Haul contemplating this new direction in my life and ministry. Now the recovery program I had started in Delaware was very loosely based on the Celebrate Recovery curriculum, and I had plans in West Virginia to veer even further off the Celebrate Recovery course. I have since discovered why I was reluctant to conform to the program. Running my own program, my way, was all about pride. Tailor-making my own recovery program elevated me to the keeper of all the keys, giving me the illusion of being in complete control and helping me stay aloof in a "therapist" role. It kept people looking to me for the answers. I wanted to be their savior. "I, even I, am the LORD, and apart from me there is no savior" (Isaiah 43:11).

After several months of running the "John" recovery program in my new ministerial role in West Virginia, with frustratingly minimal success, my wonderful little church sent me to my first Celebrate Recovery Summit.

It was during those three days in August 2006 that I felt challenged to make a commitment to run this ministry by the letter. I had been fighting it, as I was to learn later, mainly because I would rather help "those people," Rather than be one of "those people." However, as I listened to the testimonies given at the Summit, as I worshiped with the thousands of lives being transformed by the power of God through the truths of this program, I felt the gentle conviction of the Holy Spirit calling me to submit and SURRENDER. I had been asking everyone to share their lives with me, to open up, be completely transparent so they could find healing and hope for their lives. However, I had never really done that myself. What hypocrisy! During a question-and-answer time at one of the Summit workshops, I made a public confession that I had been using the Celebrate Recovery name, but had not been following the model. It was at that vulnerable place, the giving up of my power, where my own healing began. You could say that my journey of discovery into my own emotional and spiritual DNA finally began when I submitted to the Celebrate Recovery DNA. While I had been trying to construct a new me through meeting the needs of others, God had wanted nothing more than to deconstruct me by exposing my own many hurts, hang-ups, and habits. Through the work of this ministry, especially going through the step study, I finally dared to get honest about my past.

Principle 5 says, "Voluntarily submit to every change God wants to make in my life and humbly ask Him to remove my character defects." "Blessed are those who hunger and thirst for righteousness, for they will be filled" (Matthew 5:6). Finally, I would have to take a real look at myself and either change or continue in my own pride and ego. Then, as I wrote my inventory, I realized something that broke me to a point where I hadn't been broken before. I started to see and feel how much my efforts to replace God with self-sufficiency and self-righteousness had grieved my God and Savior Jesus Christ. After sharing my inventory, with the help of another minister, I made my first heart-wrenching amends. My first amends were offered to God, and through that process I felt His forgiveness, mercy, and love for me like never before.

In that place of grace, He gave me a new awareness of a value I could never earn, and a value I will never lose. "How deep the Father's love for us, how vast beyond all measure that He would send His only Son, to make a wretch His treasure." Today I have come to a new realization and reliance on His economy. It is not by my strength, not by man's might, but truly by His Spirit that I (and others) find true recovery. My wife and I celebrated our twelfth anniversary in June.

I have four beautiful daughters. (Yes, I am powerless and my life is truly unmanageable.) My family has now become my most important and cherished ministry.

I want to encourage anyone who is feeling the overwhelming weight of insecurity to let go, get vulnerable, and trust in the Lord. In Principle 7 we are taught: "Reserve a daily time with God for self-examination, Bible reading, and prayer in order to know God and His will for my life and to gain the power to follow His will." Celebrate Recovery rightly emphasizes this complete dependency on Christ as the only opportunity we have for true peace, security, and salvation.

I thank God for His love, and I thank God for my family; I thank God for this program and for my incredible Celebrate Recovery family; and I thank God for the opportunity to share my testimony with you.

Thank you for letting me share.

Jacki's Testimony

My name is Jacki, and I am a grateful believer in Jesus Christ who struggles with sexual addiction.

I was born and raised in a typical middle-class family, in a small town, in the high desert of Southern California. I am the youngest of five children. My dad was the breadwinner of the family and my mom worked inside the home as a full-time wife and mother. I have a lot of great memories of my childhood. My dad would always make us laugh by telling us captivating stories of lizards drag racing across the dry lakebed, or how Santa Claus once stole his toys on Christmas Eve. We'd have neighborhood football games in the street in front of our house until well into the night. And then there was my mom, who'd pile a bunch of us into the station wagon and take us on some of the wildest adventures. Those were good times.

Some memories of my childhood are not as enjoyable. When I was six years old, two teenage neighbor boys began molesting my sisters and me. As we'd ride our bikes or roller-skate up and down the sidewalk, the two of them would lure us into their garage and begin touching us inappropriately. After the second or third incident, I told my parents. Without hesitation, my dad promptly marched down to their house and confronted the boys and their parents. They were never a problem again. For reasons I couldn't comprehend, I had the courage to tell my parents about the situation with the neighbor boys, but I was too frightened to tell them about the abuse that was happening within our family. My eldest brother was molesting me as well.

It became a fairly common thing; my parents would leave the house and my brother would abuse me. I don't remember when it started or why it finally stopped. I never felt like I could tell my mom and dad. We were a very "emotionally dysfunctional" family. On the one hand, there was my mom, who taught us to find humor in virtually everything. Then there was my dad, who taught us "never to air our dirty laundry," or let anyone see us hurt. Instead, we'd focus on something that would make us laugh; that way we could avoid feeling pain and there'd be no need to cry.

I don't recall the last time I told my parents I loved them, or hearing either one of them saying it to me. Love was always one of those "understood" things. I can remember as a small child, kissing my parents good night, and hurrying off to bed. In contrast though, I don't recall embracing either one of them. It just wasn't something we did. I knew that they loved me, and I thought that was enough.

I had my first encounter with pornography when I was seven years old. I was playing with my dad's tools in the garage and found some adult magazines under his bench. I was intrigued by the images I saw. As I got a little older, I'd go to the local drugstore and sneak an adult magazine to the back of the store so I could look at the pictures without anyone knowing.

Even at such a young age, I was discrete so that no one would find out my secrets. I started attending church with a friend of mine when I was fifteen. After about a year, I prayed to receive Christ as my personal Lord and Savior. My relationship with the Lord really began to grow while I was in high school. When I graduated from that Christian school, I naively thought that I'd be "exempt" from the typical challenges of young adulthood. Several years later, my mom was diagnosed with a neurological disease. I had a very difficult time coping with the idea of watching this disease rob my mom of her independence. I felt utterly helpless. I didn't know how to express feelings of pain or fear, so I turned to alcohol and began drinking in an attempt to eradicate the pain.

As my addictive lifestyle was beginning to take shape, I accepted an information security position at work. My new job would be to monitor the networks and to investigate cases of personnel accessing pornography over the corporate networks. For more than eight years, from eight to five, my job was to go through each and every downloaded image and evaluate the content. I also had a second job as a bartender at a local restaurant. After some time, I began dating some of my customers. In the beginning, I told myself that I would just go for the casual dinner and that would be it. But eventually, I ignored the boundary I had set for myself and began taking customers home. When I wasn't working, I'd be at home drinking or surfing websites on the Internet. I'd spend between four and five hours per night, visiting the online dating services, adult chat rooms, and the telephone to act out with people all over the country. While all of this was going on, I continued keeping up the variety of appearances that had sustained me throughout the years. At work, I was the professional. To my family, I was strong and responsible. To my church, I was a devoted Christian who never missed a Sunday. I had everyone fooled, including myself. I honestly believed that I could stop acting out any time I wanted.

I set many "boundaries," telling myself that I would do "this" but definitely not "that." I crossed every one of those boundaries and eventually entered a whole new realm of acting out. I began having sexual relationships with women. I had become so disconnected from reality that it didn't matter who the person was, where they came from, if a spouse was involved, or even if the person was healthy. Reality as I knew it was gone.

As things appeared to be spiraling out of control, I began to realize that I needed help, but I didn't know where to turn. A short while later, a pastor from out of town came to my church. Ironically, that night he preached on the "woman at the well." At first I thought that was simply a peculiar coincidence, that is, until his wife was called up to the pulpit and mentioned she was a Christian family therapist. I felt as though God had just dropped these two people out of the sky for me. Once the new pastor and his wife, Susan, moved to town, I began seeking counseling. From the beginning, I was honest about where I was at in my life and what I was doing.

After a year or so, it became clear that my counselor and I saw my self-created dilemma differently. I knew I had "issues," but I was absolutely convinced that I could stop whenever I wanted to. My counselor, on the other hand, had the audacity to ask me if I thought I could be sexually addicted. Without hesitation, my response was, "Are you out of your mind? That's ridiculous!" Even though I was seeking counseling, I made the decision to walk away from the church.

I drank more than ever and was having countless encounters with people I didn't even know. The guilt of this lifestyle was becoming unbearable, but I finally realized that maybe my counselor was right. I was struggling with sexual addiction. Several months went by, and I started attending church again, but my relationship with the Lord was nonexistent. I couldn't accept that Christ could still love me. It was clear that my sin not only interrupted my fellowship with God, but it distorted my vision of Him as well. The truth of Scripture applied to everyone else but not me.

In the midst of this period of discovery in my life, the Celebrate Recovery ministry started at my home church. I attended a few times, but I did not feel safe. I live in a rural area and feared the gossip that often comes from a small town. I just could not take that risk. Before too long, I gave up on the possibility of recovery.

So, I continued to act out and got to a place where the fear of stopping was much greater than the fear of being "found out." I just didn't care anymore. The addiction in my life had taken me on a journey that I never thought was possible. I am reminded of the Scripture reference found in Deuteronomy 30:4, "Even if you have been banished to the most distant land under the heavens, from there the LORD your God will gather you and bring you back." I knew that it would take something huge for me to change.

Then on my birthday weekend, three years ago, the bottom seemed to fall out of my world into a cloud of deceit and lies. I was devastated by the person I was involved with. Over the years, I had isolated myself from nearly all of my Christian friends. I couldn't bring myself to call anyone and explain my circumstances. I began feeling this heart-wrenching pain, so I locked myself in my house for three days straight, closed the blinds, and did nothing but drink alcohol and watch pornography. I honestly didn't care if I lived or died. I had finally reached my bottom.

A few days later I met with my counselor, and she suggested I drive down to Saddleback Church and attend Celebrate Recovery. It took a few more weeks, but I reluctantly agreed to check it out. This was no small feat for me, for you see, I still live in that same small town, 180 miles away. Despite the three-and-a-half-hour commute, I knew that I had exhausted all of my other options.

I had finally come to the realization that I couldn't stop acting out on my own. I knew I needed help, and I had to go to any length to get it. My first visit to Saddleback Church, Celebrate Recovery was nothing short of terrifying. It was scary to sit in a room with a bunch of people that I didn't know. I vividly remember sitting there and listening to the small group leader read the definition of women's sexual addiction, and thinking, That sounds exactly like me. When the realization finally sank in, part of me wanted to crawl under the chair and hide. The only thing that brought me solace was listening to the women in the group share, knowing they understood what was going on in my head and heart, and realizing I wasn't alone. Even though I didn't share that night, I knew that I had come to the right place. But that, in itself, was a scary admission for me. As I pulled out of the parking lot that night, I remember saying to myself that I would never come back.

While I was driving home the next morning, I had a lot of time to think about the night before, and I couldn't help but reflect on my life and what had brought me to Saddleback Church in the first place. The life that I had been leading was nothing but a Pandora's box of lies. Over the next few weeks, I thought a lot about my trip to Celebrate Recovery and decided that I would return.

On my second or third visit, I picked up a Celebrate Recovery Bible and a set of Celebrate Recovery participant's guides. As I began working through the lessons in the participant's guides, I remember feeling as though it was such a futile effort. Every time it seemed as though I was gaining a "foothold" in my recovery, inevitably an ex-affair partner would knock on the door, a tempting email would arrive in the inbox, or a voice from the past would call me on the phone. For several months, I'd find myself at home alone in the evenings or late into the night, wanting so badly to act out. I felt as though my own home wasn't safe for me to be in. But I did feel safe with the godly women I had met at Celebrate Recovery. I found it relatively easy to pick up the phone and let one of my accountability partners know that I was struggling. The one thing I couldn't do was pray. I couldn't bear the thought of looking God in the eye and telling Him where I had been. For years I had filled my head with images and now that was all my eyes could see. It didn't matter what time of day or night it was, or who I was with, all I saw was this filth of my past. It was as though I was being mentally tortured by my thought life. It was these very thoughts that kept me from experiencing any healing in the first part of my recovery. Principle 3 says, "Consciously choose to commit all my life and will to Christ's care and control." "Blessed are the meek" (Matthew 5:5).

It was at this point that I knew I had to make a choice: I could choose life, or I could choose death. I chose life. I made the decision to turn my life and will over to the care of God. I finally accepted that He really does love me. Despite my past failures, He did just as He promised; He met me where I was and offered abundant forgiveness and grace. "He saved us, not because of the righteous things we had done, but because of his mercy. He saved us through the washing of rebirth and renewal by the Holy Spirit" (Titus 3:5).

When I walked through those doors three and a half years ago, I never dreamed that the next few years of my life would be so eventful. This journey has certainly provided its share of ups and downs. Yet the Lord always reminds me of something extremely important: "For I know the plans for you . . . plans to prosper you and not to harm you" (Jeremiah 29:11).

Over the past year, I've found myself being wheeled through the doors of an operating room on more than one occasion. Each time, I was forced to reflect on my entire life, but more importantly, on how the Lord had used such incredible dysfunction in my life to bring me into a Christ-centered recovery program that would reinstate in my heart and mind the all-important, never-ending truths of Scripture. Celebrate Recovery brought me to a place where the longing to be pure and right with the Lord became so much bigger than my weak and selfish desires.

Had I never gone through the pain of my past failures, I don't believe that I would've come to a place that I was secure enough to trust the Lord for my physical and spiritual health, but more importantly, for my future, whatever that may look like.

Over these past three and a half years, my biweekly trips to Saddleback Church have become an integral part of my recovery. And in recent months, I've taken the Celebrate Recovery model back to my home church and worked with the ministry leaders to revitalize the program, creating a safe environment where people from my own community can come and experience genuine recovery for themselves. I've started the very first women's step study group, which meets in my living room on Thursday evenings. Recently, I felt led to start Newcomers 101 and have found it to be an exciting opportunity to share about this ministry and how it has quite literally transformed my life.

Last month, I celebrated three years of sobriety. I couldn't possibly have reached this milestone without each of the incredibly brave women in my open share group, who are so dedicated to working their programs and sharing every Friday night. It is because of each one of them, in their individual significant ways, that I can share my recovery story. I can most assuredly say that I wouldn't be here if it weren't for Tina and Marnie. For over three years now, I've been their shadow, quietly walking behind and observing the miracle of recovery in action. They have often opened their homes to me, which have made my trips to Saddleback logistically simpler. They both fill many roles in my life—as sponsors, accountability partners, nurses, friends—but most importantly, they have become my family away from home.

Thank you for letting me share.

Mac and Mary's Testimony

Mac: My childhood was pretty uneventful in terms of abuse. My parents loved me and set good standards to live by. So I can't look back to blame others for my actions, actions that brought great shame. Today because of Jesus Christ, I don't have to live in the past anymore. I am free! Ironically though, I spent a lifetime searching for freedom in all the wrong things. My dad was in the military, so by the time I was fifteen, I had moved eight times. I learned to blend in and make friends quickly.

My dad preached wherever he was stationed. So I knew about God, heaven, and hell. I was taught that unless you were a Christian you would go to hell. I remember fear being the motivating factor for being baptized when I was twelve. I appeared to enter a relationship with God, but for all the wrong reasons. Two weeks later at summer camp, I was introduced to marijuana by one of the counselors. I found a group of people who looked like they were having a lot of fun, so I decided, "Who needs to live in fear? These people aren't worrying about anything!" I became fearless and believed I was invincible, not realizing I had set the pace for eventual destruction.

My dad retired from the military and went to seminary to become a full-time pastor, so we moved to Louisiana when I was fifteen. I hated the fact that we were moving and I wondered how I would ever find friends who liked doing what I liked to do now. Amazingly within the first week, I found the same people there. I never ran out of drugs, and acceptance was immediate.

Once we arrived, my parents sent me to church summer camp to straighten me out and that's where I met Mary.

Mary: My name is Mary. I am a grateful believer in Jesus Christ who struggles with codependency.

I grew up an elder's kid. My parents lived out the Deuteronomy verse: "to tie God's word as symbols around your hands and teach them to your children as you walk by them day after day." There were always guests at the dinner table in our home. Missionaries from foreign countries stayed with us for recharging, while others flocked to our home seeking wise counsel, Bible study, and to repair wrecked marriages.

During my childhood, my mother would write Bible verses on three-by-five cards and tape them up all over our bathroom walls. As I would get dressed in the morning, there staring me in the face would be several verses I would read over and over. It just became a habit without me even realizing it. My sister and I would throw our heads under the covers at night and giggle, thinking how silly it was having our mama reciting those verses to us, never realizing the impact they would have on me in years to come. I confessed Jesus as Lord of my life when I was twelve years old and was baptized, telling myself I would never sin again! I wanted to please God with all my heart.

Mac: A new school year began; Mary was a senior and I was a junior. Life was great! After a few months of dating, I talked her into having sex, the first time for both of us, by using the manipulative "if you love me" line. Two weeks later, she didn't start her period, but we thought, "No way; surely one time can't get you pregnant."

Mary: Four months later I finally consulted a doctor and, yes, I was pregnant. No one had been pregnant outside of marriage in our church, so we had a secret. I felt alone and was convinced Mac couldn't support us. He was only sixteen at the time.

By the time I was five months pregnant, I decided it was confession time to my dad. During my childhood, my mother had a mental illness. Doctors put her through experimental procedures such as electric shock treatments. She suffered in mental hospitals and was a test subject for drugs that often kept her debilitated. So needless to say, my sweet mother who loved me the best she knew how didn't notice I had a growing belly.

I had always been able to talk to my dad, and I knew I couldn't keep it from him any longer. I walked into the den where my dad was taking a nap. I had snuggled up next to him many times throughout the years on that big old, flowered sofa, while he read Bible stories to me and we talked about God's love.

I knelt down next to him, eye to eye, and said softly, "We need to talk, Daddy." I was prepared for him to point his finger and say all kinds of harsh words. But tears began streaming down his cheeks as he said he would support and love me always. I told him my plans for moving out of town and giving my baby up for adoption.

I left home for my secret summer trip. Three months later it was August 17, 1975. That date is significant later in our story. The doctor left me in a tiny room all alone. Labor lasted for twelve hours with no anesthesia and no family. As they rushed me into the delivery room, a nurse shoved a gas mask over my face. I thought they were suffocating me to punish me for what I had done.

I awoke later in bed sheets soaking wet from perspiration and tears. I experienced emotions that were alien to me. A time that was supposed to be the happiest time of my life was my saddest. I moved to a Christian college out of state. My dad was hoping to get me away from Mac.

Mac: But I followed her there. My parents thought by sending me to a Chris tian college, they would fix me. Guess what? I found the people who loved to party my first day on campus. In fact, I found the guy who first introduced me to pot six years earlier at church camp. Halfway through the semester, I was kicked out of college after sneaking out of the dorm past curfew to smoke a joint with a friend. Mary and I both went home and married three weeks later.

Married life was great. We partied all the time. Later we would come to understand it helped us to mask the guilt of giving up our baby. When we had been married three years, we started trying to have another baby. Mary told me she was quitting the partying. I said, "Go ahead, but I'm not." Even in the midst of my addiction, I set a boundary and decided to quit everything except smoking pot. I convinced myself that marijuana wasn't so bad.

As I continued down the road of drug addiction, the conflict began between us. Our two daughters were born during this time. However, we lived separate lives under the same roof while growing further apart. I stayed away from the house as much as possible, working over-time to pay for my drug habit. By this time, meth had become my drug of choice.

Mary: In time, I came to the realization that our marriage was totally unmanageable, and I couldn't survive without turning my life and hurts over to God. I had to quit trying to be Mac's Holy Spirit and fix him and instead work on my own shortcomings. I started seeking the path-way to peace while Mac continued to run down the path to destruction. This pattern continued for seven years.

I held on to the verses I remembered reading as a child on my bathroom wall. In Isaiah 55:11, it says when God's word is spoken, it does not come back empty but will accomplish what He desires and achieve the purpose for which He sent it.

I would also repeat Isaiah 41:10 to myself the way I remembered my mother quoted it slowly and distinctly. I felt God was speaking to me.

"Do not fear for I am with you. Do not be dismayed, for I am your God. I will strengthen you and help you. I will uphold you with my righteous right hand."

All those Scriptures I heard as a child were coming back to me, comforting me during the dark and lonely nights. Now I had two secrets I carried. We had a son we would never know and I had an insane husband! I say insane because I didn't know all the drugs he was doing and their effects.

So I walked on eggshells to keep peace. I wore my mask to church every Sunday. I just wanted my insides to feel like everyone else looked on the outside, perfect, I thought.

Mac: Amazingly enough, even as a drug addict, there was a line I said I would never cross. The last two years of my addiction I was shooting up ten to twelve times a day. I wore long-sleeve shirts all the time so no one would notice the marks on my arms. I slept only about sixteen hours a week.

One Sunday morning, God gave me a great gift at the time and I didn't even realize it. It was a moment of clarity. I was crashed out in the bed, and our four-year-old daughter stood beside the bed and said to her mother, "Why doesn't Daddy go to church with us anymore?" Mary said, "He's been working hard. He needs sleep." Our daughter replied, "If he doesn't go to church, then I'm not either!" I pre-tended to be asleep and not hear what she said.

They left for church and then all of a sudden I felt like I ran into a brick wall. God used a little girl to break my heart. I realized I was killing every-body I claimed to love. It was as if my eyes were opened for the first time seeing the insanity of it all. So I collected all my drugs and paraphernalia and burned them.

Mary: I was crushed realizing our children were being affected. That Sunday the sermon was on confession and how good it is for the soul. I remember the song "It Is Well with My Soul." The words hung in my throat. I couldn't breathe. I wanted to just run out of the building. Arriving home, I found Mac sitting in his recliner with tears in his eyes.

Mac: I was raised to believe that men shouldn't cry or show any weakness. But what I found in those tears that morning was relief like I'd never known. I told Mary all that I had done and that I wanted to start a new life. For the first time, Mary stepped out of her codependency and said,

Mary: "Who are you going to call? I'm tired of keeping secrets."

Mac: "I told you I'm through with that life. What more do you want?"

Mary: "We need someone to help us. Would you talk to our pastor?"

Mac: Our pastor had been coming to my cabinet shop for years, getting me to build things for him, only to find out later they were things he really didn't need. He saw something in me that nobody else did. So he came over to pray with us. He said I didn't have to confess before the church, but I might help someone else if I did. I knew I needed to be held accountable.

Mary and I responded to an altar call that Sunday night, expecting to be shunned by people. The whole church came down afterward and cried with us. They didn't know what to do with me—I was their first drug addict—but they loved me and said to keep coming back.

There was one lady who said I needed to go to AA. I thought she was talking about some kind of car club. She said, "Not triple A, but double A—Alcoholics Anonymous."

Mary wanted me to talk to someone at a rehab center the next day. I told her I wasn't crazy and didn't need that. I finally agreed to talk but nothing more. After much discussion with the head guy, he asked if I would stay. I said, "Okay, I guess I'll stay. But I've got to go home and get my stuff."

Mary: "That's okay; your stuff is in the trunk!"

Mac: Our life became a whirlwind with rehab, ninety meetings in ninety days, Bible studies, and making new friends. A whole new life had begun for us.

We started Overcomers two years later, which we led for fourteen years. We had approximately twenty to thirty people who came on a regular basis.

Mary: The only other people who knew about our son were my dad, my brother, and his wife. Fast-forward to spring 1988, one month after Mac yielded to God, when God gave us a surprise gift. Our church youth group was going to a rally five hours away and my sister-in-law was one of the chaperones.

They were assigning groups to stay in homes and by the time they got to my sister-in-law's group, they had run out of homes. So they were asked if they would mind staying in a town close by. As the suitcases were being loaded into the car of a friendly couple, my sister-in-law asked if they had any children. When the woman said they had a son named Heath, a funny feeling came over my sister-in-law. So she asked his age. Heath's mother said he was twelve. So my sister-in-law went one step further and asked, "When is his birthday?" Heath's mother said August 17—the date our firstborn, Heath, arrived on August 17, 1975! At 2:00 a.m. our phone rang. My sister-in-law whispered, "You'll never imagine where I am." I said sleepily, "Where?" She replied, "Heath's bed!"

A family at our church has the last name, Heath, so I questioned her, "What are you doing in Mr. Heath's bed?" She exclaimed, "No, no—Heath, your son!" Mac and I feel God gave us that gift at that time in our lives to reassure us our son was loved and cared for in a Christian home.

After waiting seven more years, in August 1994 we got the call we always hoped we would get. When Heath was about to turn nineteen, his parents contacted us that he would like to meet us on his birthday. My dad was in charge of videoing the momentous occasion, but as we sat down later to view it, the whole first part of the reunion video was showing the ground. My dad was so excited he forgot he was holding the camera! It's been seventeen years now since we first met Heath.

We didn't get to see Heath's natural birth, but we were blessed with witnessing his spiritual birth as Mac baptized him! In 2005, Heath's parents moved to our city and Heath's mother and my mom became best friends as she took care of my mom after my dad died. We also attend the same church and celebrate holidays together. Our family continues to grow as God has blessed us now with eight grandchildren!

Mac: After leading Overcomers for thirteen years, Mary's brother "happened" to be at Saddleback Church and told me about a ministry called Celebrate Recovery and said I ought to check it out. So in 2004, we attended the Summit. During the second day I told Mary, "We're stopping what we're doing and starting this! Look how many more people we can help—more than just drug addicts and alcoholics, anyone with a hurt, hang-up, or habit!" After 120 days of prayer and preparation, we started Celebrate Recovery at our church on New Year's Eve 2004! During this preparation time, I learned about Principle 8 and realized that this is exactly what God had in mind for us.

Principle 8 states: "Yield myself to God to be used to bring this Good News to others, both by my example and by my words." "Blessed are those who are persecuted because of righteousness, for theirs is the kingdom of heaven" (Matthew 5:10). This is why we went through all of these trials and then we found out there was more!

I love watching God's plan for our life unfold. A few years ago, a pastor of forty years tried to commit suicide. The "Pharisees" in the church finally got to him. And the only way he could get through his week was by doing something he said he would never do—take a drink. That one drink turned into every Monday. He had been drinking the last ten years and nobody knew except his wife. Finally he couldn't take the hypocrisy of his own life anymore and that's when he attempted suicide. Along with the bottle, he took a handful of pills. He was moved from pastor to one of "those" people. So I got the call to go visit him.

I visited him in ICU and even though he was unconscious, I prayed over him and said, "Don't give up. God still has a plan for you." Over the next few weeks, I was able to share with him about the hope that God still had for him. He later became a part of our Celebrate Recovery ministry. While at one of our small groups, he shared with me that he had just met our son's parents at church on Sunday. I said, "Everybody has; they go to church here now!" And he said, "No, no, you don't understand. Forty years ago when I first became a pastor I performed their marriage ceremony!"

Before our son was conceived, God had a plan to use this man to marry the couple that would adopt our son! And then later, allow me to be instrumental in giving him the hope that his relationship could not only be restored, but also that God would continue to use him! God always sees the big picture, and He is always right on time!

Mary: We went from the twenty to thirty people attending our Overcomers' group, a ministry that was already working to an average attendance of over 250 every Friday night at Celebrate Recovery. Our children are a part of Celebrate Recovery. They serve in roles of state rep, ministry leader, training coach, open share group leaders, nursery worker, videographer, and youth minister.

Twenty-four years ago, I prayed God would just keep Mac awake in church. God has truly taken the ashes of our lives and turned them into something beautiful. I believe when God said in Joel 2:25, "I will repay you for the years the locusts have eaten."

We can't keep quiet about what the Lord has done in our lives and in the lives of our Celebrate Recovery Forever Family! If there is restoration for us, there is hope for you too! Don't give up; put your faith in action by making life's healing choices.

Mac: Being on the front line of what I believe is THE outreach ministry of the church, we are able to bind up the brokenhearted, to proclaim freedom for the captives of sin in Jesus' name, and release from darkness the prisoners of hurts, hang-ups, and habits.

Celebrate Recovery has helped us reach more hurting people to find healing than we could've ever imagined. How can we repay the Lord for His goodness! We share the hope we've found in Jesus! Today we are making life's healing choices and that's Celebrate Recovery!

Thank you for letting us share.

Appendix 5

Celebrate Recovery®
Welcome Newcomers!

The purpose of Celebrate Recovery is to fellowship and celebrate God's healing power in our lives through the eight recovery principles found in the Beatitudes and Christ-centered 12 Steps. This experience allows us to be changed. We open the door by sharing our experiences, victories, and hopes with one another. In addition, we become willing to accept God's grace in solving our life problems.

By working the Christ-centered steps and applying their biblical principles found in the Beatitudes, we begin to grow spiritually. We become free from our addictive, compulsive, and dysfunctional behaviors. This freedom creates peace, serenity, joy, and, most importantly, a stronger personal relationship with God and others.

As we progress through the principles and the steps we discover our personal, loving, and forgiving Higher Power—Jesus Christ.

Welcome to an Amazing Spiritual Adventure!

Celebrate Recovery Small Groups WILL:

- Provide you a safe place to share your experiences, victories, and hopes with others who are going through a Christ-centered recovery.
- Provide you with a leader who has gone through a similar hurt, hang-up, or habit, who will facilitate the group as it focuses on a particular principle each week. The leader will also keep Celebrate Recovery's "Five Small Group Guidelines."
- Provide you with the opportunity to find an accountability partner or a sponsor.
- Encourage you to attend other recovery meetings held throughout the week.

Celebrate Recovery Small Groups Will NOT:

- Attempt to offer any professional clinical advice. Our leaders are not counselors.
- Allow its members to attempt to fix one another.

Appendix 6

Celebrate Recovery® Things We Are, Things We Are Not

Things We ARE:

- A safe place to share
- A refuge
- A place of belonging
- A place to care for others and be cared for
- Where respect is given to each member
- Where confidentiality is highly regarded
- A place to learn
- A place to grow and become strong again
- Where you can take off your mask
- A place for healthy challenges and healthy risks
- A possible turning point in your life

Things We Are NOT:

- Therapy
- A place to look for dating relationships
- A place to rescue or be rescued by others
- A place for perfection
- A place to judge others
- A quick fix

Appendix 7

Celebrate Recovery® Gratitude List

Principle 7-Step 11

I'm thankful to God:

I'm thankful to God for placing others in my life:

I'm thankful for my recovery program:

I'm thankful for my church:

Remember, maintaining an "attitude of gratitude" is the best prevention against relapse.

"Do not be anxious about anything, but in every situation, by prayer, and petition, with thanksgiving, present your requests to God. And the peace of God, which transcends all understanding, will guard your hearts and your minds in Christ Jesus" (Philippians 4:6–7).

Appendix 8

Celebrate Recovery DNA Group Formats

DNA Format for Large Group: One Hour

(The order of the format is flexible. As long as the components are included, you may adjust the flow of events as you desire.)

- Welcome and Open in Prayer
- Worship music
- Read the 8 Principles or Christ-centered 12 Steps, with Biblical Comparisons
- Lesson or Testimony[1]
- Member, and must be reading and using the approved edited version.
- Closing Prayer (It is optional to close with the Serenity Prayer; however, it is highly
- Recommended.)
- Dismissal to Open Share Groups

Optional best practice elements:

- Announcements
- Chip ceremony
- Special music with offering or invitation
- Guest speaker or special lesson a few times a year.

DNA Format for Open Share Groups: One Hour

1. Welcome and Open in prayer
2. Leader Introductions
3. Read the CR Small Group Guidelines
4. Group Open Sharing
5. Wrap-up and close in prayer

---

1. Testimonies are to be written in advance, edited and approved by the Ministry Leader or Team

Optional best practice elements:

- Focus Question
- Read issue pamphlet for that group
- Share written prayer requests
- Invite Participants to your fellowship event following group
- Chips

DNA Format for Step Study Groups: 1 ½ to 2 hours

1. Welcome and Open in Prayer
2. Leader and Participant Introductions
3. Read the 8 Principles or Christ-centered 12 steps
4. Read the CR Small Group Guidelines
5. Read the lesson acrostic from the Participant's Guide (when starting a new lesson) and take turns sharing answers to the questions.
6. Wrap Up and Close in Prayer

Optional best practice elements:

- Small Group Expectations (Initially when a new meeting starts, can be found in the ALT.)
- Worship song at the beginning of the meeting
- Share a devo from the *Celebrate Recovery 365 Daily Devotional* or the *Celebrate Recovery Study* Bible (no more than 5 minutes, remember, no outside curriculum).
- Assign the homework questions from the workbook for next week's meeting.
- Announcements
- Share Written Prayer Requests

Appendix 9

Yearly Lesson and Testimony Schedule

Week	Principle	Large Group Teaching
1		Introduction/Overview of Program
2	1	Lesson 1: Denial
3	1	Testimony
4	1	Lesson 2: Powerless
5	1	Testimony
6	2	Lesson 3: Hope
7	2	Testimony
8	2	Special Music, Lesson, Event or Speaker
9	2	Lesson 4: Sanity
10	2	Testimony
11	3	Lesson 5: Turn
12	3	Testimony
13	3	Lesson 6: Action
14	3	Testimony
15	4	Lesson 7: Sponsor
16	4	Testimony
17	4	Lesson 8: Moral
18	4	Testimony
19	4	Lesson 9: Inventory
20	4	Testimony
21	4	Special Music, Lesson, Event or Speaker
22	4	Lesson 10: Spiritual Inventory Part 1
23	4	Testimony
24	4	Lesson 11: Spiritual Inventory Part 2
25	4	Lesson 12: Confess

Appendix 10

Celebrate Recovery Small Group Guidelines

1. Keep your sharing focused on your own thoughts and feelings, using "I" and "me" statements. Please limit your sharing to three to five minutes.
2. There is NO cross talk please. Cross talk is when two individuals engage in conversation excluding all others. Each person is free to express his or her feelings without interruptions.
3. We are here to support one another, not "fix" one another.
4. Anonymity and confidentiality are basic requirements. What is shared in the group stays in the group. The only exception is when someone threatens to injure themselves or others.
5. Offensive language has no place in a Christ-centered recovery group.

The following guidelines are to be used in all online Open Share Groups and Step studies.

6. **All members must use headphones.** This will ensure that no one else can overhear what is shared in the group.
7. **All members must be on camera and alone in the room,** with the camera facing them the whole time. If the group leader asks, they must show the rest of the group that no one else is in the room.
8. **The meetings will not be recorded.** This protects the confidentiality and anonymity of the meetings.

Emphasize at the close of your meeting that Guidelines stay intact as participants fellowship with each other after the meeting.

Celebrate Recovery Extended Small Group Guidelines

1. **Keep your sharing focused on your own thoughts and feelings, using "I" and "Me" statements. Limit your sharing to three to five minutes.** This is a very important guideline. Using "I" and "Me" statements keeps us focused on our own thoughts, feelings, and actions, allowing us to take responsibility for our own recovery. Please adhere to the three-to-five-minute rule, so that everyone has an opportunity to share; and to ensure that one person does not dominate the group sharing time.

2. **There is NO cross talk. Cross talk is when two individuals engage in conversation excluding all others. Each person is free to express his or her feelings without interruptions.** Cross talk is also making comments or asking questions while someone is sharing, speaking to another member of the group while someone is sharing or responding to what someone has shared during his or her time of sharing. This guideline is about respect. When other participants are sharing, we don't want to interrupt their thoughts and feelings, which may be very deep, painful, scary, sad, etc. It's their time about them, not us. Basically, anything that would give the speaker the impression that we don't care about what they have to share, could be considered cross talk.

3. **We are here to support one another, not "fix" another.** We do not give unsolicited advice or attempt to solve someone else's problems. This includes sharing scriptures for the purpose of preaching or teaching, during our time of sharing. We also do not offer book recommendations or counselor referrals. This helps us stay focused on our own issues.

4. **Anonymity and confidentiality are basic requirements. What is shared in the group stays in the group. The only exception is when someone threatens to injure themselves or others.** It can be very hurtful to discover that someone's sharing is being discussed outside of the group time. Most of the people in recovery have never been able to "tell the secret"—they need to be assured that this is the safe place to do it. When communicating with group members, be careful about protecting anonymity and confidentiality. Please be advised, if anyone threatens to hurt themselves or others, the group Leader has the responsibility to report it to the Celebrate Recovery Ministry Leader.

5. **Offensive language has no place in a Christ-centered recovery group.**

The main issue here is that the Lord's name is not used inappropriately. We also avoid graphic descriptions. If anyone feels uncomfortable with how explicitly a speaker is sharing regarding his/her behaviors, then you may indicate so by simply raising your hand. The speaker will then respect your boundaries by being less specific in his/her descriptions.

The following guidelines are to be used in all online Open Share Groups and Step Study Groups.

6. **All members must use headphones.** This will ensure that no one else can overhear what is shared in the group if others are present in the home. Even if you are alone in your home/car it helps all participants feel safe as they cannot ensure you are completely alone. So, we just keep this guideline consistent for everyone.

7. **All members must be alone in the room with their camera on and facing them during the entire meeting.** If you have any backgrounds on, please turn those off. However, a blurred background is fine. Again, we ask that your camera be on, and that you face the camera for the entire group time.

8. **This meeting will not be recorded.** This protects the confidentiality and anonymity of the participants.

Appendix 11

Inventory Worksheet

Principle 4 Inventory Worksheet

1. Who hurt me?	2. What happened?	3. How did you feel?	4. What was the damage?	5. What was/ What is my part?
Who is the object of my resentment or fear?	What specific action did that person take that hurt me?	List any emotions that you felt.	What did this action make me believe is true about myself, others, or God?	As a result of that action, what action did I take? What behaviors did I develop as a way to cope?
			What damage did that action do to my basic social, security, and/or sexual instincts?	What part am I responsible for?
				Who are the people I have hurt?
				How have I hurt them?

Principle 4 Inventory Worksheet

1. Who hurt me?	2. What happened?	3. How did you feel?	4. What was the damage?	5. What was/What is my part?